The Industrial Revolution
in World History

Essays in World History

William H. McNeill and Ross E. Dunn, *Series Editors*

The Industrial Revolution in World History
Peter N. Stearns

FORTHCOMING

Coming Full Circle: An Economic History of the Pacific Rim
Eric L. Jones, Lionel Frost, and Colin White

The Horizons of Hellas
Charles D. Hamilton

**Christian Missionaries and European Expansion:
1450 to the Present**
Roger B. Beck

The New World Civilizations
Richard E.W. Adams

**Sailors, Ships, and the Sea:
Seafaring Technology in World History**
John F. Guilmartin, Jr.

The Islamic Gunpowder Empires in World History
Douglas E. Streusand

The Rise of Europe in the Middle Ages
William D. Phillips, Jr.

Energy in World History
Vaclav Smil

THE INDUSTRIAL REVOLUTION IN WORLD HISTORY

✛

Peter N. Stearns
Carnegie Mellon University

✛

Westview Press
Boulder • San Francisco • Oxford

Essays in World History

All rights reserved. No part of this publication may be reproduced or transmitted in any form or by any means, electronic or mechanical, including photocopy, recording, or any information storage and retrieval system, without permission in writing from the publisher.

Copyright © 1993 by Westview Press, Inc.

Published in 1993 in the United States of America by Westview Press, Inc., 5500 Central Avenue, Boulder, Colorado 80301-2877, and in the United Kingdom by Westview Press, 36 Lonsdale Road, Summertown, Oxford OX2 7EW

Library of Congress Cataloging-in-Publication Data
Stearns, Peter N.
  The industrial revolution in world history / Peter N. Stearns.
    p. cm. — (Essays in world history)
  Includes bibliographical references and index.
  ISBN 0-8133-8596-2. — ISBN 0-8133-8597-0 (pbk.)
  1. Industry—History. 2. Economic history. I. Title.
II. Series.
HD2321.S74   1993
338.09—dc20   93-18719
                                                                                           CIP

Printed and bound in the United States of America

The paper used in this publication meets the requirements
of the American National Standard for Permanence of Paper
for Printed Library Materials Z39.48-1984.

10   9   8   7   6   5   4   3

For Deborah and Duncan
as they launch their research careers

Contents

Illustrations

Introduction:
Defining the Industrial Revolution

T HE INDUSTRIAL REVOLUTION began in Great Britain almost 250 years ago—
the starting point was the 1760s. Within a half century it started to spread, first to
most parts of northwestern Europe and also to the new United States. Early
industrialization in Belgium, France, and the American northeast dates from the
1820s. By the 1880s industrial revolutions had begun in Russia and Japan as well as
in several parts of southern and east-central Europe, such as Catalonia, Poland,
and the Czech area around Prague. Canada, Australia, and parts of South Africa
also undertook serious industrial development around this time. In a third wave,
industrial revolutions had been launched by the 1960s in South Korea and other
parts of the Pacific Rim and, more tentatively, in Turkey and Brazil.

The industrialization process had international ramifications from the first. It
resulted from massive changes in world economic relations that had given western Europe access to capital and markets almost literally around the globe. World
historical shifts thus enabled a few societies to pioneer in the new economic and
technical forms industrialization entailed. The force of change embodied in the
industrial revolution could not, in turn, be contained in modern Western
societies. Even as industrialization caused massive upheavals in each society directly involved, the process quickly spilled over to alter basic economic and social
relationships from Latin America to China. Intensifying industrialization and the
accession of ever more societies to the ranks of industrializers amplified the world
historical impact of the process. Thus, looming large among the many ways to
characterize the twentieth century in world history is the power of the industrial
revolution. If the nineteenth century sketched a first set of international reactions
to industrialization in Western society, the twentieth century has been determined in substantial part by the impact of industrial techniques around the
world and by specific efforts to industrialize in many different societies.

The industrial revolution occurred in particular places, such as Britain or New
England or Japan, and therefore must be studied and compared in those places at

1

the appropriate points in time. However, the same industrial revolution has also been reshaping the world at large for 200 years. Ultimately, its role in changing the framework of world history shows its most important face.

From the beginning, industrialization has been a set of human changes. Early developers in factory industry had to depart from their parents' habits, an approach that often required considerable personal sacrifice and generated familial strain.

> For example, in northern France in the early 1840s, Motte Bossut set up a large mechanical wool-spinning factory. His parents had run a much smaller, more traditional textile operation, manufacturing with only a simple sort of machinery; they prided themselves on being able to watch over every detail of their operation and directly supervise a small labor force. Motte Bossut, in contrast, aspired to make France the factory equal of England—during a visit there he had smuggled out illegally the plans for state-of-the-art factory equipment. His large factory quickly became one of the leaders in the region, but his parents would not set foot in it, judging its scale and its riskiness to be genuinely immoral.

> In Germany, Alfred Krupp was born in 1812 into a successful merchant family in the city of Essen. His father, a poor businessman, had decimated the family fortune, however; Friedrich Krupp had twice set up steel manufacturing plants with swindling partners, which had led to failure and public disgrace. Alfred was sent to work in a factory at age thirteen, while his sister labored as a governess. In 1826 Alfred began his own firm on the basis of his father's meager inheritance, manufacturing scissors and hand tools. No technical genius, Krupp applied a single-minded devotion to his firm's success, bent on avoiding his father's mistakes. As a result, he built one of the giant metallurgical firms during the crucible decades of German industrialization.

> Chung Ju Yung was a South Korean villager who in the 1940s, at age sixteen, walked 150 miles to Seoul to take a job as a humble day laborer. He soon moved into modest business activity and began to help build South Korea's industrial revolution. By the 1980s, when Chung was in his sixties, his firm, Hyundai, had 135,000 employees and 42 overseas offices, engaging in activities ranging from automobile manufacture to the construction of huge petroleum supertankers.

The entrepreneurs who masterminded part of the industrialization process came from varied backgrounds. Rags-to-riches stories were not unknown, but the most consistent thread involved these individuals' ability to recognize the potential of new technology and break through some of the economic habits that had dominated the previous generation. This was as true of factory owners from business families, like Motte Bossut, as of manufacturers from peasant or worker origins.

Factory owners formed only part of industrialization's human story, of course. Workers also shaped the industrial revolution, and they too faced change, sometimes involuntarily, in making their contribution. This was true for men, who were most directly involved in new work forms, but it applied to children and women as well.

- Children had always worked, in most social groups. They assisted their parents on the farm and in the household and provided some of the menial labor for craft manufacturing, often under strict employer control. They continued to work in the early factories but in a much less personal atmosphere, amid the dangers of powered machinery and new demands for physical exertion or unrelenting pace. Government hearings held in Great Britain a few decades after the industrial revolution began pinpointed what was probably the most shocking exploitation of child labor: Children had moved in work status from being supplemental labor to being beasts of burden. For the growing cotton factories in Lancashire, greedy for workers and particularly interested in the "small and nimble fingers" of children to help tend the machines at low cost, gangs of children were recruited from the urban poorhouses. Many came from families displaced from rural manufacturing by the expansion of the very factories they now served. As factory hands, they were housed in miserable dormitories and often beaten to spur production. Shifts of children worked day and night, alternating with time in the dormitory; as an 1836 report suggested, "It is a common tradition in Lancashire that the beds never get cold." Not surprisingly, some suicides were reported, by children driven to physical and emotional despair.

- Persis Edwards came to the new textile factories of New Hampshire in the 1830s from a farm background. Like most of the new factory hands, she expected to work only a few years, saving most of her wages to send back to her rural family or to accumulate a nest egg for her marriage. In 1839 she wrote a cousin that she liked her job "very well—enjoy myself much better than I expected." However, she complained (doubtless judging by the standards of labor she had grown up with) that the work made her feel "very much confined, could wish to have my liberty a bit more." Another female relative commented in a letter a bit more bleakly, noting that factory women had lower status than their peers who taught school or made dresses in an artisanal shop; her personal reaction was equivocal: "I was so sick of it at first. I wished a factory had never been thought of but the longer I stay the better I like [it]."

∼ By 1907, during the first phase of Japanese industrialization, 62 percent
of the factory labor force was female, mostly drawn from distant agricultural villages. As in Europe at an earlier time, a growing population plus
the decline of rural manufacturing jobs made peasant families eager to
send some of their number to the cities, regardless of the stress involved
in adjusting to new settings and new work. Factory recruiters contracted
with fathers or brothers in Japanese peasant families, giving them a fee
for the commitment of a daughter or sister to what was a system of near-
slavery. Factory women worked twelve hours a day, received food and
dormitory housing, and had to buy most of their goods in the company
store. They were granted itemizations of what supplies their labor had
earned and a small amount of spending money, because the factory directors had found that any financial latitude prompted the women to
run away. Most of the women probably hoped to return to their native
village to marry a farmer, but more often they stayed in the cities, marrying a male worker or falling into prostitution. An English social worker
visiting Tokyo commented on the lives of these industrial women: "Female factory workers not only lived in a desert of thought but also their
physical environment [was] a kind of desert as well."

The human meaning of the industrial revolution obviously varied by far more
than time and place. Industrialization that occurred early, like Britain's, faced the
strains of sheer novelty, as techniques were explored that had no precedent. Later
industrialization could copy, but it faced the competition of existing industrial
nations; this imposed stresses as well. Industrialization in the context of Japanese
culture had an impact different from that in France, with a distinctive mix of opportunities and problems in each case. Overwhelmingly, however, the industrial
revolution varied with the type of group and type of individual involved. Factory
owners could see industrialization in terms of progress and opportunity, though
they might, depending on personality, have anxieties and worries as well. Newly
recruited or compelled workers had less margin in their adjustments to the industrial economy, and they were readier to think in terms of deterioration and disorientation—though, as the New England factory women suggested, adjustments
were possible, and real benefits were discernible. Finally, a third group, initially
the largest, saw industrialization developing around them—in Britain in 1800, in
Japan in 1900—and had to decide how it would alter their lives even as they remained in the countryside or labored in traditional artisanal shops or commercial
businesses.

This book deals with the unfolding of the industrial revolution in its various
major settings around the world and with its international impact outside leading
centers. Discussed are the processes industrialization involved, the causes that
promoted it, and the ways in which it transformed a range of international relationships. This survey will not, however, lose sight of the human dimension: The

industrial revolution meant change—a more decisive set of changes than most people ever experience historically. It meant opportunity, excitement, stress, and degradation, and these diverse features formed an essential part of the conversion from an agriculturally based to an industrially based society.

Technology and Work Organization

The industrial revolution constituted one of those rare occasions in world history when the human species altered its framework of existence. Indeed, the only previous development comparable in terms of sheer magnitude was the Neolithic revolution—the conversion from hunting and gathering to agriculture as the basic form of production for survival. Both the industrial revolution and the Neolithic revolution brought fundamental changes in the ways people worked, where they lived (settled communities rather than nomadic bands, then cities instead of rural communities and farms), the potential economic surplus available, and the numbers of people who could be supported around the world. These changes inevitably had ramifications reaching into almost every aspect of human experience—into the habits of thought and the relations between men and women as well as into systems of production and exchange. The full story of the industrial revolution is precisely the examination of these multiple impacts.

The essence of the industrial revolution, however, was fairly simple. Stripped to its bare bones, the industrial revolution consisted of the application of new sources of power to the production process, achieved with transmission equipment necessary to apply this power to manufacturing. And it consisted of increased scale in human organization that facilitated specialization and coordination at levels preindustrial groupings had rarely contemplated.

The industrial revolution progressively replaced humans and animals as the power sources of production with motors powered by fossil fuels (supplemented by water power and, very recently, by nuclear power). The key invention in Europe's industrial revolution was the steam engine, which harnessed the energy potential of coal. Later industrial revolutions also used electric and internal combustion motors (developed by the 1870s) and petroleum as well as coal. Before the industrial revolution almost all production in manufacturing and agriculture relied on equipment powered by people or draft animals, with some small assistance from waterwheels. Except for waterwheels, used mainly to mill grain, almost all tools were designed for manual use. Animals often pulled plows for farming, but planting and harvesting were done by hand, with workers aided by simple tools like sickles. Looms for weaving cloth were powered by foot pedals, and the fibers strung by hand. The industrial revolution progressively introduced steam or other power to the production process and steadily increased the proportion of the process accomplished by equipment without direct human guidance. Power looms thus not only replaced foot pedals but also crossed threads automatically after a worker initially attached them to the frame. Machine tending involved making sure the thread supply remained constant and dealing with snapped threads or other breakdowns; the cloth itself did not have to be touched by hand until it was gathered. Dramatic new sources of power—vastly more potent than what people and animals could provide and transmitted to the product by semiautomatic machinery—were the technological core of the industrial revolution.

The organizational facet of the industrial revolution was initially symbolized by the factory, but the organizational principles spread beyond the factory itself. The industrial revolution brought together groups of people in the production process. Most production operations before the late eighteenth century centered on the household, with collaboration and specialization among ten or fewer people. Even though many early industrial factories were small, they promoted the grouping of greater numbers of people for the production process. They also increased the amount of specialization; tasks were subdivided, which increased the total production even aside from new technology. Even most large work gangs before the industrial revolution, like slaves in the mines and agricultural plantations of the Americas, had been relatively unspecialized. Finally, industrial-style organization involved more conscious management of workers toward a faster as well as a more fully coordinated work pace. Here too was a contrast with the more relaxed work styles characteristic of much preindustrial labor, including a good bit of slave labor. Thus, redefined work discipline and specialization, along with growth in the size of the work unit, defined the organizational core of the industrial revolution. Labor systems that could not match these organizational characteristics, including slavery and purely household production, declined or even disappeared during the industrialization process.

The two central features of industrialization—revolutions in technology and in the organization of production—yielded one clear result: a great increase in the total output of goods and in individual worker output. Per capita productivity went up, in some cases massively. A spinning worker in 1820 France or Britain using steam-driven spindles instead of a manual spinning wheel could produce literally a hundred times the thread of a preindustrial counterpart. This productivity gain was unusual—the doubling of per capita output possible with early mechanical looms had already potentially transformed the material framework of the society involved. Increased output could and often would be used in various ways: to increase inequality in the standard of living, to support higher tax revenues, to provide for rapidly growing populations, or to change and possibly improve material conditions for the masses. These varied results and the balance among them form vital topics to explore in dealing with the impact of industrialization on individuals and societies.

The risk in analyzing the essential features of the industrial revolution is that they seem deceptively simple. Exploring the history of industrialization involves multiple tasks—tracing why certain parts of the world were open to new technologies and new organizational forms; analyzing why different industrial societies established somewhat different policies (for example, varying the role of government in triggering and guiding the industrialization process); and understanding the host of different human reactions that emerged, even in a single industrial society, as people adjusted to innovations like steam-driven machines and factories. The full history of the industrial revolution, in other words, involves variety and complexity. Nevertheless, even as we probe these richer human meanings, the bare-bones definition must not be forgotten: In any industrialization process, the technological and organizational substratum inevitably looms large.

Issues in Interpretation

Before grappling with the history of industrialization, we must sketch a second level of definition; our effort should take into account a few crucial arguments among historians who continue to try to determine the best way to come to terms with this watershed in the human experience.

The industrial revolution was a human phenomenon, involving individuals touched by events on a personal level, but it consisted more of certain general processes than of tidy historical signposts. Participants in industrialization had to deal with work systems, with the rise of new kinds of stores, with new habits of time. These changes involved hosts of individual events: a manufacturer deciding on his factory rules, a peddler realizing that the quantity of goods required a village shop instead of itinerant hawking, a manufacturing worker learning to listen for the clock-based factory whistle. These events, multiplied by the hundreds of thousands of individuals involved, constituted the new work processes, the rise of new kinds of shopkeepers, the sense of a new urgency in work time.

The essence of the industrial revolution does not, however, flow from very many clearly labeled seminal events, such as the advent of a new president or the signing of a major treaty. Event-based history proceeded as industrialization took hold: Britain fought the armies of Napoleon, Japan installed a new constitution, Russia was battered by the 1905 revolution. The industrial revolution was involved in these events and had some obvious events of its own: James Watt's invention of the steam engine, the passage of new child labor laws, the establishment in Japan of a ministry of industry. But fitting industrial history and event-based history together is not easy, and most students of industrialization deal with a somewhat distinctive set of historical markers. Great individuals and decisive events are less important than in some other kinds of history.

The industrial revolution is also an odd type of revolution. The kinds of revolutions easiest to define are political upheavals, like the French Revolution of 1789 or the Russian Revolution of 1917. Revolutions of this sort seem to have defined beginnings and endings (the French Revolution, launched in 1789, went through identifiable phases until the advent of Napoleon in 1799, and the active revolutionary period ended either at that point or with Napoleon's defeat in 1815). In fact, current thinking about political revolutions introduces some new fuzziness: The Russian Revolution, seemingly over at the end of the civil war in 1921, actually lasted at least into the 1930s, with Stalin's consolidation, and recent events suggest that basic debates launched by the revolution continue in the 1990s. Nevertheless, the active upheaval of most revolutions, from the first riots to the firming up of a new regime, rarely lasts more than a decade.

The industrial revolution is another matter, for it clearly spread over many decades and had no tidy beginning or end. For example, Great Britain started opening steam-powered factories in the 1780s. The change quickly swept through a few important industries—cotton spinning was almost entirely mechanized within a decade—but the economy as a whole changed far more slowly. By 1850 there were still as many craft workers as factory workers and as many rural people as urban. Industrialization had changed the work lives as well as the prospects and outlook of the nonfactory majority, but it had not yet revolutionized them. And while productivity had exploded in a few sectors, again as in cotton spinning, overall per capital output grew only gradually (about 2 percent per year) because so much of the population still worked in traditional settings.

Industrialization, in fact, frequently gained momentum several decades after the first serious introductions of new equipment and factories. Some societies, as we will see, experimented with a few factories and had no subsequent industrial revolution at all. But even many regions that did industrialize in some manufacturing sectors saw a greater wave of change forty or fifty years after their initial engagement. The "second industrial revolution" in western Europe, late in the nineteenth century, thus perhaps brought more changes to more people than the first revolution did. Both Japan and Russia redefined and accelerated their industrialization processes in the 1920s and 1930s, a half century after their serious involvement began. Industrial revolutions, clearly, are long, recurrent, and hard to pinpoint.

Is this revolution at all? Some historians have recently argued that it is not. They point to the modest pace of change in the initial decades of a so-called industrial revolution and emphasize also that significant changes were taking place well before steam engines and factories hove into view. Industrialization as a process—a very long, drawn-out process—they will allow, but an industrial revolution seems to this revisionist group a very misleading concept.

Arguments of this sort have certainly dented an earlier schematic image of the industrial revolution. In the 1950s economic historian W. W. Rostow sought to create something of a model of industrial revolution, abstracted from particular historical developments but fitting all industrial revolutions—from Britain's first effort through Japan's more recent drive to possible revolutions in the future (he wrote before the Pacific Rim's surge to the fore). Rostow emphasized a few "take-off" decades in which the initial introduction of new technology spurred particularly rapid change in the relevant sectors. More recent work on industrialization points instead to the variety of changes that occurred even as the first factories were introduced: Some craft sectors grew, some industrial sectors remained atypical and small, and no precise pattern of industrial dynamism existed from one region to the next. Furthermore, preliminary phases did not lead, lockstep, to some general maturation. Whereas Germany moved quickly to a focus on relatively large factories in heavy industry (though this accompanied maintenance of a substantial artisanal sector), France achieved impressive manufacturing growth rates through a different blend, combining some factories with pressures to speed up craft operations in industries such as furniture making. When a single-standard industrial revolution served as the model, France seemed simply to be an industrial laggard. New understandings of diverse paths of change and of the gradualness of transformations even in dramatic cases such as Germany combine to muddy the picture: France experienced a nineteenth-century industrialization but a French one, not some all-purpose process that in three decades would generate the triumph of factory industry across the board.

But if industrial revolutions are uneven, slow, and particular, with no one case quite like the next, there is no need to discard the term "revolutionary." After all, political revolutions sometimes prove slow, and they certainly never change as much or as rapidly as proponents imagined. Industrial revolutions spring from previous changes—this is an obvious aspect of causation and helps explain why some societies have industrial revolutions and others, despite considerable effort, do not. Industrial revolutions take time, and they involve different parts of the labor force in quite different degrees of change. They do, however, produce some fundamental shifts, building from the increasing introduction of new technologies and new organizational forms even if (as in the French case most obviously) the introduction is not only gradual but somewhat idiosyncratic.

The revolutionary quality of industrialization becomes still more obvious in the world context. British and even French industrialization proceeded, as we shall see, from earlier patterns of economic and social change. The introduction of steam-driven equipment denoted a real shift, but one occurring within an already dynamic context. Industrial revolutions later on, based in large part on imitation of earlier developments elsewhere, had revolutionary implications more quickly. Russia began to form a factory labor force within the same generation as it abolished rural serfdom and began to spread literacy; Japan produced a new entrepreneurial class only a generation after abolishing feudalism; South Korea launched its industrialization only a generation after the economic and political oppression of Japanese occupation. Change in cases of this sort moved with bewildering speed, and the industrial revolution formed a central part of massive social and political transformations.

In sum, the variety and unevenness of industrial development make the concept of industrial revolution undeniably slippery. No initial definition can substitute for exploration of actual cases, and no orderly schema fully captures reality. Nevertheless, the phenomenon does involve revolutionary levels of change, which is why societies that have generated a real industrial revolution differ from those contemporary ones that have introduced some mechanized manufacturing but not a full revolution. The debates about the concept properly remind us of its complexity but need not distract from the fundamental—indeed, revolution-ary—alterations the process generates over time. The huge differences between the Britain of 1880 and that of 1780, the United States of 1900 and that of 1820, or the Japan of 1960 and that of 1880 took shape gradually and unevenly—but they unquestionably occurred. Indeed, the first use of the term "industrial revolution," by a British observer in the 1880s, belatedly reflected the powerful alterations in the basic structures of that society and implicitly anticipated comparable sea changes in other societies in which the force of new technology and new organi-zational principles took root.

The Range of the Industrial Revolution

The sheer potency of the industrial revolution raises several other definitional is-sues, though they can be more quickly handled. First, if an industrial revolution begins (though often in societies already changing rapidly) with the widespread adoption of new equipment and the factory form in several key industries, when does it end? This issue is closely attached to the warnings against oversimplifica-tion. Because many industrial forms spread gradually, the process does not have a neat termination point. French peasants, for example, began widespread use of tractors only after World War II. They had previously adopted new kinds of hand tools and some new processing equipment; they had certainly increased their pro-duction for the market; and they had used mechanical transportation like trains and steamships. But their substantial commitment to mechanization in the pro-duction process came surprisingly late (though it was quite enthusiastic when it finally arrived). Could France be regarded as industrialized before its vital peasant sector was fully engaged? Clearly, the unevenness of industrialization means that fundamental changes may continue for well over a century after the process iden-tifiably began. Furthermore, the industrial revolution generated recurrent change even in the sectors it first affected. Many British cotton workers, faced in the 1890s with new American-devised machines that allowed a single worker to tend eight to sixteen mechanical looms rather than the two to four of early industrialization, judged that their work lives were changing in a far more radical fashion than those of their predecessors. They were probably wrong, but they had an arguable case. Industrial societies accept, whether they like it or not, a commitment to re-current cycles of technical and organizational innovation, which means periodic renewal of a sense of unsettled upheaval.

The most revolutionary period of the industrialization process ends, however, when most workers and managers (whether in factories or smaller workshops) use some powered equipment and operate according to some of the principles of industrial organization. At this point, the larger society has gained an ability to apply industrial procedures to most branches of the economy, and although it may not fully have done so (as with the somewhat laggard French peasants), virtually every major group has faced some serious adjustment to the impact of the industrial revolution. Historically, this point has been reached seventy to a hundred years after serious technological innovation first began. Thus, for example, it is legitimate to peg the end of the U.S. industrial revolution at about 1920, when factory production overwhelmingly dominated other forms in manufacturing and when half the population lived in cities. Vast economic changes were to occur after 1920, extending the transformations the industrial revolution had wrought, but the industrial context was set.

The definition of the industrial revolution, thus, includes: a massive set of changes that begin when radical innovations in technologies and organizational forms are extensively introduced in key manufacturing sectors and that end, in the truly revolutionary phase, when these innovations are widely, though not necessarily universally, established in the economy at large. Subsequent changes, often quite unsettling, are virtually assured, but they arise within the contours of an industrial society.

But what, then, is an industrial society? This is a second definitional issue in expanding the idea of industrial revolution beyond its most basic elements. What kinds of social alterations followed from new machines, factories, stores, and offices? The industrial revolution was a systems change: New technology and organization boosted production and propelled manufacturing over agriculture as the industrial society's greatest source of wealth and employment. To handle factory and related jobs, and because industrial machines began to take over some of the production previously performed in the countryside, cities grew rapidly. By 1850 half of Britain's population lived in cities, the first such urban achievement in human history—for even the most effective agricultural societies had never been able to free up more than 20 percent of a population from the rural economy.

A systems change of this sort inevitably, though again gradually, affected every aspect of human and social life. Personal habits changed as people learned a new sense of time and discipline. The status of old people changed. The industrial revolution in Europe and the United States gave the elderly some new functions, such as babysitting for their working adult children, but it diminished their status: Jobs became associated with high energy and the ability to learn new techniques, and the elderly were culturally downgraded because they seemed to lack these qualities. The industrial revolution changed the nature of war, as was obvious from the U.S. Civil War (1861–1865) onward: Industrial war meant more rapid and massive troop movements, devastating weaponry, and greatly increased death and maiming in battle.

Because of the power of the industrial revolution, virtually everything was altered: relationships between parents and children, art, politics, and diplomatic relations, to name some areas of change. By the 1850s the industrial revolution was beginning to encompass the whole of history, particularly in societies that were directly industrializing but also to some extent around the world. Change was not complete; otherwise, we could expect to see in the 1990s each industrial society virtually identical to the next, which is not the case. Continuities from preindustrial cultural and political patterns plus different experiences in the industrial revolution process itself maintained important differences. Nevertheless, in a real sense the history of the industrial revolution is the history of the modern world; no factors even remotely rival industrialization's impact in explaining what has gone on in the world—and what still goes on as adjustments to the alteration of basic human systems continue. Even sweeping shifts in human loyalties, like the rise of nationalism, though they follow from new ideologies, can be traced directly to the disruption of local ties and the intensive contacts among different parts of the world that industrialization fostered: People became nationalistic to provide themselves identities that might replace meanings the industrial revolution destroyed.

Yet a focus on the industrialization phenomenon itself must be somewhat selective. To gain a sense of what it involved, in terms of new stresses and new opportunities, we need not march through every subsequent war in which new ships, cannon, and industrially produced propaganda were put into operation. The focus must be on the most direct human and institutional impact and on some general patterns in areas such as combat or human aging. This understanding can then be put into play in dealing with the specifics of the world's military history or of social welfare developments over the past century and a half. The emphasis on the kinds of changes that most directly, almost inexorably, resulted from new technology and new organization of production during the century or so in which major societies were intensively engaged in the industrial revolution provides the guidelines for the most meaningful analysis.

The industrial revolution as an international development raises the final set of complexities. The revolution quickly affected the whole world. As early as the 1820s, Latin American economies, newly freed from Spanish control, began to suffer from competition of machine-made goods from Britain; both local manufacturing and merchant activity declined. In the 1830s the economic pressures of industrialization pried open China as industrializing Western nations insisted on access to Chinese goods and markets and had the industrially generated military might to drive home their demands. Yet the industrial revolution occurred in individual societies and must be understood in this context as well. Because industrialization first occurred in the West, it is sometimes traced there and then dropped. Even in Western history, British industrialization, because it came first, is sometimes sketched as if it preempted the field. Yet it is obvious that the industrial revolution does not fit conveniently into the 1760–1850 time slot that might indeed be used for Britain. Nor did British patterns prove to be entirely typical of the process elsewhere, even in other European nations. The industrial revolution must be seen as a basic development that occurred in many different places and, of course, at many different times—indeed, it continues today. Particular national or regional patterns of industrialization must be compared, even though some key ingredients are the same.

Furthermore, industrialization both united and divided the world, and this tension also continues. Industrial technologies and expanding manufacturing output quickly brought all major areas literally closer together. This is why China found its traditional isolation impossible by the 1830s and why Africa, its rivers newly penetrable by steamboats, opened perforce to new levels of international trade. The shrinkage of the world through industrial forms of transportation and communication has intensified with every passing decade. Yet the industrial revolution created new division, separating countries engaged in the process from those that for many reasons, including the pressures placed upon them by the industrial states, were unable to join the parade. The split between "have" and "have-not" regions was and is primarily a split between industrial and (at least as yet) nonindustrial, and it is a novel and nasty kind of division. The cast of characters is not constant. Japan, definitely a have-not nation extensively bullied by the industrial West in the 1870s and 1880s, obviously managed to grab a seat at the industrial feast with a vengeance. Nevertheless, the overall tension industrialization generated in the world at large, simultaneously drawing regions into closer contact while creating new and agonizing differences among them, continues to describe much of the framework of world history. Both aspects, the shared systems and the stark divisions, must be captured when the industrial revolution is understood as it should be—as a world process.

The industrial revolution formed one of the central transformations of human history. Like all major shifts, it brought advantages and disadvantages in its wake. Industrialization has improved human health, for example by dramatically reducing infant mortality rates around the world. Yet industrialization has worsened the natural environment and continues to do so. Industrialization, finally, is recent and ongoing; we are still adjusting to its implications. Understanding the industrial revolution and its diverse results not only is essential in dealing with recent world history but can help us gain insight into ourselves.

PART ONE

The First Phase, 1760–1880:
The West Leads the Way

1

Britain's Revolution: New Processes and Economic Transformation

BEFORE the eighteenth century the most advanced economies in the world featured a combination of craft manufacturing (its most skilled components based in cities) and a large labor force committed to agriculture. Most production, both manufacturing and agricultural, was based on manual household labor, with larger village groups combining for certain operations like harvesting and road building. The use of slave crews for commercial production of key agricultural goods like sugar and tobacco had spread, particularly in the Americas, though there were no major changes in technology. Several societies had developed sophisticated craft skills for the production of luxury cloth, metal goods, and other items. China, Japan, India, the Middle East (including North Africa), and western Europe stood at the forefront in terms of artisanal technology and the vital capacity to produce iron and iron products. Africa had a well-established ironworking tradition, and metallurgy and armaments manufacturing were advancing in Russia by 1700.

West European technology had gained decisive ground from the fifteenth century onward. Western production of guns, based on earlier skills in ironworking developed initially for the production of great church bells, provided a crucial military edge, particularly in naval conflicts. Western metallurgy generally led the world by the sixteenth century. During the seventeenth century growing dominance in world trade spurred the growth of textile production in many parts of western Europe, and here too technological refinements occurred that made the West effectively an international leader. Western biases concerning the rest of the world began to take on a technological cast, with scorn for the many peoples slow to imitate Western developments. A Western missionary in the seventeenth century described how, in his opinion, the Chinese could not be persuaded "to make use of new instruments and leave their old ones without an especial order from the Emperor to that effect. They are more fond of the most defective piece of antiquity than of the most perfect of the modern, differing much in that from us who are in love with nothing but what is new."

With all these developments, however, Western technology and production methods remained firmly anchored in the basic traditions of agricultural societies, particularly in terms of reliance on human and animal power. Agriculture itself had scarcely changed in method since the fourteenth century. Manufacturing, despite some important new techniques, continued to entail combining skill with hand tools and was usually carried out in very small shops. The most important Western response to new manufacturing opportunities involved a great expansion of rural (domestic) production, particularly in textiles but also in small metal goods. Domestic manufacturing workers used simple equipment, which they usually bought themselves, and relied on labor from the household. Many combined their efforts with farming, and in general their skill levels were modest. The system worked well because it required little capital; rural householders invested a bit in a spinning wheel or a hand loom, while an urban-based capitalist purchased the necessary raw materials and, usually, arranged for sale of the product. Output expanded because of the sheer growth of worker numbers, not because of technical advancement; indeed, the low wages paid generated little incentive for technical change.

Western Europe in 1700 was an advanced agricultural society, with an unusually large commercial sector and a great deal of manually operated manufacturing. The region was developing a certain fascination with machines but most decidedly was not industrialized.

Three changes began to combine during the eighteenth century to generate the world's first industrial revolution. Two of them affected several parts of western Europe, but one was more particular to Britain, where the revolution first took shape.

New agricultural methods came into use in the late 1700s. Peasants in many parts of Europe, including Ireland, France, and Prussia, began to grow potatoes, a New World crop long regarded with suspicion. Potatoes offered several advantages over the grains Europeans had traditionally relied upon as staple food: Higher caloric value could be produced from smaller and sometimes less fertile plots of land, and for many decades potatoes were less subject to periodic diseases than were grains. Increasing adoption of the potato supported the beginnings of rapid population growth in Europe by the 1730s. Britain's population, for example, doubled between 1750 and 1800, while that of France rose by 50 percent. The potato also freed up a percentage of rural labor for work in other areas, again because of its caloric yield on small plots. At roughly the same time, farmers in Holland began to develop new drainage systems by which swampland could be converted to agricultural use, and they introduced nitrogen-fixing crops that enabled them to keep fields in use every year rather than being rested every third year to regain chemical fertility. With less fallow land and more land in use overall, food production expanded, which also contributed to population growth and to re-lease of new workers for other potential work activities.

While agricultural improvements took shape in various places, they received enthusiastic support in Britain, where aristocratic landlords were particularly interested in new and more rewarding production for market sales. Draining of marshes added cultivable land in eastern England. Innovators like "Turnip" Townshend spread the word about using nitrogen-fixing crops to increase production by eliminating fallow land. Increased food supplies spurred British population growth and reduced the percentage of the labor force required in agriculture.

Massive strides in European science, in an already active commercial economy, encouraged attention to new technology in the manufacturing field. A host of scientific societies took shape that combined researchers with merchants and manufacturers, which led to excited discussions about down-to-earth technological possibilities. Advances in chemistry helped trigger the discovery of new techniques for manufacturing and glazing pottery in eighteenth-century England. New scientific knowledge about the behavior of gases set a context for considering the possibility of harnessing steam to provide a moving force to replace unreliable water and wind as power sources. The first steam engine was invented by a French refugee in Holland in the late 1600s; several Dutch scientists discussed the prospect of propelling a boat by steam. Around 1700 the engine was improved in England by Thomas Newcomen, who applied it to drainage pumps for coal mines. A steam truck was invented in France in the 1760s, though was never put to use. The engine was perfected in the 1760s by James Watt, a Glasgow craftsman who produced scientific instruments, and could be applied for industrial use. In a poem written in 1789, the English scientist Erasmus Darwin (grandfather of the evolution-theory biologist Charles) ecstatically praised the engine's possibilities:

> *Soon shall they arm, unconquer'd steam! afar*
> *Drag the slow barge, or drive the rapid carp;*
> *Or on wide-waving wings expanded bear*
> *The flying chariot through the fields of air.*
> *—Fair crews triumphant, leaning from above,*
> *Shall wave their handkerchiefs as they move;*
> *Or warrior bands alarm the gaping crowd,*
> *And armies shrink beneath the shadowy cloud.*

Along with changes in agricultural production and a stream of new inventions and attendant intellectual enthusiasm came some less dramatic shifts in England's domestic manufacturing system. The nation was already a leader in world trade. It had a growing population by the 1730s, and the public was expressing interest in more fashionable clothing—an early manifestation of new consumer tastes. This setting prompted a handful of domestic producers to think about expanding their operations, in a gradual shift that proved to be the forerunner of a new organization of manufacturing labor. For example, the Halifax area in York-shire in the late seventeenth century was a significant center for the production of wool cloth by local artisans in the countryside who often combined their manu-facturing with farming. Output from each worker was low, though the profits could provide some useful supplementary income. Even substantial farmers put their hand to the loom from time to time or used family members as workers. In the 1690s a few workers began buying more wool than they could handle them-selves; they hired other workers to work the wool at home for them and, without abandoning their own labor at first, were on the route to becoming manufactur-ers. By the next generation, these same manufacturing families, a minority of the wool workers in the region overall, were beginning to separate themselves socially from their employed labor. They were no longer willing to share a beer; they were thinking of their workers as a class apart. One of them wrote in 1736 during a trade depression, "I have turned off [laid off] a great many of my makers and keep turning off more weekly." His "makers," clearly, had become disposable sub-ordinates in the process of production, and a traditional manufacturing system was beginning to yield to a more structured hierarchy.

By the 1730s several of these strands of change were beginning to combine in England. Growing numbers of workers sought jobs as the population increase and some new agricultural methods reduced opportunities in farming. Although the total number of agricultural workers increased, even as aristocratic landlords consolidated their holdings and sponsored more efficient methods, the percent-age of a rapidly growing population employed in agriculture declined. Market op-portunities for manufacturing production rose, however, despite frequent slumps, through population growth, expanding international trade, and the growing appetite for consumer goods like fashionable clothing. As more and more workers and small businesses began expanding their operations by hiring wage workers, the profile of a new manufacturing middle class began gradually to emerge. Finally, new technology began to be developed for the sector that most obviously invited it—the domestic production system. In 1733 an English artisan, James Kay, invented the flying shuttle, a new kind of loom for weaving cloth that automatically moved thread horizontally through a frame when activated by a foot pedal. This machine was nothing fancy, and no new power was involved, but one worker with a child as assistant could now do the work of two adults. Inven-tions for automatically winding fiber to make thread followed in the 1760s. New opportunity and evolving attitudes on the part of the growing manufacturing class, plus the excitement surrounding technological change and the resultant en-couragement to invention, were pushing the traditional production system well beyond its former bounds.

By the 1760s, then, the ingredients of the industrial revolution had been assem-bled in England, after several decades of changes within the domestic manufac-turing system. New entrepreneurs were ready to manipulate workers in novel ways. Inventions increased the number of industrial processes handled automatically. The manufacturing sector and its labor force were growing steadily. Then came a usable steam engine, which by the 1770s could be hooked up to some of the semiautomatic inventions already devised for manual textile workers. Because steam power was concentrated and could not be transmitted over long distances, workers had to be assembled near the engines to do their work; small factories had to replace household production sites. This final change, too, was developing rapidly in certain key sectors by the 1770s. Britain's industrial revolution was under way.

Britain Becomes the Workshop of the World

The initial explicit stages of the world's first industrial revolution—as opposed to the previous preparatory decades—involved a number of elements. Rapid innovation transformed several sectors of industry, with new technology and organization at the core of change. Without this, the industrial revolution could not have been identified. At the same time, many branches of the economy were affected only slightly, and thus some overall measurements of industrialization remained modest. Within the innovative sectors, intense misery pervaded the experience of many of the human beings involved; the industrial revolution was built on the backs of exploited labor. Finally, as the revolution caught on, it inevitably brought in its wake further change in both technology and business practices. Most of these developments occurred during decades when Britain nearly monopolized the new processes, winning a growing world role on the strength of its industrial lead.

The cotton industry commanded the central role in Britain's early industrialization. Cotton, as a fiber, had characteristics relatively easy to mechanize; it broke less often than wool and, particularly, linen. Further, cotton was a new product line in Europe, more open to innovation. It had been widely used in India, and an Asian market for cotton cloth already existed. In England, however, its novelty facilitated the introduction of new machines, though the raw fiber had to be imported. Workers were displaced indirectly by the rise of cotton because traditional linen production declined. The lack of a large established labor force in cotton obviated the need to prompt many traditional workers to change their ways, and this fact limited resistance. At the same time, cotton had great appeal as a product: It could be brightly colored for a population increasingly eager to make a statement through clothing, and it was easily washed for a population some segments of which were developing more stringent notions of personal cleanliness. Cotton was in demand, and this invited new techniques to produce the cloth in quantity.

By the 1730s a series of inventions began to shift cotton manufacturing increasingly toward a factory system. The flying shuttle, designed originally to improve hand weaving, was refined over another thirty years sufficiently in accuracy to

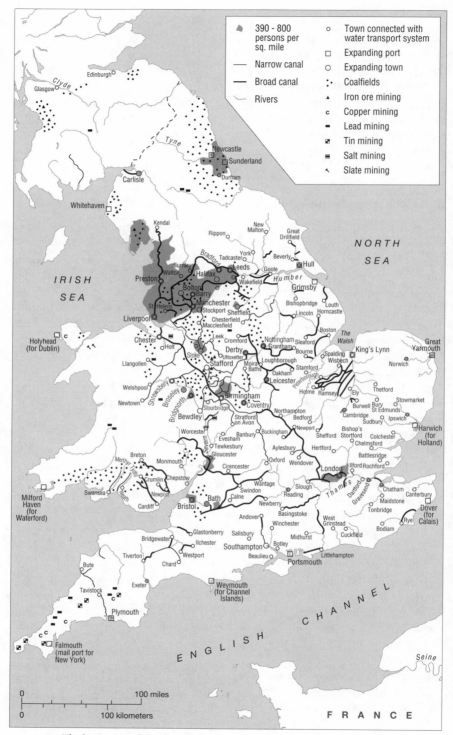

MAP 1.1 *The beginning of the industrial revolution: Great Britain, c. 1750–1820.*

make possible the application of nonhuman power. Edmund Cartwright patented a power loom in 1785; his description of his procedures revealed the new kind of thinking being applied to technical issues: "It struck me that as plain weaving can only be three movements which were to follow one another in succession, there would be little difficulty in producing them and repeating them." Indeed, mechanization involved isolating parts of the production process that could be accomplished through highly standardized, accurate motion and then applying to such motion equipment that could be linked to power sources. Weaving turned out to be among the more complicated stages to mechanize, and Cartwright's loom had to undergo substantial improvements before, by around 1800, it could be widely used.

More impressive developments occurred in the preparatory phases in cotton. James Hargreaves invented a spinning jenny device about 1764, which mechanically drew out and twisted the fibers into threads—though this advance too initially was applied to handwork, not a new power source. Carding and combing machines, to ready the fiber prior to spinning, were developed at about the same time. Then in 1769 Richard Arkwright developed the first water-powered spinning machine; it twisted and wound threads by means of flyers and bobbins operating continuously. These first machines were relevant only for the cheapest kind of thread, but other inventions by 1780 began to make possible the spinning of finer cotton yarns. These new devices also could be powered by steam engines as well as waterwheels. The basic principles of mechanized thread production have not changed to this day, though machines were to grow progressively larger, and a given worker could tend a greater number of spindles. Other inventions pertinent to the industrialization of cotton production included new bleaching and dying procedures (in the 1770s and 1780s) and roller printers for cloth designs that replaced laborious block printing by hand—another new method that increased production a hundredfold while reducing workers' skill requirements.

Cotton production by the 1790s was advancing with extraordinary rapidity. New machines required a factory organization, for the power could not be transmitted widely. Workers had to be removed from their homes and clustered around the new machines. Cotton spinning was entirely concentrated in factories by the 1790s. Because mechanical weaving lagged, this initial industrialization spurred a massive expansion of domestic looms; the thread produced was distributed from huge warehouses in the new factory centers such as Manchester. Power weaving came into general use in the Manchester area only after 1806, then began the full conquest in cotton after 1815—to the immense distress of the hundreds of thousands of workers who had been drawn into the surrounding countryside to do the weaving. There were massive fortunes to be made in the industry. Robert Owen, a store assistant, began his Manchester factory in 1789 by borrowing £100, and by 1809 he was in a position to buy out his partners in his New Lanark Mills for £84,000 in cash—this in a country where only about four percent of the population earned more than £200 per year.

Sales of manufactured cotton goods soared, for with the new machines not only did output increase, but prices plummeted. Exports were essential, and by 1800 approximately four pieces of cotton cloth were sold abroad for every three disposed of at home. As late as 1840 cotton continued to provide about half of the entire value of British exports. Continental Europe was a major market, but it consumed only about a third of Britain's export production in this field. Latin America was seized by British cotton exports after Spanish rule was cast off early in the nineteenth century. By 1820 the impoverished continent was buying a quarter as much cotton cloth from Britain as was Europe, and by 1840 the figure had risen to a full half. India and Southeast Asia were deindustrialized by a combination of British factory competition and colonial policy as machine products beat out hand labor; cotton imports from Britain rose by 1,500 percent between 1820 and 1840. Africa was another major market. Of the major nations, only China held out until its economy was forced open in the early 1840s.

Britain's industrial revolution consisted until about 1840 primarily of changes in the cotton industry, with its massive results in terms of expanding production and world outreach, but other developments were vital as well. Mechanization of wool spinning and weaving was well under way by 1800, impeded only by the higher cost and greater fragility of wool fiber. New machines and procedures were introduced into beer brewing; the big factories established included the great Guinness brewery in Dublin. Pottery manufacturing concentrated important developments in industrial chemistry during the late eighteenth century, while new methods reduced the work required in processes such as glazing and cutting. Several of these innovations created major health hazards for the workers involved— new grinding methods, for example, "hath proved very destructive to mankind, occasioned by the dust suckled into the body which ... fixes so closely upon the lungs that nothing can remove it"—but productivity per worker expanded immensely, to the benefit of new pottery magnates such as Josiah Wedgwood. In the 1830s new printing presses were developed that could be powered by steam engines, which greatly expanded production in such fields as daily newspapers. A few commercial bakeries also introduced important new methods.

The most striking mechanical strides outside the growing textile sectors occurred in metallurgy and mining. During the eighteenth century British manufacturers learned to produce coke from coal (by heating and concentrating it in special ovens) and to use coke instead of wood-derived charcoal for smelting iron ore. Coke production in turn depended on advances in furnace design and steam blasting (introduced by John Wilkinson in 1776). As coke supplies grew, furnace design for smelting and refining iron was also reconsidered; the result was larger furnaces and higher output per worker. Henry Cort's reverberatory furnace for refining iron (developed in 1784) saved fuel but above all increased productivity by 1,500 percent. Steam-powered machines to roll metal, replacing manual hammering, soon followed. The iron industry began to expand rapidly. Britain had produced 25,000 tons of pig iron in 1720; by 1796 the figure was 125,000 and by 1804 was 250,000 tons.

The growth of the iron industry had two further consequences. Coal mining surged to provide the fuel for iron smelting and for steam engines generally. Major advances in work methods at the coal face did not develop, though there were important improvements in timbering mine pits to allow deeper shafts. Transportation from the coal face did demand attention. Wooden and metal rails were laid down to facilitate carts of coal being pulled by horses or people; soon after 1800 experiments with steam-driven engines to pull the carts began. At the same time, the number of miners increased rapidly because this vital industry remained extremely labor-intensive.

At the other end of iron production, machine building expanded steadily. Inventions of new equipment, from spinning machines to the steam engine, did not always translate readily into production methods beyond the prototypes. Twelve years passed, for example, between Watt's construction of a working model engine (1765) and usable cylinders that could be widely manufactured. Before 1800 machine building was scattered in small shops and was performed with hand methods, and even after this date the industry long demanded highly skilled workers laboring with relatively little sophisticated equipment of their own. But attention in France and the new United States to the manufacturing of guns led to the development of precise patterns for designing machine parts, such that these parts could be interchangeably used on a given machine. Several machines were designed to bore and turn the machine pieces, and their industrial use gradually spread in Britain (and the United States and western Europe) during the early decades of the nineteenth century.

Headed by advancements in the cotton industry, Britain's early industrial revolution featured dramatic new methods that subsequently generated improved productivity and more standardized products in a host of industries. Heavy industry—mining and metallurgy—gained ground rapidly, though the importance of the labor force and the total product long lagged behind textiles. Vast numbers of new workers were drawn into factories and mines. Some of these people were relatively unskilled, for many of the new processes required only modest training compared with older methods, but some, as in machine building, applied extensive skills to new products. Developments were not uniform: Many production branches, as in the manufacturing of brass and other small metal goods, were scarcely touched, though they often expanded given growing demand. Nor was progress steady: Great lags often intervened, as in mechanical weaving, between initial devices and widespread applicability. Britain's industrialization was a revolution, but it neither occurred overnight nor was tidily packaged.

The revolutionary quality, however, showed through in a host of ways. Urban growth was one of these. Cities of various sorts exploded in Britain in the late 1700s and early 1800s, the result of burgeoning banking operations, growing port activities, and so on. The biggest expansion, however, occurred in the factory centers as factories located near energy sources and a large labor force accumulated to facilitate factory operations. Manchester, Britain's cotton capital, grew from a modest town of 25,000 in 1772 to a metropolis of 367,232 by 1851. Leeds, Birmingham, and Sheffield, centers of textiles or metalwork, grew by 40 percent between 1821 and 1831 alone. Britain's industrialization revolutionized where many people lived by drawing work increasingly into the big-city context (and of course by making agriculture more efficient, thus less labor-intensive). During this period the majority of British families changed their residence and much of their framework of daily life as they shifted from reliance on agriculture to involvement with industry.

Industrialization Exacts a Price

The industrial revolution, even in its early phases, prompted major changes in business scale. Many operations started small; because initial textile machinery, in particular, was not costly, many small-scale innovations could draw on a wide array of available business talent. But there was obvious challenge. Traditional textile equipment for a home manufacturing operation cost a fraction of what was required to set up an early factory: By the 1780s British textile mills were valued at £3,000–4,000, many times the £25 cost of a good hand loom. The first multistoried factory powered by steam, established in 1788, was valued at £13,000; its steam engine alone, large for the time at thirty horsepower, cost £1,500. Plants for metallurgy and mining operations were more expensive still.

Businesses did not immediately have to adopt radically new methods of capital formation and management systems, but the pressure to innovate was quite real. Many firms were established as partnerships because necessary capital was unavailable otherwise. Many factories, launched under the eye of an ever-present owner, had to generate a small bureaucracy when it became clear that directing the labor force, providing necessary technical expertise, arranging for purchase of raw materials, and selling the goods simply escaped the capacity of any one individual. Borrowing arrangements became steadily more elaborate, although abundant capital kept interest rates fairly low in early British industry. Family firms had to branch out to hire outsiders to participate in more specialized management structures. And while massive profits were possible—Robert Owen's achievement was replicated in a host of cases as a new class of wealthy factory owners began to emerge in the 1820s—the possibility of failure was very real as well. Sales recessions were frequent, particularly in industries like cotton that depended on exports. Poor harvests reduced income at home and cut deeply into industrial sales. Significant economic crises occurred at least once a decade; a particularly severe recession followed the end of the Napoleonic Wars in 1815. Workers suffered most in these catastrophes as unemployment soared, but many manufacturers collapsed financially as well.

The early industrial revolution in Britain was built on the backs of cheap labor driven mercilessly hard. The standard of living fell for many workers in rural regions, who were pressed both by population growth and by competition from machine-made goods that cut into branches of domestic manufacturing. Many rural women, for example, lost their manufacturing income when spinning was mechanized. With less land available for small farmers, less supplementary employment, and competitive pressure on agricultural wages, stark misery spread in many agricultural districts. While hand weavers enjoyed some real prosperity before 1800, when thread production soared but mechanized weaving had yet to take hold, their pay began to plummet thereafter. By 1811 wages were down one-third from their 1800 levels, and by 1832, when hand weaving in cotton was dying out in Britain, they had fallen by a full 60 percent. Industrialization was not fully to blame for this collapse—population pressure and displacement of small farmers by aristocratic landlords played a role—but there can be no doubt of the massive hardships involved. Further, although the worst misery was centered in areas remote from the factories, the widespread deterioration also cut into the standard of living of industrial workers, who faced a growing amount of potential competition for jobs.

In the factories proper, however, wages in some sectors held up somewhat better, for new workers had to be drawn in. Mining wages, for example, seemingly improved in Britain's early industrial revolution. Skilled workers, needed to set up and maintain the new machines, also did well, often winning long-term contracts and other benefits. On the other hand, many employers, desperate for workers but desperate also to keep costs down to protect their expensive investments and allay their fears of business failure, looked for labor shortcuts. This was the inspiration for hiring groups of orphans from London and other large towns, who were shipped in droves to the factory centers in return for employer provision of food and barracks housing. Extensive use of child and female labor was not in itself novel—families had always depended on work from all its members to survive—but use of children and young women specifically because of the low wages they could command reflected the pressures of early industrial life and unquestionably constrained the nascent working class in the factories. To be sure, factory-produced goods such as clothing and utensils fell in price; but there were drawbacks too: Urban housing often was costlier than the preindustrial rural counterpart, and food costs fluctuated. Historians of Britain's industrial revolution have debated the standard-of-living question for many decades without definitively agreeing about whether conditions grew worse or better. Certainly there was variety, and factory workers were not the worst-paid group in the British population. Certainly also, however, particularly before about 1819, there was widespread suffering in the factory cities, where few workers were able to afford much above a bare subsistence even as more of their employers grew fat from the fruits of the new industry.

Other pressures added to the burdens on the new factory workers. No regular provision for illness or old age cushioned industrial life, and factory workers, unlike many small farmers, had no plot of land to fall back on for at least a modest food supply if their strength began to fail. The frequent economic slumps often caused unemployment rates, even for skilled workers, to soar as high as 60 percent for several months or even a year, and food prices often went up in these periods. Not surprisingly, many workers, even those capable of improving their earnings, found industrial life extremely unpredictable, even nerve-wracking, and in the worst slumps, death rates rose in the factory centers. Furthermore, and again even for workers whose pay might have increased modestly, the industrial revolution cut into leisure time. The labor force was prodded to work harder than its preindustrial counterpart, and work hours inched up as employers sought to maximize use of the expensive machinery. Some textile factories drove their workers sixteen hours a day, Saturdays included. Traditional festival days, when rural workers had taken time off, came under attack as the new factories fined workers for unauthorized absences. Finally, factory jobs exposed many workers to new physical dangers: dust from textile fibers, accidents in the coal mines, and maimings from the fast-moving—usually unprotected—machinery.

The early industrial revolution depended on the need that growing numbers of workers had for jobs in order simply to survive. Necessity, not attraction, lay at the root of the formation of Britain's new factory labor force. Relatively low pay—declining pay in some circumstances—helped subsidize the investment in new machinery and supported the gains that motivated successful entrepreneurs, and increased work time contributed to growing output along with the machines themselves. And while the misery was worst in the early decades of industrialization—real wages and urban health conditions began to improve in the 1820s or at least in the 1830s—and while debate continues about exactly how bad things were, there is no doubt that desperately hard work and scant reward constituted key ingredients in the early industrialization process in Britain.

Not surprisingly, conditions of early manufacturing generated serious protest among many British workers, though labor organization was illegal and poverty limited the resources available for protracted struggle. Many workers struck or rioted against cuts in pay or high food costs. Beyond these specific efforts, a number of factory hands articulated a larger sense of the exploitation to which they were in their judgment subject and about the gap that had opened between them and the factory masters. A Manchester cotton spinner in 1818 condemned his employers for their "ostentatious display of elegant mansions, equipages, liveries, parks, hunters and hounds ... they are literally petty monarchs, absolute and despotic, in their own particular districts; and to support all this, their whole time is occupied in contriving how to get the greatest quantity of work turned off with the least expense." The spinner also excoriated the "terrible machines" that had so worsened the quality of work as compared with preindustrial life. Some workers did far more than talk. In a series of riots between 1810 and 1820 hand workers attacked and destroyed the textile equipment that threatened their jobs or at least their accustomed wages. These Luddite workers claimed inspiration from a mythical leader, Ned Ludd, whose office was supposedly in Sherwood Forest, and they pointed to a world of work in which skills would be valued, workers treated as equal producers rather than factory "hands," and machines outlawed. Their efforts failed, as did more ambitious unionization attempts in textiles and mining during the 1820s and early 1830s. But the resentment of the new working class that the factories had assembled could scarcely be denied. The industrial revolution created a new division between the directors of manufacturing, the owners, and the workers they sought to control. To many observers, this was one of the essential and deeply troubling features of the wider industrial revolution. A middle-class traveler to Manchester in 1842, W. Cooke Taylor, put it this way in a published travel account:

> As a stranger passes through the masses of human beings which have accumulated round the mills and print works ... he cannot contemplate these "crowded hives" without feelings of anxiety and apprehensions almost amounting to dismay. The population, like the system to which it belongs, is NEW; but it is hourly increasing in breadth and strength. It is an aggregate of masses, our conceptions of which clothe themselves in terms that express something portentous and fearful ... as of the slow rising and gradual swelling of an ocean which must, at some future and not distant time, bear all the elements of society aloft upon its bosom, and float them Heaven knows whither. There are mighty energies slumbering in these masses. ... The manufacturing population is not new in its formation alone; it is new in its habits of thought and action, which have been formed by the circumstances of its condition, with little instruction, and less guidance, from external sources.

Change Generates Change

By the 1820s, then, Britain's industrial revolution had introduced new technologies in cotton and other textiles, in pottery and metallurgy, and in aspects of coal mining. It had generated an unparalleled export surge that brought Britain's achievement home to peoples almost around the world. It had destroyed several traditional manufacturing sectors at home and abroad. It had introduced factory organization to many branches of production and had prompted a massive growth in British cities. It had created a dynamic new business class and an even more novel as well as more numerous working class. Even in a society already heavily commercial, with an important manufacturing sector, it had fundamentally altered the framework of social and economic life.

And the revolution would not stop. Innovations were not constant, but they recurred. Existing machines became more refined; the number of spindles on a cotton-spinning machine, for example, increased periodically, which greatly heightened production per worker. The number of workers in major industries grew inexorably. So did the average size of factories and firms, which permitted greater specialization of labor and more bureaucratic management. These developments brought innovation in business practices and labor conditions beyond what the initial industrial revolution had required. A measure of the persistent change was output: In 1830 Britain produced about 24 million tons of coal, four-fifths of the world's total; by 1870 the figure was 110 million, still half of all the coal mined around the world. British pig iron production was 700,000 tons in 1830; thirty years later it had more than quintupled, to almost 4 million tons. Raw cotton imports rose sixfold in the twenty years after 1830; in this period also, average productivity per worker doubled. All this meant steadily rising exports. By 1870 British exports exceeded those of France, Germany, and Italy combined, and they were three times the level of exports from the United States. Rising output boosted industrial profits, which provided additional capital for still further changes, and began to permit some definite if modest improvements in the standard of living of most workers even as income inequality continued to increase.

The ongoing industrial revolution in Britain involved more than expansion from an earlier base. It also meant radical new directions. A new breakthrough in metallurgy in 1856 brought changes greater in many ways than those previously created by use of coke and coal. Henry Bessemer (along with inventors in other countries) worked on the problem of removing chemical impurities, in particular carbon, from raw iron (called pig iron). The conventional procedure demanded extremely labor-intensive operations, as highly skilled workers called puddlers stirred molten ore to remove the carbon. After repeated experimentation, Bessemer found that altered furnace design could accomplish the same results automatically; a blast of compressed air passed through the molten iron would extract the carbon. Not only were labor costs reduced, but the Bessemer converter made possible the construction of much larger blast furnaces, another huge productivity gain. Finally, the same procedures enabled industry to use the controlled reintroduction of carbon to make steel, a much tougher metal than iron but previously extremely expensive to manufacture. An industry already transformed was transformed anew, in a pattern that would be repeated often as the industrial revolution proceeded.

The most dramatic extension of industrialization in Britain after the initial decades occurred in the field of transportation. As output grew, pressure on transportation facilities inevitably increased: Goods had to be carried to market, raw materials to the places of manufacture. Improved roads and, especially, the spate of canal building helped, but inventors—aware from prior industrial experience that concerted experiments could produce dramatic results—looked for more genuine innovation. Initiatives with rail transport had already begun in the coal mines; the first steam engine for hauling coal out on tracks was introduced in 1804. In 1821 a group of inventors and entrepreneurs chartered a railway line between Darlington, a mining center, and the port of Stockton. Some of the wagons were pulled on rails by horses, but locomotives were also developed, under the guidance of George Stephenson. The first full-scale locomotive was unveiled in 1825, but its frequent breakdowns almost resulted in cancellation of any further experiments. An improved model featuring a larger boiler that could produce greater heat was tested in 1827 and put to regular use just a few months later. With this success established, a more ambitious rail line was opened in 1829 between the cotton port of Liverpool and the great factory center in Manchester. A contest was set up for locomotive design, and one model attained a speed of twenty-eight miles per hour—an achievement marred, however, by a breakdown before the test was completed. More reliable models operated at about sixteen miles per hour, but this was sufficient to launch a spate of railway building in Britain and, soon, elsewhere.

Developed at about the same time were steam-driven ships (the first transatlantic steamship lines opened in 1838), and these and railroads plus faster communication via the newly invented telegraph truly revolutionized the conveyance of goods, people, and information. More bulk could be transported over longer distances at greater speed than ever before. This result of industrialization also generated additional change. Labor recruitment could reach out more widely. Coal and iron (soon steel) production had to expand simply to meet the demand generated by railroad construction and operation. The industrial revolution was beginning to feed itself, sprouting new branches to deal with opportunities presented by prior developments. This same acceleration inevitably attracted attention elsewhere to the wonders of Britain's achievement. A growing number of countries judged the power of Britain's transformation not only in economic but also in military terms, and this dual interest was yet another spur to the ongoing momentum of the revolution.

2

New Causes: Why Did the Industrial Revolution Happen, and Why Did It Happen in Eighteenth-Century Britain?

EXPLAINING the industrial revolution is a challenge to analysts of history. Identifying the factors that caused the industrial revolution is a complex task because no one development stands out. The task is vital not simply as a historical exercise but as the basis for understanding the complexity of the challenges awaiting societies that tried to establish an industrial revolution even after Britain showed the way. The variety of developments that combined to create the first industrial revolution had somehow to be replicated, though not necessarily in identical fashion. This same daunting variety helps explain why a number of regions have not managed to launch full-scale industrialization to this day. Complex causes persist as a factor in world affairs.

Not surprisingly, historians have offered different emphases. Occasionally, industrialization is presented as flowing from a few dramatic inventions and from some new thinking about the economy, notably Adam Smith's market-oriented theories issued in 1776 that stressed the importance of vigorous economic competition free from government controls as a means of generating innovation and growing prosperity. Inventions of course were involved—but why did they occur? And why did Britain produce more inventions than other countries (followed, in the formative decades of industrialization, by France and the United States)? New economic theories helped produce some policies favorable to industrialization, but these did not cause it; they came too late, and they affected too few people. Any explanation of the industrial revolution must account for new behaviors on the part of literally thousands of people: entrepreneurs who gradually moved toward a factory system, workers who staffed the factories, investors who provided capital, consumers who eagerly accepted the machine-made products. A number of powerful factors had to combine to generate a change as substantial as even the early phases of industrialization.

For the industrial revolution to occur, considerable investment funds were required—the new machines were expensive, far costlier than any manufacturing equipment previously devised, even in the very small factories that characterized much early industry. Also needed was access to raw materials, including textile fibers but particularly coal and iron, the sinews of the industrial revolution. Government interest in supporting economic innovation was a factor, though various kinds of specific government policies could do the job. Of major importance was an available labor force that did not have more agreeable employment options, for while some workers might be attracted to the industrial life because of high pay for their particular skills, the excitement of innovation, and greater independence from traditional family and community controls, most workers entered factories because they had little choice. Finally, industrialization, particularly in its first manifestation in Britain, required an aggressive, risk-taking entrepreneurial spirit that would drive businesses to venture into innovation. All these ingredients must be considered in dealing with the causes of the industrial revolution. To be sure, recent reminders of how gradual the process was—how factory firms developed often as part of a very slow, multigenerational evolution from domestic manufacturing operations to a new willingness to organize and subordinate manufacturing labor—affect analysis. The industrial revolution need not be explained as a dramatic single eruption or a rapid, coordinated set of changes; early steps in industrialization help account for later ones, as the revolution rippled out from the minority of the population initially involved. Still, the challenge of explaining the process remains considerable.

Several basic factors were generally widespread in northwestern Europe by the eighteenth century; others were more particular to Britain. A large seam of coal ran from Britain through Belgium and northern France to the Ruhr valley in Germany, and the most intense early industrialization developed along this coal seam. Iron ore deposits also existed in western Europe, in some cases close to the coal sources. Without these raw materials—and especially coal as the energy source for smelting metal and powering the steam engine—early industrialization would have been impossible. Western Europe also had abundant wool and, through already established colonial trade, initial access to cotton (grown in the southern colonies of British North America and in parts of Asia).

The key resources that had of course been sitting in the ground for many millennia facilitated the industrial revolution by their presence, but they did not cause it. Far more important was the impact of the scientific revolution in western Europe during the seventeenth century. Few scientific discoveries directly affected early industrial technology, though the work on gases and chemicals was relevant; the fuller marriage of science and industry occurred only after the 1830s, when the industrial revolution was already well advanced. Science did, however, help persuade people that nature could be rationally understood and controlled. It promoted an outlook attuned to change and generated widespread new interest in technical experiments. Definitions of science, from the pens of such experimenters as Francis Bacon in England, had urged its potential application to material conditions. It was no accident, then, that a vast refocusing of Europe's intellectual orientation preceded the industrial revolution itself.

Europe's commercialization also helped set the context for the industrial revolution. Many Europeans were familiar with production for the market or were accustomed to buying some of the goods they needed rather than manufacturing every subsistence item locally. Habits of this sort were obviously essential to the industrial revolution, during which they were greatly extended. As with the scientific revolution, the expansion of commercial activities in seventeenth century formed a vital precondition for industrialization. Through the domestic manufacturing system, direct links followed from commercial endeavors more generally. Further, during the eighteenth century Europe's increasing commercial system generated important changes in banking. National banking systems were established in England and several other countries, which facilitated nationwide marketing and thus expanded the opportunities for manufacturing and sales.

Commercial experience as a factor should not be overly stressed, however. Even in business-minded Great Britain, the new banks rarely lent money to industrial firms; they focused on merchant and real estate operations. Nor did many established merchants become involved in the early factories. Factories were regarded as risky and dirty, and respectable people, even in the business community, kept some distance. Early industrialists most commonly came from artisanal or manufacturing backgrounds, though the collaboration of individual merchants and landlords, particularly in the expensive operations of metallurgy, was vital. Commercial experience and commercial institutions prepared the industrial revolution, but some gaps remained to be filled before striving industrialists linked up with existing commercial operations.

Another vital ingredient of Europe's industrial context—this one also taking shape before the industrial revolution but gaining ground steadily immediately before its advent—involved Europe's growing role in world trade. From the late fifteenth century onward, west European countries, ultimately headed by France, the Netherlands, and Britain, had won increasing control over international commerce. European ships and merchant companies dominated international trade, even in some cases in which exchange did not directly involve Europe at all. Increasingly, a hierarchy emerged in the international economy in which Europeans acquired minerals and agricultural goods from other areas (including their colonies in the Americas, India, and elsewhere) and in return sold manufactured products, including fine furniture, cloth, and metal goods such as guns. Because Europeans could price their goods to include the cost of processing, they were in general able to profit from the exchange. Not all parts of the world actively engaged in trade with western Europe at this point, but parts of eastern Europe (which sent grain, furs, and timber supplies), the Americas (precious metals, sugar, and tobacco), and India and Southeast Asia (spices, tea, and gold) added steadily to western Europe's wealth. The active slave trade that Europeans ran between Africa and the Americas was another source of profit.

Europe's role in preindustrial world trade set up the industrial revolution in several ways. Growing amounts of commercial experience developed through the trading companies, and new technologies relating to shipbuilding and warfare received impetus. Governments were encouraged to pay attention to the importance of fostering trade, though this at times also led to heavy-handed efforts at control. Trade leadership helped stimulate a taste for new products. Growing interest in cotton cloth originated first from trade with India, particularly in Britain. The British government then sought (from the 1730s onward) to encourage cotton manufacturing at home and to prevent undesirable dependence on foreign manufacturing by banning cotton imports, which had the additional effect of reducing India's economic vitality and opening this area to British goods. At the same time, Britain used its holdings in India and particularly the southern colonies in North America to provide raw cotton for its new textile branch. Above all, foreign trade, including colonial trade, expanded the markets for European manufacturing and thus contributed directly to one of the obvious reasons to seek more productive technologies. Trade also provided capital through the growing wealth of many business and landowning groups. Thus, Europe's industrial revolution, which was to have such dramatic effects on the wider world, stemmed in great part from Europe's ability to draw disproportionately on world resources.

Population and Capital as Triggers for Industrialization

The several changes in European society and economy, combined with the availability of underground mineral resources, provided most of the specific ingredients needed for an industrial revolution. These preindustrial changes already were accelerating by the early eighteenth century when the population explosion developed in western Europe and added the final general factor.

Rapid population growth resulted from new food supplies and other developments such as a temporary lull in major plagues. There was also a pause in the most devastating kinds of warfare between 1715 and 1792. Increased population pushed workers to seek new, even unpleasant, kinds of jobs, provided growing markets for inexpensive manufactured goods, and prodded even some prosperous families to seek economic innovation. An eastern French family, the Schlumbergers, was a case in point. In the 1760s the head of the family ran an artisan shop, producing cloth but displaying no particular business dynamism. He had twelve children; that all of them lived to adulthood was somewhat unusual but illustrative of the impact of population growth in a single-family context. Simply in order to provide for his brood in the accustomed respectable middle-class fashion, Schlumberger had to expand his textile operations, hiring domestic manufacturing workers and then tentatively introducing some powered equipment. His children, building on their father's example, became dynamic industrialists in the early nineteenth century, creating large textile and machine-building factories and sponsoring the first local rail line. Population upheaval promoted economic dynamism in a number of ways and at various levels of the initial industrialization process in western Europe.

Industrial revolutions require capital. This was not easy to find in western Europe—many sectors of established wealth shied away from the risk and grubbiness of the factory system—but capital resources had expanded steadily on the strength of growing internal and especially international trade. New technology rested on the more gradual prior improvements in European manufacturing techniques before 1700 and on the spread of scientific ideas and the new confidence in mastering the forces of nature. Necessary labor derived from the growing manufacturing force in crafts and domestic manufacturing, which provided relevant basic skills as well as sheer numbers, and then from the population surge. Once factory industry began, furthermore, it increased the number of workers seeking urban jobs by rendering many sectors of domestic manufacturing obsolete. An entrepreneurial spirit, evidenced as an interest in innovation and organizational expansion, resulted from prior growth in the business class, from the challenge of population increase in certain favorably positioned families, and from the increasing cultural emphasis on science, material progress, and control over the environment. None of this assured easy industrialization, but the combination overall was powerful—as it had to be to launch the first industrial revolution the world had ever experienced.

Britain as a Special Case

Finally, why was Britain, among the several areas of western Europe in which relevant changes had been taking shape, in the vanguard? Within the larger west European context, there were several special features in Britain. Population growth was extremely rapid in the eighteenth century. Its effects, in terms of freeing up available labor, were magnified by major changes in agriculture. British landlords successfully pried land away from smallholding farmers through the government's Enclosure Acts. These required farmers to enclose their fields, usually by planting hedges, but the expense was beyond many small farmers, who had to sell out to the landlords. British agriculture became dominated by large estates, and while these employed many workers, they did not absorb a growing population as readily as peasant-dominated agriculture proved able to do elsewhere. Thus there were hungry workers eager for new options. The enclosed estates, in turn, increased market production, providing food for growing cities.

British artisans were also unusual. Most urban artisans in western Europe belonged to guilds, which tried to protect members' working conditions by limiting new technology and preventing any employer from creating undue inequality or threatening wage rates by hiring too many workers. Guilds were ideal for a relatively stable economy, but they definitely inhibited both rapid labor mobility and changing techniques. Britain had once boasted a guild system, but it had virtually disappeared by the eighteenth century. The result was twofold: Employers had unusual freedom to bring new workers into established branches of production, and were at liberty to tinker with new methods—perhaps the most important single source of Britain's lead in inventions.

Britain's extensive international trade provided capital and markets and also supplies of vital materials such as cotton. The British aristocracy was more favorable to commerce than its counterparts on the European continents; some British landlords directly participated in setting up new mines and manufacturing, and tolerance for commercial development was high. The British government favored economic change. Tariff regulations in the eighteenth century, such as the barriers to the importation of cotton cloth from India, spurred new industries. Other laws that discouraged the export of new machinery or designs impeded rapid imitation elsewhere of British gains. Laws made the formation of new companies relatively easy and officially banned combinations of workers—what we would call unions—which in turn constrained protest. During the eighteenth century a number of local governments began to build better roads, and then a wave of canal building developed at the end of the century. The new infrastructure facilitated the movement of both raw materials and finished goods. At the same time, the British government did not attempt to regulate manufacturing extensively. Other European governments, though often eager to promote economic growth, tended to control manufacturing with regulations about product quality, techniques, and some working conditions. The British state was less interventionist. This was not always an advantage, as we shall see in other industrialization cases, but it perhaps served well in setting a favorable framework for the first industrial revolution.

Simple luck in terms of natural resources also aided Britain. It had excellent holdings in coal and iron, which were often located quite close together. The island nation had not only coastal waterways but good navigable rivers, which further facilitated the transport of the two materials so vital to early industrialization but extremely heavy and costly to move over land. Britain was also running low on timber supplies by the early eighteenth century, which encouraged the search for alternative fuels, notably coal. This in turn spurred industrial development, from the adaptation of the initial steam engine for mine pumping to the use of coal for smelting iron.

In the 1800s England's industries expanded and improved, causing towns such as Sheffield, located in northern England, to grow in population and importance. Sheffield factories produced high-quality steel, silver-plated items, and other metal goods. (Courtesy of the Mansell Collection Limited. Reprinted by permission.)

Finally, Britain apparently provided an optimal setting for producing individuals inclined to taking risks in business. Good market opportunities and an extensive preindustrial manufacturing system formed part of this framework. New ideas about science and material progress spread more rapidly in Britain than in most other European countries. A relatively small government meant limited chances for success by seeking bureaucratic jobs. Furthermore, Britain tolerated a number of Protestant religious minorities such as the Quakers, though this indulgence was incomplete: Protestants who were not members of the established Anglican church could not attend universities or gain government employment. This ambivalent situation encouraged members of these minorities, eager to demonstrate God's favor, to seek opportunities in business. Certainly the Protestant minorities produced a disproportionate number of early manufacturers, who were stimulated by a belief that disciplined work, frugality, and economic drive were pleasing in the sight of God and who were eager to get ahead where the chances lay—through entrepreneurial initiative.

In sum, Britain concentrated many of the changes developing generally in western Europe and added an array of special factors ranging from flukes of nature to new forms of callous manipulation of agricultural labor. Quite possibly the more general shifts taking place throughout Europe would have generated an industrial revolution elsewhere by the early nineteenth century; the uniqueness of the British combination should not be exaggerated. Nevertheless, the fact was that Britain came first and that its leadership can be explained.

For at least a half century the nation's effective monopoly over the industrial revolution was scarcely challenged. British industry enabled the country to hold up against the much larger population of France during the wars of the French Revolution and the Napoleonic era. By the 1830s Britain's industrial lead was so obvious, and its related need and ability to export cheap machine-made manufactured goods were so great, that the government changed its basic tariff policy. Britain became a pioneer in free trade, allowing imports of food and raw materials that helped keep prices (and wages) down while relying on manufacturing exports to balance the trade exchange and even to show a tidy national profit.

Britain was indeed pouring manufactured goods into the markets of the world. Machine-made textiles cut into customary production not only in Latin America but also in Germany. British iron products undersold traditional charcoal-smelted metal in France. Here, obviously, was a rude challenge. But here also was an opportunity. Britain's success in industrialization added another ingredient to the changes taking place in western Europe. Continental businesses and governments began to wake up to the possibility of copying British machine design and factory organization, realizing they must stir themselves lest they be engulfed in a British industrial tide. The industrial revolution began to spread.

3

The Industrial Revolution in Western Society

 AM HERE in the centre of the most advanced industry of Europe and of the Universe." So wrote the young French textile entrepreneur Motte Bossut during a visit to England in 1842. He was not exaggerating. A few years later, in 1851, when Britain celebrated its industrial might in the Great Exhibition at Crystal Palace, it had no peer in any of the principal phases of mechanical production. Several European countries were superior in textile design and the United States led in a few minor categories such as machine stitching. But the British lead in textiles, metallurgy, mining, and machine building seemed insurmountable.

Britain's industrial superiority inevitably affected the next phase of industrialization: A list of causes of all the industrial revolutions launched between 1820 and 1870 has to include both the example of Britain and the international activities of British businesses. The countries that first imitated Britain did so not only because they shared many of the same features that had produced the British surge but also because they were geographically close (or in the case of the United States, historically and culturally close) to the industrial island. French textile factories surged in the north, which abutted the English Channel, and in Alsace, where the leading industrialists were Protestant and therefore shared contacts with England.

The industrial rise of Britain spurred west European and American businesses. There were profits to be made and industries to defend lest British exports overwhelm the entire manufacturing base. Foreign governments had to take an interest as well. British economic might during the Napoleonic Wars demonstrated the relevance of industrialization to power politics. Gains in metallurgy and machine building had direct links to armaments. The obvious potential of the railroad moved government officials interested in better political and military contacts who otherwise would have preferred to keep society immune from the upheavals of economic change. Britain's success, in sum, was an active cause of the subsequent round of industrialization in societies having many of the same commercial, scientific, and social features that had spurred the British. Foreigners began to flock to Britain to learn, and British entrepreneurs and workers began to set up operations abroad.

There were three principal stages in the wider Western effort to copy Britain's mechanical advances. Before 1789 European governments sent over a few observers to learn about British technology. The French in 1764 dispatched a scientist to study British metallurgy, and on his return he used the new methods to develop one of France's great iron manufacturing firms, the de Wendel company. The French government also paid a British metallurgist to set up a cannon foundry. Various German and Swiss states sent students also, and some of them brought back new textile equipment. Such transfers of technology were unusual, however, partly because British law forbade the export of new technology or the emigration of skilled workers.

Then the French Revolution exploded in 1789, and its turmoil and the ensuing European war interrupted major developments for over two decades. Yet the revolution also introduced important new legislation that (though the drafters largely did not so intend) helped pave the way for industrialization in Western Europe. In France and also neighboring territory like Belgium and western Germany, guilds were abolished, which removed restrictions on the movement of labor and technical innovation. Western Europe in this way became more like Britain. Internal trade barriers were removed in countries like France, and commercial law was regularized. Other laws prohibited combinations of workers—these too emulated the British lead and inhibited labor protest against change. Although those who launched the French Revolution did not intend to promote industrialization (and the ensuing disorder actually delayed it), the new laws and a general enhancement of the power of the middle classes, along with Britain's display of industrial success during the battles with Napoleon, completed the causation for western Europe's economic transformation.

When war ended in 1815, Europeans intensified their study of British ways, seeking to circumvent British laws prohibiting technology transfer. In 1819 the Prussian government sent a locksmith to study British machine building, and he returned to form a major plant in Berlin. The French and Dutch governments bribed British entrepreneurs to set up modern metallurgical factories directly; the French steel industry took shape under James Jackson as a result, and it was a Jackson grandson who in 1861 set up the first Bessemer converter in France. Belgian businessmen smuggled British machinery out of the country in rowboats and in a few cases literally kidnapped skilled British workers. Francis Cabot Lowell, an American, visited Britain in 1810–1812 and two years later established the first power looms in the United States and the first major textile plant that combined mechanical spinning and weaving. French and Swiss metallurgists visited frequently. Alfred Krupp, a German, made his study trip in 1838, by which time

Germans and others were also studying British railroads and mining engineering. The Belgian government directly hired George Stephenson to set up railroads there, and all the European states, plus the United States, imported British locomotives.

European and American businesses also hired British workers. By 1830 there were at least 15,000 British workers in France, serving mainly as skilled technical personnel in textile and metallurgical plants. Employers offered huge bonuses and wages sometimes double the local rate to induce the vital British workers to emigrate. The results were not always happy, for some of the British workers involved were inferior types. A Swiss engineer complained:

> Not only do they cost a damned lot of money, but they are often drunkards. English workers who are both efficient and well behaved can earn a very good living at home. … British workers seldom fulfill the sanguine expectations of their foreign employers because they are handling materials to which they are not accustomed and because they are working with different people than they would be at home.

Needless to say, most European industrialists trained a local labor force as quickly as possible. Nevertheless, the British ingredient was often central to the process. French metallurgists, for example, found that it took at least a decade to teach French workers some of the necessary skills, mainly because their rural background did not generate the requisite motivation. British workers, accustomed to industry, were also attuned to the idea of innovating in return for making more money, an outlook that did not immediately arise elsewhere.

Also important was the direct emigration of British industrialists. Samuel Slater, an apprentice in one of the Arkwright textile plants, emigrated to the United States in 1789 under the sponsorship of a Rhode Island merchant; he soon established the first textile factory in the country. The first Swiss cotton factory was set up by two Britons, and another Englishman, along with a few imported British skilled workers who taught mechanical weaving, revolutionized Dutch cotton production after 1830. No English family did more for European industrialization than the Cockerill clan in Belgium. William Cockerill brought modern textile machinery to France in the 1790s—Napoleon made him a citizen in 1810, which allowed him to continue operations. A Cockerill machine-building plants in Liège employed 2,000 workers by 1812. By the 1830s the Cockerill operation included the largest integrated metallurgical and machine factory in the world, its owner boasting that "I have all the new inventions over [at Liège] ten days after they come out of England." Mining, shipbuilding, and railroad development fanned the Cockerill empire, which also expanded into Germany. A Belgian observer noted that the Cockerills saw "a mission to extend manufactures everywhere and to fill the whole world with machinery"—profit possibilities and a genuine missionary zeal made a heady combination.

The British role in stimulating wider industrialization was particularly crucial into the 1840s. Individual Britons continued to contribute thereafter, but by this point the industrial revolution was firmly anchored in Belgium, France, the United States, and Germany and was developing deep native roots. British industrial adventurers began to work farther afield, in Russia and Austria for example, where full industrial revolutions were yet to emerge.

Even the British role before the 1840s should not be exaggerated, for it obviously combined with the emergence of new business interests in western Europe and the United States and with shifts in government policy. Furthermore, imitation was never precise. Each subsequent industrial revolution had its own flavor, sharing many features with the British process because of the intrinsic nature of industrialization as well as emulation but also responding to local constraints and opportunities. The sheer difference in timing was a factor as well. The British industrial lead forced some later industrial revolutions to develop different emphases. Textiles, for example, played a less prominent role in German industrialization partly because British imports had made major inroads before the German process gathered momentum. This was one reason Germany's industrial revolution stressed heavy industry from the first. In addition, the possibility of imitating Britain meant that many west Europeans and Americans required less time for experimentation; they could begin with more sophisticated and productive machinery from the start. Thus, the next round of industrial revolutions did not impose quite so much new misery on the labor force as had been forthcoming in early British industrialization. French or German industrial workers were not well paid, and wages had been traditionally lower in these countries in any event, but the intense deprivation of the British industrial slums and the reliance on virtual slave gangs of children were largely avoided.

In addition to coal-rich Belgium's rapid transformation, three follow-up industrial revolutions in Western society were particularly important. France, Germany, and the United States joined the industrial parade between 1820 and 1840, and each displayed distinctive features in the process. In combination, their industrial revolutions essentially completed the industrialization of the Western world by the 1870s, increasing the worldwide impact of the industrial revolution while cutting into Britain's preeminence. By then all three countries, though in particular Germany and the United States, were also spearheading further transformations of the industrial economy that extended the process of technological and especially organizational change well beyond Britain's first stages.

France: An Eclectic Course

France, western Europe's richest and most populous country in the eighteenth century, faced several drawbacks in attempting to imitate the British achievement. Recurrent revolutions into the 1870s were not helpful to the business climate and perhaps even encouraged several French governments to be somewhat more protective of traditional economic groups than were their counterparts elsewhere.

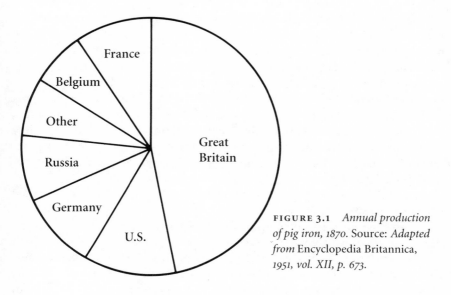

FIGURE 3.1 *Annual production of pig iron, 1870.* Source: *Adapted from* Encyclopedia Britannica, *1951, vol. XII, p. 673.*

Certainly the French were fiercely protectionist in their tariffs against foreign (notably British) goods, a move favoring inefficient, old-fashioned textile and metallurgy firms that would otherwise have perished. But most countries seeking to emulate the British had a long protectionist phase to help safeguard their manufacturing, so the French tactic probably was not decisive. Far more important were deficiencies in natural resources. The French simply did not have the large coal reserves of Britain, Germany, or the United States. By 1848 they were in fact exploiting a higher percentage of their reserves than any other country, but they could not keep up. To do so they needed to import coal, which resulted in higher costs, particularly in metallurgy. France's ability to compete in heavy industry was further weakened after its war loss to Germany in 1871, when it surrendered most of its iron-rich province of Lorraine. Finally, French population growth, though substantial, was lower than that of most other Western nations, which meant less spur for workers to flock into factory centers. French factory cities grew but far less than their counterparts elsewhere, and difficulties in recruiting labor—workers were able to indulge a preference to remain in the countryside—played a substantial role.

Because of these limitations, French industrialization was less impressive than that of several other countries, and the nation's relative economic strength declined as a result. There was a real industrial revolution nevertheless. About 20 percent of all manufacturing workers were employed in factory industry or coal mines by 1850. Cotton and wool production was substantially mechanized, and several new metallurgical centers featuring large factories and advanced techniques had developed. The French introduced a number of important inventions, including a mechanical loom for fine cloth, the Jacquard, that helped spread mechanization in textiles and ultimately helped inspire twentieth-century advances in circuit-board technology. French output began to expand rapidly. Coal production rose thirteenfold between 1820 and 1870, while iron production sextupled. The pace of French industrialization increased after 1842 when the national government agreed on a railroad system and sponsored its rapid development. Unlike in Britain, where most railway initiative lay in private hands and the government provided only its right of eminent domain to aid in property acquisition, the French government built the rail systems, then turned over most of the lines to private companies on ninety-nine year leases; the companies provided the rolling stock. France's national system was completed in the 1860s, and an active program of local development went forward thereafter, boosting French heavy industry in particular and making a major contribution to the transportation needed for industrialization more generally.

The French industrialization process featured some relative lags and a greater degree of government involvement than the British model. It also emphasized concurrent transformation of craft production. France had a well-established craft tradition, with export markets in such goods as fine furniture and silk cloth. Because of some limits on industrialization in other areas and as a means of circumventing British competition, many French manufacturers worked to expand craft output without totally revolutionizing the technology. Furniture makers, for example, began to standardize design and production, which allowed workers to be trained more quickly and increased their output. They still worked in small shops with largely manual techniques, but they were almost mass-producing tables, cabinets, and other items that could be sold to middle-class households not only in France but abroad. The workers involved keenly sensed and resented the changes, lamenting a faster pace of work and a decline of creative artistry.

Through the rise of factory industry and the emphasis on substantial transformations within the craft system, France increased its annual per capita economic growth almost as rapidly as Britain in its industrial revolution period. Indeed, France pioneered in one of the obvious outcomes of the industrial revolution: a major innovation in distribution systems. More goods to sell and a growing urban market meant traditional small shops no longer sufficed. The first department store, aimed at high-volume sales, opened in Paris in the 1830s.

Germany: Trend to Big Business

German industrialization got under way later than the French version. Absence of tariff protection for textiles perhaps hampered early development and certainly fostered a tremendous sense of industrial inferiority. Germany was also divided into separate states and industrialized only after a customs union created a larger national market in the 1830s. Full abolition of the guilds and serfdom also came late in Germany; these institutional features reduced labor mobility into the 1840s. Finally, unlike France and the United States, Germany contributed almost no new inventions to the early industrialization process and remained highly dependent on foreign technologies into the 1870s. Simply locating adequately trained skilled workers was a problem; one manufacturer complained in the 1830s that it was impossible to find a single German worker capable of making a machine screw.

Nevertheless, coal-mining output began to expand rapidly by the 1830s, almost doubling in that decade alone. Between the 1840s and 1870 German coal production expanded sevenfold as deep mines were sunk, particularly in the rich Ruhr valley coal basin. A few coke furnaces in metallurgy were installed early, but before 1850 only 10 percent of all iron was coke-smelted. In the 1850s, however, iron production expanded at a rate of 14 percent per year. By then the German states were also actively expanding their railroad network; most of the lines were built and operated by the governments involved. In the 1870s Germany benefited from the acquisition of Alsace and Lorraine, which had strong concentrations of industrialized textiles and of metallurgy respectively. Development of new smelting processes facilitated fuller use of phosphorus-rich Lorraine ore, another boost for Germany's ascendant heavy industry. By 1913 Lorraine alone was producing 47 percent of all iron ore mined in Europe, and most of this fell to Germany's benefit.

From the 1850s onward, German industrialization displayed several distinctive features. Sheer speed was one important point. So too was the unusual concentration of heavy industry, which followed from Germany's excellent resources in coal and iron and from the fact that Germany's industrialization was the first to take shape almost exclusively after railroads, with their huge demand for coal and metal, were introduced. In addition, the German government was extensively involved in supporting industrialization; an example of this was its state-based railroad policy. Because Germany had a smaller preindustrial middle class and less capital than Britain or France, government operations helped make up the difference. State backing for investment banks, for example, promoted the accumulation of investment funds.

Germany also quickly became a center for business combination. Many small firms continued to operate in crafts and retailing, so the picture should not be overdrawn. But Germany's stress on capital-intensive heavy industry, plus state backing, provided favorable conditions for experimenting with new kinds of big companies and cartels. By the 1870s gigantic firms like Krupp dominated much of German metallurgy and mining, with branches extending from the mines through smelting and refining of metal to the production of armaments and ships. Huge capital demands in these industries encouraged German investment banks to facilitate large business combinations to help assure profits. Newer industrial sectors like chemicals and electrical equipment were quickly dominated by two or three large firms, in part because of the backing of the investment banks. Two companies, the Allgemeine Elektrizitaets Gesellschaft and Siemens, controlled over 90 percent of the German electrical industry and developed extensive branches abroad. Firms of this size not only accumulated massive capital; they were also in a position to set prices somewhat independently of market forces. Combinations of big business units also occurred in Germany. Several steel cartels formed that allocated market quotas for certain products to ensure the price held up; a coal cartel set production limits for each member for the same purpose. By the late nineteenth century there were 300 cartels in Germany, many with extensive market control and political influence. Germany was not alone in the rise of big business, but it emphasized such arrangements more than Britain or France did.

The United States: Dynamism of a New Nation

Along with the German version, American industrialization formed the great economic success story in world history between 1850 and 1900. U.S. industrial growth began in the 1820s with importation of technological systems from Britain. Although American inventors contributed significantly to the industrialization process through such achievements as the mechanical gin for removing seeds from cotton fiber and the major strides in devising the system of interchangeable parts, the United States remained dependent on European technological advances throughout the nineteenth century—British and French at first, then German and Swedish in industries like chemicals. American businesses were quick to imitate: Construction of locomotives began just a year after the first British model reached the United States. Only local lines were laid before 1830, but 3,000 miles of track were set out in the following decade, mainly in the Northeast, and major interregional lines were launched by the 1840s. As usual, the new infrastructure generated increased demand in heavy industry and facilitated other industrial operations. Extensive canal building also contributed to the burgeoning process.

Textile factories, which used water as well as steam power, formed the core of initial American factory industry, and factory towns spread across New England. But there were advances in machine building, printing, and other manufacturing sectors. The invention of the sewing machine in the 1840s initiated a transformation in clothing manufacture from handwork to faster-paced mechanized output, not only in New England but in midwestern factory centers like Cincinnati (by 1840 the nation's third largest industrial city).

In its first stage U.S. industrialization increased the amount of manufactured goods in circulation and encouraged the further development of market specialization in other areas such as agriculture, even as the bulk of the nation's economy remained nonindustrial. The process was also marked by relatively favorable labor conditions. Workers were in short supply, and recruitment required paying relatively high wages. Many women were drawn from farms into the factories in expectation of working a few years and then returning with a nest egg. Skilled male workers were also relatively well treated. Unlike their counterparts in Europe, they also had the vote, which fostered their sense of connection to the larger society. Worsening conditions in the 1830s provoked a number of labor strikes; then in the 1840s growing numbers of immigrants, Irish in particular, fed the urban labor force, and standards of living deteriorated in many factory centers.

The second stage of U.S. industrialization took off with the expansion of war industries during the Civil War. American arms manufacturers extended their operations, beginning a tradition of arms sales abroad when the domestic market shrank after 1865. Development of intercontinental rail links spurred industrial growth on another front. Railroad companies were in private hands and pioneered in a number of aspects of American big business: huge capital investments, a large labor force, and attempts to assure regional monopolies over service. As early as the 1850s American railroads began to devise appropriate forms of organization for a large company, commissioning engineers to plot out management structures and information flows. The railroad age in the United States also involved massive government support, including federal land grants that helped provide capital to the growing network.

It was in this context in the 1870s that Andrew Carnegie introduced the Bessemer process into steel manufacturing on a large scale, lowering prices substantially in the bargain. Expansion of mining fed the growing use of steam engines in manufacturing and transport. The manufacturing labor force expanded rapidly as well through the growing recruitment of immigrant workers from southern and eastern Europe and, for a time on the West Coast, from Asia. Average factory size increased: By 1900 over 1,000 American factories employed between 500 and 1,000 workers, and 450 more had over 1,000. Not only heavy industry but also textiles experienced this growth in factory size.

U.S. industrialization obviously displayed much the same surge toward big business that characterized Germany in these decades. Investment banks helped coordinate the growth of multifaceted companies. As in Germany also, the sheer speed of the American industrial explosion altered the world's economic context with dizzying rapidity. Indeed, it was through industrial expansion that the United States began to make an independent mark in world history by the 1870s. Several American companies began establishing branches abroad. Two American firms, in sewing machines and agricultural equipment respectively, were the largest industrial enterprises in Russia by 1900. More than in Germany, much American public opinion remained committed to a rhetoric of free enterprise even as big business grew and the government actively contributed to industrial expansion not only through grants of land but also through high protective tariffs.

The industrial revolution in the United States had three other distinctive features. First, what amounted to an industrialization of agriculture occurred along with the transformation of manufacturing. The vast lands of the westward-ex-

BOBBIN & DRAWING FRAMES.

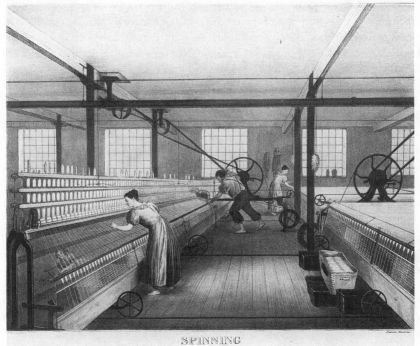

SPINNING

PROGRESS OF COTTON No 9

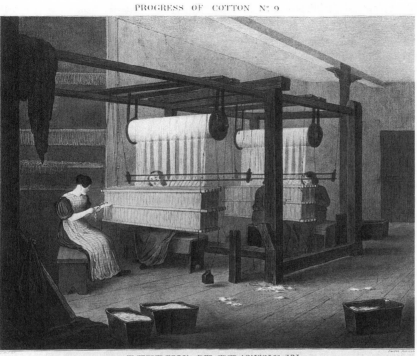

REEDING OR DRAWING IN

These lithographs are from an unusual series called The Progress of Cotton, *published in the early nineteenth century, which shows all the steps in the processing of cotton from field to finished product. (Courtesy of the Yale University Art Gallery. Reprinted by permission.)*

panding nation encouraged the development of new equipment, from horse-drawn harvesting machinery to tractors that were in growing use by the end of the nineteenth century. Agricultural output expanded rapidly, providing the nation with vital export commodities by the 1870s. American farmers often warred with big business (over railroad rates, for example), but there was less disjuncture between the rural and urban economies than in France and Germany. The United States also avoided the outright shrinkage of the agricultural sector that came to characterize Britain, which traded industrial exports for dependence on food imports.

The United States also relied unusually heavily on foreign capital. The nation was rich in resources but lacked the funds to develop them as rapidly as industrialization required. Huge investments from Europe, in particular Great Britain, fueled American industry throughout the nineteenth century, and the nation remained in international debt until World War I.

American industrialization contributed important organizational innovations in addition to the growth of big business. Because of an initial potential labor shortage and then the importation of immigrant workers regarded by many American industrialists as racially inferior to Anglo-Saxon stock, American factory managers devoted great thought to the conscious control of their labor force. They developed factory police forces to quell strikes and by the late nineteenth century were experimenting with engineering research, called time-and-motion studies, designed to calculate the movements of workers so that they could be systematized and sped up. Time-and-motion engineers set pay rates on the basis of optimal worker efficiency and subdivided tasks so that more and more workers performed in a routine, almost machinelike fashion. European factories quickly introduced some of the same thinking, but the initiative in new organizational techniques came disproportionately from the United States. The world's first large political democracy ironically pioneered in rigid workplace hierarchies, building on the implications of the factory system to create greater management control.

The Industrial West by the 1880s

The spread of rapid industrial revolutions to Belgium, France, Germany, and the United States effectively converted the bulk of Western society to an industrial economy by the 1870s. Industrial revolutions were also under way in Scandinavia, northern Italy, and the Netherlands. A few regions, of course, were largely unaffected: southern Italy and much of Spain, for example, as well as regional pockets within industrial nations. Ireland, under British rule, industrialized little; it served as a cheap source of agricultural goods and labor. The American south was largely nonindustrial even after slavery was finally abolished; it too served as a dependent economy providing cotton and other raw materials while buying manufactured goods from the north.

Nevertheless, the expansion of industrialization altered the economic balance both among Western nations and between the West and the world. Britain's huge industrial lead progressively dwindled as the German and American share of the industrial pie expanded. The British found it difficult to accommodate to some of the forms the industrial economy began to take by the 1870s. Britain provided less technical training for workers and managers than Germany did, relying instead on more traditional kinds of skill and initiative, and moved into the big-business age less comfortably than its new rivals did, partly because of its established pattern of family-owned factories. Industrialization in Britain continued—history reveals no instance of a retreat from industrialization save in wartime, at least until the collapse of the Soviet economy in the 1980s—but its relative share declined.

Overall industrial output elsewhere in the West continued to increase. The expansion of railroads and the focus on heavy industry in Germany and the United

States prompted strong growth in metallurgy and related branches such as armaments. New electrical and chemicals industries took off, the latter on the basis of new manufacturing needs and techniques in dyes, chemical fertilizers, and explosives. The organizational thrust of the industrial revolution took on new contours with the rise of big business and the development of new methods of disciplining and arranging the factory labor force. In sum, the rapid change in the cast of industrial actors made clear what British industrialization had already taught: The industrial revolution involved ongoing change, not simply an initial conversion to new techniques.

The expansion of Western industrial society also brought growing international rivalry. The British worried increasingly about competition, particularly from Germany. A major depression in the 1870s, not fully resolved until the 1890s, resulted in part from international pressures and also worsened those pressures. The "great depression" of the 1870s, as it was then called, was a new kind of slump. Traditionally, depression had begun with agricultural failures caused by bad weather or crop disease; food prices then rose, which cut demand for manufactured goods. By the 1850s the expansion of agricultural production plus transportation improvements that made widespread food shipment possible reduced the prospect of this kind of collapse in the industrial areas. Recessions in the new context began with a failure of demand for other reasons, which led banks to cut their industrial loans and produce yet another reduction of industrial demand. The resulting spiral of declining production and growing unemployment caused less dire want than had the old agricultural failures, but the cycle also tended to be more prolonged. The crisis of the 1870s, triggered by several bank failures in the United States, stemmed from a growth in industrial output that often exceeded demand. Workers' wages were low. The incomes of European peasants were declining because of competition from cheap food imports from the Americas. In this context came a major industrial pause: Sales plummeted and manufacturers tried desperately to find new outlets for their goods while cutting wages and jobs in the process.

The 1870s depression did not permanently interrupt Western industrialization. It did, however, generate new demand for an increase in protective tariffs against foreign goods, a movement that swept over all industrial nations except Britain in the next two decades. The crisis also gave rise to urgent efforts, avidly supported by many industrialists, to seek new market security internationally. Interest in expanding imperialism increased, in part because of a desire to monopolize potential markets in Africa and Asia and to insulate these markets against growing international competition. Thus, the advent of new rivalries within the industrial world helped escalate the impact of industrialization in the world at large. This in turn helped move the Western-dominated first phase of the industrial revolution into a more fully international setting.

4

The Social Impact of
the Industrial Revolution

THE INDUSTRIAL REVOLUTION was an intensely human experience. Its technological and organizational core had ramifications reaching into almost every facet
of society. Specific impacts varied somewhat with each region's industrial revolution. The experiences of women in France, for example, differed somewhat from
those in Britain because a larger number of French women stayed in the labor
force; by the late nineteenth century about 23 percent of the French labor force
was female compared with about 15 percent in Britain. Nevertheless, in broad
outline the social impact of industrialization was similar in most Western countries. This impact changed somewhat with time: Initial results did not always persist as the industrial revolution matured, and although these variations proved
more substantial than regional differences, the theme of major change applied to
both time and place. No society managed to industrialize without massive social
dislocations.

Life on the Job

One fundamental transformation involved the work experience. Factory workers
sometimes faced an increase in poverty, as wages were kept low and prices of
some goods rose. Other workers, as we have seen, won modest benefits from the
industrial revolution, and certainly the tendency after the initial decades was for
standards of living to improve. Constraints remained very real. The new working
class had little margin over subsistence, and various crises such as illness, a recession, or old age had potential to bring extreme misery. Furthermore, reactions to
other features of the industrial revolution often were colored by initial suffering.

Nevertheless, the exiguous standard of living was not in itself the most important difficulty facing the labor force.

Job conditions imposed many hardships. Factory life subverted the traditional work rhythm the labor force brought from craft or agricultural backgrounds. Machines worked quickly, and employers believed (or professed to believe) that hard work was the stuff of life. New shop rules attempted to bring a new pace of work to the factory hands. Workers had to arrive when the factory whistle blew; if they were late, they would be locked out, lose half a day's pay, and be fined as much in addition. Workers could not wander around the factory, chatter, or sing (even if the constant din of the new machines permitted). The typical unevenness in the former work pace was explicitly attacked: Work was meant to be steady as well as fast, with no whimsical interruptions, for if one worker stopped, a whole machine might shut down. Rules, fines, and layers of supervisors were devices aimed at imposing an unfamiliar sense of time and coordination on the factory hands.

The development of factory supervision followed from the struggle to reshape a whole labor force. Many early factories decentralized supervision considerably. A skilled spinner might directly hire the two or three assistants he required, often employing members of his own family. If the crew did not work well, the spinner himself would lose pay, so he had a stake in proper discipline. Fairly quickly, however, this system was replaced with more formal direction. Decentralized operations did not assure fast, regular work, given the huge increase in pace that employers sought. Further, many workers lacked adequate knowledge about their machines to tend them reliably; more skilled, technical direction was required—not for the sake of workers or safety but for the machinery itself. (One French factory owner each week decorated the most productive machine in the plant with a garland of flowers, a clear indication of where priorities lay in the work process.) Thus most factories after a decade or two introduced foremen designated to hire and fire workers and to keep the work going properly. Many of these foremen were drawn from the worker ranks, but they were expected to represent management interests and to drive their workers hard. With this innovation, the factory system not only introduced a new pace and discipline but also a new experience of being bossed. For the first time in Western history (aside from American slavery), a growing minority of people were working under the daily control of someone else and not simply for a few years of youthful apprenticeship but for a lifetime. Later developments that restricted the foremen themselves, such as the rise of industrial engineering and formal time-and-motion regulations in American factories, carried the loss of control over daily work life even further.

Some employers modified the sense of strangeness with active policies of paternalism. Because of humanitarian sentiments but even more because of the need to attract and retain skilled miners or metallurgists, often in remote areas, heavy industrial firms in particular adopted such policies, but textile companies often tried the approach as well—like the Massachusetts companies that built and supervised attractive barracks for their initial female factory hands. Paternalistic firms constructed worker housing, provided some medical care, and in other ways extended assistance beyond the wage to certain workers. Many workers viewed paternalism as an appropriate from of treatment, reminiscent of the attention landlords or artisans masters provided in the old days. Paternalism was not uniformly beneficent, however. Companies that provided housing could use the threat of eviction to discipline potential strikers. Furthermore, many paternalistic benefits proved meager or deteriorated when a company had assembled an adequate labor force. For various reasons, paternalism did not basically modify the growing formality and impersonality of direction in the factories: Most workers saw themselves as separate from the employing class, and many resented this along with so many other novelties.

Industrial work also became steadily more specialized. As more procedures were carried on by machines, a growing number of workers did small, repetitious tasks. There were important demands for considerable skill, but the semiskilled ranks grew most rapidly overall, particularly as the industrial revolution wore on. These semiskilled workers required training but of a limited sort, and they had little sense of contributing much to a final product that they might see as their own. This was one reason many factory workers worried about their demeaned status in society—a pervasive theme around the world during industrialization.

New pace and discipline, a lifetime of supervision by a separate management group, and a limited sense of achievement—these were the hallmarks of the factory work experience, and they differed from the standards workers might have recalled from rural or craft backgrounds. Furthermore, they tended to extend beyond the factory to other work settings. Artisans, in particular, found themselves confronted with attempts to speed up work, even when technology had not greatly changed. And they watched their employers, once fellow workers though also owners of the shop, turn into owners of small businesses. Many artisan masters increased their shop or crew size—construction work experienced this trend especially—and withdrew from the production process to concentrate on directing work and arranging sales. Many masters also stopped housing and feeding their employees as craft workers gradually became part of a permanent working class.

Workers experimented with various kinds of adjustment to the new work setting. Some liked it, at least for a time. Many workers expected to remain in the factories for only a few years, then to return to the countryside with some savings. A few workers enjoyed gaining new skills or were fascinated by new equipment such as the powerful railroad locomotives. A number of workers profited from the possibilities for upward mobility. While only a handful of workers actually rose from rags to riches, becoming factory owners in their own right, a larger number were encouraged to acquire greater skill or to become foremen. Mobility was not, however, open to most workers, and many did not find the prospect relevant.

A larger number of workers sought ways to modify the new work regimen and regain some control. They wandered around the factory or stole or dirtied materials, regardless of what the rules said. Many took unauthorized days off after their earnings built up a bit. Employers who expected workers to maximize their pay found that most preferred to earn less but have more free time. Artisans especially but also some factory workers often took Mondays off to extend their Sunday leisure—French workers called the practice "holy Monday"—and defended it for some time. Workers changed jobs frequently, particularly when they were young, single, and in their prime earning years, believing they possibly could improve conditions and gaining an illusion of choice and defiance. In new employment they could vary their routine for a few days at least. Not surprisingly, many new factories faced up to 100 percent turnover in a given year as the majority of workers indulged in transiency around a core of more stable personnel.

Factories during the industrial revolution formed something of a battleground between the growing labor force with its work habits and expectations and the new factory owners with their demands. The owners progressively managed to reshape work habits—many noted that even the second generation of workers, born and bred in the factory shadow and often beginning work as children, were less intractable than their parents. Certainly specific habits, such as returning to the countryside during harvest, declined rather quickly. But employers did not win the battle to their full satisfaction. One French owner complained that his workers labored only 72 percent as hard as his factory rules required, and while the claim was self-interested, it perhaps approached the truth. Workers maintained a distinctive conception of work, and they did not give up this conception entirely.

With time, workers also began to develop another strategy: to accept changes in the work situation in return for higher pay. Skilled British workers—what some have called the "aristocracy of labor" in the factory economy—began to articulate this bargain by 1850. They (and workers later in other countries) essentially conceded that they could not control their labor in traditional ways. If they had to accept a faster pace and recurrent changes in techniques, they felt entitled in return to a share in rewards in the form of higher pay and shorter hours. This approach—called "instrumentalism" because workers were accepting their work less as an end in itself and more as an instrument to a better life off the job—was one of the novel results of the factory environment.

A serious constraint on the work experience, particularly in the early decades of the industrial revolution, came from limitations in recreational opportunities. The new industrial cities were bleak places. Hours of work were very long, and many workers had neither time nor energy for much entertainment off the job. Employers and other officials also directly attacked many popular leisure customs. Traditions of village festivals, which had dotted the preindustrial calendar for ordinary people, faded quickly, partly because workers lived and labored among strangers and could not replicate the festival setting but even more because city governments actively opposed traditional processions as dangers to public order. Employers, too, in their desire for regular work habits, fined workers who took traditional days off, though this tactic was not always fully successful.

Police forces, newly created in European and American cities, spent up to half their time trying to regulate popular leisure habits in the interests of maintaining what was now defined as public respectability and creating a more punctual, docile working population. Much worker leisure focused on the tavern. Drink provided an escape from the tedium of work life. Even more important, the neighborhood tavern offered workers a chance for some sociability as they struggled to form new ties in a difficult environment. In sum, the period was a low point in the history of popular leisure. Only when the factory system was well established did a greater range of opportunities develop that allowed workers to define more clearly a nonwork portion of their waking hours.

Forging the Industrial Family

The industrial revolution had an immense impact on family life. Observers in all the industrial societies began worrying about the fate of the family institution early on, in what has become a consistent theme in industrial history. By some measurements many families managed to survive the transformations surprisingly well. Rates of marriage, for example, went up in western Europe during the nineteenth century because more people could hope to support a family and because marriage seemed to offer important advantages. There was no simple equation between the industrial revolution and a decay in family life. Unquestionably, however, industrialization strained many families and forced virtually every group to redefine the basic functions the family was to serve.

The biggest jolt the industrial revolution administered to the Western family was the progressive removal of work from the home. Families were no longer centers of production, though the transition was gradual and remnants of older domestic activity persisted into the twentieth century. Families retained a host of economic functions, which was one reason marriage remained vital for so many people. But the functions were more diffuse than when the family had served as the fundamental economic unit in which husbands and wives contributed tangibly to the family's subsistence and children began to assist the family economy from an early age.

Two visions of the industrial family developed in western Europe and the United States during the nineteenth century. Middle-class commentators increasingly saw the family as an emotional haven, an essentially spiritual refuge deliberately separate from the new stresses of economic life. Home was a sanctuary in which innocent children could be taught morality. Marriage was a loving partnership between two people who shared a pure affection that could rise above petty material concerns. As an American writer put it, "True love—that which abides—has its foundation in a knowledge and appreciation of moral qualities." The family ideal offered purpose and justification for the messy competition of the business world. This sanctification of the family was a statement of ideals, to be sure.

But the interest in separating family qualities from industrial life had some genuine reality among the middle class as emotional and moral satisfactions were sought even while family economic functions declined. Many middle-class families became centers of sedate leisure, and women enhanced family time playing the piano and reading aloud uplifting stories. Along with the leisure function came a new interest in family-oriented consumption, for the focus on the home easily translated into desire for better and more comfortable furnishings and decorations. Thus emerged a growing market for a variety of manufactured products, such as wallpaper, furniture, and carpeting.

The second definition of the industrial family, common in the urban working class, stuck closer to tradition. The family remained an economic unit, though it no longer was the center of production. Families could serve new economic needs by providing supplementary wage earners, particularly children. They could provide additional earnings from home-based activities such as taking in boarders or doing laundry. A more extended family that linked several adult relatives, not just the married couple, could aid with loans to tide through unemployment and provide information about available jobs.

Both visions of the functions of the family required substantial reshuffling of familial roles. The overarching need to adjust to the removal of production from the home created even greater pressures in the same direction. The task of the man of the family was to generate primary economic support. In working-class households other family members contributed some wages, but the breadwinning capacity of the husband/father was vital. A good family man was, above all, a man who fulfilled his obligation to provide. Women had to spend growing amounts of time organizing family consumption. In the middle class this meant running a fairly complex household, usually with the aid of an employed servant. In the working class this meant shopping and trying to stretch a tight budget simply to keep food on the table. Many a working-class housewife had to feed her husband all the meat she could afford because his stamina was so essential to the family's survival. Working-class wives also took on new responsibilities for maintaining contact with other relatives, for in contrast with more traditional families, in which husbands' relatives loomed largest, the kinship ties of wives now predominated if only because they had more opportunity than their husbands to socialize.

Women's work roles declined substantially during the industrial revolution. They might have acquired other family responsibilities—like their role as moral arbiter in the middle-class household—but their sheer economic importance dropped. Industrial technology attacked women's work early on, as it did in displacing domestic spinning. Because men had, on balance, performed more skilled manufacturing tasks before the industrial revolution, their work was somewhat more sheltered from mechanical competition. Furthermore, when production did move outside the household setting, many families faced a genuine dilemma: How could child care, shopping, and housework be taken care of? The answer, generally, was to emphasize a new and sharp kind of labor division between adult men and women: Men worked and earned while women took care of domestic duties.

The economic decline of women was long masked by their importance in the early factories, particularly the textile centers. Well over half the early labor force in cotton production, from New England to Belgium, was provided by women. Many employers argued that women's willingness to work for lower wages, their nimble fingers amid the machines, and their docility were essential for industrial success. But the absolute numbers of factory women were small compared with the hundreds of thousands of female domestic manufacturers being pushed out of work. Furthermore, most factory women were young, in their teens and early twenties, and intended to work for only a few years before marrying and quitting the factory scene. Finally, the percentage of women in the textile factories declined somewhat with time; the mechanization of weaving, for example, brought more men into the factories. An even sharper displacement process occurred in the business class. Many early factories maintained an older tradition of family management. Women kept accounts and supervised sales, while their husbands bought supplies and directed the labor force. Very quickly, however, with any success at all, the wife was moved off the premises to direct the domestic haven.

Within a generation, a clear pattern of gendered work developed throughout the industrial West. Middle-class women did not hold jobs at any point in their lives. Only unmarried adults could, with great difficulty, find respectable work as governesses for children. Working-class women commonly held jobs from late childhood until marriage in their early twenties; their earnings contributed significantly to the family economy. The majority worked as domestic servants, for there were not enough factory jobs to go around, but the contribution of young women to manufacturing remained considerable. After marriage a minority of women continued working, particularly in the textile centers. In general, however, it was taken as a sign of a man's failure if the wife had to work outside the home: Drunkenness, disability, or death were the obvious culprits. Working-class women did earn in the home as babysitters, laundresses, or boardinghouse keepers; some even manufactured small items like artificial flowers. But they were outside the mainstream of wage-earning labor.

Men vaunted the new economic division between the genders. This was one principle on which businessmen and many male workers readily agreed: Respectable adult women should not work. Increasing emphasis on women as the frailer sex followed from this categorization. Because the organizations of working-class men typically excluded women, a new gender basis for protest activity arose. Early unions regarded women as unreliable members—for were they not willing to accept low wages? Thus emerged the start of a vicious circle: Because men's groups excluded women, many female workers turned against budding unionism, which further incensed the male leadership. Additionally, many male workers hoped to gain better wages for themselves by limiting competition from women. Hence many worker leaders joined middle-class humanitarians in urging legal limits on women's hours of work, like the twelve-hour law passed in Britain in 1847; the avowed purpose was to protect women from strain, to safeguard the home, and to make a source of labor competition less desirable to employers.

Some working-class men also assaulted or taunted women on the job, seeking to demonstrate by means of abusive sexual prowess a masculinity that was being challenged by loss of skills and authority in the factory. Abuse in the family almost certainly increased as well, founded on the new differential in economic power between men and women and men's effort to compensate for demeaning jobs by assertiveness in other areas. A British worker stated a common theme: "I found my wife was out when I returned home after closing hours [of the local tavern], so when she did come in, I knocked her down; surely a man can do a thing like that to his wife." Middle-class gender relations were less candid, though some factory owners sexually abused their female workers. But in the middle class also, assumption of women's weakness and irrationality followed from the loss of economic place.

The challenge to traditional roles in the family economy extended to children, for whom the industrial revolution also ushered in a fundamental transformation. Children had always begun to work early in life, both in agriculture and in craft shops; child labor was not an invention of the industrial revolution. Both employers and workers found it normal for children to labor in the early factories—workers because of the pressing need for supplementary income and a sense that early work would prepare children with skills for later use in the traditional economy, employers because they clearly benefited from the low wages of the children.

Child labor in the factories was not, however, merely traditional, a fact various groups began to realize early on. Some children were mercilessly exploited, especially in British industrialization, and the pace of work put unusual strain on young workers. Accidents were common, particularly because children often worked as the machines were operating; cotton spinning had a category of labor called bobbin boys who tied broken threads while the machine ran on. As the supervision of labor became more formal, child workers were increasingly separated from their parents or other relatives and placed under the direction of strangers. Their treatment might not have deteriorated—uncles or fathers often drove children hard—but parents became increasingly uncomfortable at this further disruption of tradition.

Improvements in machinery made child labor increasingly unnecessary. Larger textile machines and more automatic processes reduced the viability of very young workers. Such changes, combined with humanitarian concerns and workers' desire to regain family control, led to a series of child labor laws, initiated in Britain in 1833. These laws limited the use of children under twelve and reduced the hours even for younger teenagers. The laws were vigorously debated; many manufacturers in particular resisted these challenges to their authority. Nevertheless, a growing number of middle-class reformers condemned the cruelty of industrial child labor. They also insisted that children needed time for schooling to prepare them more adequately for industrial work later because on-the-job training was declining with the dilution of craft traditions. Many workers agreed, seeking better treatment of their children and a reduction of low-wage competition. The British example finally helped spur child labor legislation elsewhere. France passed its first law in 1841, and German states introduced similar measures. The early laws were not well enforced—France, for example, installed paid inspectors to regulate the use of children only in the 1870s—but the trend was clear.

In the long run, obviously, the chief impact of the industrial revolution was to dissociate children from productive labor. Middle-class families did not put their sons to work until their later teens; working-class children were increasingly held out until at least age twelve or fourteen. Children's roles were redefined by the growing belief that the task of childhood was education, not contribution to the family income. By the 1830s in the northern part of the United States and by the 1870s in France and Germany, this belief had been converted to legal mandate in the form of compulsory primary schooling. Children were removed from much potential abuse through this shift, but they also became progressively more separated from the adult world and from direct contact with the roles they would have as adults. New concepts such as adolescence came into play in acknowledgment of the in-limbo stages of development between literal childhood and a life of work.

The redefinition of childhood obviously had further impact on the family itself. Created was another barrier between fathers and their children, as the separation of work and family meant an increasing day-to-day gap between men and their offspring. Families also had to reconsider how many children to have. First in the middle class, then after about 1870 in the working class in western Europe and the United States, the birthrate began to plummet. If children were no longer a resource but rather an expense—the cost of maintaining them and readying them for school actually went up—parents fairly quickly realized that a smaller family made stark economic sense. The industrial revolution thus led quite directly to a demographic revolution in which the average family size shrank to unprecedented levels. By 1900 families in most groups throughout the Western world expected to have two to four children rather than the six to eight regarded as the norm just a century before. This change had further implications for adult sexuality and birth control, for the functions attached to motherhood, and for family interactions with children themselves. The spiral of changes launched by industrialization required a host of subsequent adaptations.

The adjustments in family roles the industrial revolution impelled varied in duration. The first impulse to heighten the division between men and women proved not to be permanent, though it lasted well into the twentieth century. Later phases in the evolution of industrial society in the West brought a subsequent transformation in women's employment that undid much of the differentiation introduced in the nineteenth century. The man/provider, woman/homemaker distinction lingered to an extent, but the constraints it imposed lessened in the late twentieth century. In contrast, the transformation of childhood steadily intensified as the length of schooling expanded and as the dissociation of children from extensive work commitment increased. On a larger scale still, the need persisted to redefine family functions—to find a basis for stability once the family stopped serving as an essential economic unit and to generate believable definitions of family success once production moved outside the home. Even though the industrial revolution in a strict sense was completed almost a century ago, many people in Western society today continue to grapple with the huge changes it introduced into personal life and private institutions.

Social Divisions and Protest

The industrial revolution divided Western society in new ways. Several traditional social classes saw their prestige plummet. Aristocrats suffered, for their economic status derived from land ownership and their ethic disdained detailed attention to commercial methods and motives. Individual aristocrats, from eastern Germany through Great Britain, benefited from increased agricultural sales or from direct involvement in setting up new mines or metallurgical plants. As a whole, however, the class declined as both its economic base and its culture were undercut by the industrial surge. A large part of the history of western Europe in the nineteenth and even early twentieth centuries followed from the maneuverings of these beleaguered aristocrats trying to compensate for their economic anachronism. The tension between established aristocracy and the industrial revolution had some constructive results: Individual aristocrats participated in many efforts to regulate some of the worst abuses of industrial labor, combining humanitarianism with social-class resentment against greedy but successful manufacturers. One reason the United States lagged somewhat in labor regulation lay in the absence of an aristocratic counterpoise. But the decline of the aristocracy also had negative effects. German aristocrats, for example, used their political power to provide tariffs and subsidies for their production of low-quality grains, a tactic that helped to keep food prices higher for the masses than they otherwise would have been.

Other established groups were gradually reduced by the ongoing revolution. Europe's peasantry shrank in relative numbers and in economic significance. The artisan class was progressively divided between the owners of small businesses and the wage laborers. Traditional economic values and settings declined along with these social classes, and the process often was painful.

The clearest direct result of the industrial revolution involved the expansion of a new middle class, spurred not only by the rise of factory owners and managers in industry but also by various professional groups such as engineers who could associate with the industrial effort and the even more rapid increase of an unpropertied working class dependent on selling its labor in the industrial market-place. Middle class and working class shared some of the experience of the industrial revolution. As already noted, both groups had to reconsider the roles of women and the appropriate size of family, though they reached somewhat different conclusions and followed a different chronology. Anxieties about change and failure affected both groups as well.

But the middle class readily saw the industrial revolution as a source of social and personal progress. These individuals accepted the ethic of hard, intense work and saw it pay off in terms of personal achievement. Even at the end of the nineteenth century, French industrial managers, graduates of schools that already had pushed them to work extremely hard, expected to work frequently on Sundays and holidays, focusing on little beyond the job—"cold to worldly distractions" was how one industrial engineer was described. Because they had succeeded in industrial life, many middle-class people were impatient with complaint. The industrial middle class exhibited some charitable inclinations—extending paternalistic aid to the workers and indeed sometimes failing to rethink a traditional sense of social hierarchy in ways that might have led to acceptance of worker initiatives—yet this group tended, from both convenience and principle, to develop a new callousness to those below it. It relied heavily on the notion that paying a wage discharged one's obligations to the labor force. If poverty existed, it resulted from poor work habits. The thinking was distinctly self-serving: Good workers could save enough to tide them and their families through bad times. The real causes of misery were excessive drinking—as one French engineer put it, workers "understood no pleasure without a drink in their hand"—and poor family habits, including breeding too many children. Any self-disciplined person could see the benefits of industrial life and use them to advantage. Throughout the Western world, middle-class readers regaled themselves with wildly exaggerated stories of rags-to-riches success. Horatio Alger in the United States, Samuel Smiles in Britain, and many others showed how hard work and technical ingenuity would bring a poor person to the summits of the business world in a single lifetime.

Both perceptions and reality differed greatly for the growing working class. For these people the industrial revolution meant, at best, some modest and uncertain gains in living standards, but it also entailed tremendous personal disruption, an alien system of work, and a tragic loss of control. Mobility was for most a chimera. Working harder might simply have led to wage cuts so that the benefits would emerge as profit for the employer, not pay for the worker. Planning for the future made little sense given frequent recessions. Many workers found it better to work their children hard (in the interests of acquiring a small home, for example) than to promote their education and advancement. Many workers opposed the idea of intense work designed to maximize productivity and turned to a concept British laborers called a "lump o' labor"—that a given day and a given amount of pay demanded so much effort and no more. Not only the interests but many of the basic ideas of the working class clashed with those of the middle class.

A new kind of class division was thus endemic to the industrial revolution in Western society. Unlike the traditional owning and laboring groups, aristocrats and peasants, who had shared a number of ideas about what work and life were all about, many middle-class and working-class people disagreed fundamentally. Furthermore, and again unlike aristocrats and peasants, the two groups were in daily contact because one class now supervised the other on a regular basis. The industrial revolution established the conditions for recurrent class conflict on both ideological and material grounds. A number of theorists were quick to define the contest. As early as the 1820s groups of utopian socialists, both in Europe and the United States, urged the establishment of new, cooperative principles of work that would replace class divisions with a new harmony. (New Harmony was in fact the name of several utopian communities established by Europeans and Americans in the United States.) More important still was the ideology Karl Marx began to develop in the 1840s. Marx described the inevitable conflict between profiteering owners and the workers who created the real value of manufactured goods. He forecast a future in which the working class would continue to expand yet become more miserable and finally turn against the exploiting class. Violent revolution would produce a new state where government would seize property from the capitalist owners and create a cooperative society in which voluntary concord and essential equality would prevail. Unlike most utopian socialists, Marx favored the industrial revolution—machines did create the potential for greater social wealth and leisure—but he identified fundamental flaws in the version of society being created under capitalism with its inevitable intensification of class warfare.

Frequent protest indeed marked the decades of industrial revolution in Western society. Many workers reacted out of sheer misery. Food riots—a traditional protest form—erupted periodically in factory cities as workers attacked bakers for raising bread prices. Other violence was directed against competing workers. Philadelphia weavers rioted against Irish immigrants who seemed to threaten their jobs, while several ritualistic associations of French workers frequently engaged in pitched battles. A more innovative form of protest centered on the strike, which withdrew labor—the only real commodity of the working class—to press factory owners for better conditions. Early industrial strikes broke out particularly when employers attempted to reduce wages during economic slumps. In the textile town of Lowell, Massachusetts, for example, managers announced a 15 percent wage cut in 1834. Female factory workers gathered immediately, despite company attempts to dismiss the ringleaders. Protest songs showed that basic issues transcended pay to include the kind of hierarchy being established in factory life:

The overseers they need not think
Because they higher stand
That they are better than the girls
That work at their command.

Strike movements occasionally spilled over into larger organizational efforts. Many British textile workers and miners gathered in national campaigns to set up labor unions in the 1820s and early 1830s, hoping to use union organization to counteract the power of employers to set working conditions. On a more local level, craft workers, increasingly alienated from their employers, frequently set up local unions that would enable them, when the economy was booming and skilled workers in short supply, to gain real bargaining power in improving wages and limiting hours of work.

Finally, workers sometimes reached out for a larger kind of protest against the industrial order itself. Some attacked machines; Luddite episodes in France in the 1820s were expressions of many of the same interests in restoring an older order of work that had sparked original Luddism in Britain a decade earlier. Others sought political means of redressing the new inequality that marked the workplace. Many American workers participated fervently in republican demonstrations in the 1820s and 1830s, seeking broader political rights that would affirm their basic equality in society. British Chartists gained millions of signatures in campaigns to grant political rights to the working class; the goal was a combination of practical gains (new state sponsorship of worker education, for example) and symbolic equality. A variety of workers, in particular from the craft sectors, participated in the European revolutions of 1848. Some German artisans sought a restoration of the guild system and other restrictions on the industrial order. Craft and factory workers in Paris rallied for what they called the "organization of work," by which they meant some immediate state measures against widespread unemployment and a larger rollback of the increasing mechanization and inequality of work.

Despite these efforts to express physical suffering and acute moral agony, none of the protest currents succeeded in deflecting the steady onrush of industrialization. The grand labor union schemes failed. The Chartist petitions were rejected. Worker participation in the revolutions of 1848 was brutally repressed. Government troops destroyed the partisans of a new organization of work in the bloody June Days in Paris. A few months later Prussian forces crushed the craft workers in Berlin and other German centers.

Workers faced impossible hurdles in seeking to slow or redefine the basic trends of the industrial revolution. Protest organizations were illegal and remained so in most Western countries until the 1870s. Troops and police were readily rallied against worker efforts. Employers had great repressive power through their ability to fire strikers and sometimes evict them from their homes. Bargaining with small groups of craft workers was necessary because their skills earned them special attention, but employers zealously attacked larger groups whose agitation challenged their authority in industry. Workers themselves were divided. Male workers tended to ignore issues affecting women. Craft workers tended to highlight their skills and traditions, rejecting the unions whose members were the growing mass of factory hands. Many factory workers relied on individual adjustments that impeded collective action. A few workers concentrated on rising to supervisory posts. A larger number changed jobs so often that they formed inadequate ties with any set of colleagues. That most factory workers labored among strangers complicated protest planning. When a growing number of workers were also immigrants—Irish workers in Britain and the United States, French Canadians in the United States, Belgians in northern France—the problem was compounded. Finally, the goals of workers were often diffuse. Their opposition to principles of industrial work might be fierce, but their alternatives were vague. Some advocated a restoration of guilds, others sought some utopian community, and others did not know quite what to claim.

Working-class protest slowed for two decades after 1848. In France and Germany many leaders were arrested or exiled after the uprisings collapsed. Police forces became more adept at riot control. Many "labor aristocrats" decided to concentrate on respectable unions that would bargain calmly for improvements and strike only as a last resort and then without violence. A New Model Unionism movement developed in Great Britain featuring skill-specific unions of craftworkers and skilled factory operatives like machine builders (called engineers in Britain). Craft unions surfaced in Germany and France. The first wave of working-class struggle had ended; dying with it were the most sweeping efforts to call the factory system itself into question. A new current of protest having as its objective important gains within the industrial system began to take shape from the late 1860s onward in the United States as well as in Europe. New organizations sought the loyalties of craft and factory workers alike; the American Knights of Labor and the Marxist Social Democratic Party in Germany were two examples. Class warfare was about to enter a second major phase associated with the ongoing industrialization of the West.

A New Political and Cultural Context

The impact of the West's industrial revolution extended well beyond work and leisure, family life, and basic forms of protest. Governments changed, though responses to the revolution were only one component in the new political systems that emerged in Western nations during the nineteenth century. The extent of state involvement in economic policy varied, from noninterventionist Britain to the much more active German government. Nevertheless, all Western governments began to participate in new activities relating to railroad expansion, industrial tariff policies, and sponsorship of technical expositions. All governments also increased their role in education, providing a growing number of primary schools for the masses and a growing array of technical schools to enhance the training of experts. With the enactment of child labor laws, governments became gradually involved in the regulation of industrial working conditions, and this in turn ultimately produced a specialist bureaucracy capable of monitoring compliance with labor and safety laws. Finally, governments began to respond to some of the special material problems highlighted by the industrial revolution and undertook new welfare functions. To be sure, Britain during the 1830s sought to make assistance to the poor less rather than more desirable, an approach reflective of middle-class interests in revising traditional notions of charity so that people would take responsibility for themselves. City governments, however, were already beginning to distribute some food to help the poor during economic recessions. Then in the 1880s the German government pioneered in state-sponsored insurance to provide modest payments to aid the sick, the injured, and the elderly; the goal was simultaneously to reduce some of the starkest problems of working-class life and to defuse growing worker commitment to socialism.

Government initiatives continued to vary greatly. In the United States, cities and states rather than the federal government responded to most industrial issues. Germany, with a greater statist tradition, innovated more extensively than Britain. Nevertheless, there was a general commitment to supporting industrial growth, providing essential educational facilities, expanding police activities, and regulating some industrial excesses. This redefinition of state functions throughout the Western world formed yet another part of the broader industrialization process.

Culture changed as well. Many artists and writers turned against the ugliness of the industrial setting. Romantic painters early in the nineteenth century concentrated on idyllic scenes of nature in part to contrast with the blight of factory cities. A bit later, many artists professed a withdrawal from their larger society, urging that art was for art's sake; this was a radical alternative to industrial materialism. On the more popular level, the industrial revolution stimulated interest in secular rather than religious culture. Religion survived, and the intensity of certain strands, like Methodism among British workers or Catholicism among many immigrant workers in the United States, formed a vital part of working-class life. On balance, however, the industrial revolution encouraged pursuit of material gains and belief in the power of science and technology. Many workers turned against established churches; allied with conservative, propertied classes, these institutions seemed deaf to workers' concerns. Interest in socialism or other protest ideas gave some workers an alternative loyalty, which reflected and enhanced the secularization process. For their part, many industrial managers, though sometimes conventionally religious, turned to growing identification with nationalism and science, including the competitive version of Darwinian theory that spread particularly in the United States. No single industrial culture emerged, but the industrial revolution had substantial impact on ongoing cultural change.

Finally as the industrial revolution solidified in western Europe and the United States during the nineteenth century, it inevitably altered relationships with other parts of the world. The power of industrial technology fed new power politics on the international scene; an explosive round of imperialism was a direct consequence of the West's industrial expansion and internal competition. Even before the imperialist outburst, however, industrialization had cut into traditional economies from Mexico to Malaya and had forced a growing number of governments to take some first, halting steps toward replicating the West's economic Goliath.

5

The Industrial Revolution
Outside the West

Before the 1870s no industrial revolution occurred outside Western society. The spread of industrialization within western Europe, while by no means automatic, followed from a host of shared economic, cultural, and political features. The quick ascension of the United States was somewhat more surprising—the area was not European and had been far less developed economically during the eighteenth century. Nevertheless, extensive commercial experience in the northern states and the close mercantile and cultural ties with Britain gave the new nation advantages for its rapid imitation of the British lead. Abundant natural resources and extensive investments from Europe kept the process going, joining the United States to the wider dynamic of industrialization in the nineteenth-century West.

Elsewhere, conditions did not permit an industrial revolution, an issue that must be explored in dealing with the international context for this first phase of the world's industrial experience. Yet the West's industrial revolution did have substantial impact. It led to a number of pilot projects whereby initial machinery and factories were established under Western guidance. More important, it led to new Western demands on the world's economies that instigated significant change without industrialization; indeed, these demands in several cases made industrialization more difficult.

Pilot Projects

Russia's contact with the West's industrial revolution before the 1870s offers an important case study that explains why many societies could not follow the lead of nations like France or the United States in imitating Britain. Yet Russia did introduce some new equipment for economic and military-political reasons, and these initiatives did generate change—they were not mere window dressing.

More than most societies not directly part of Western civilization, Russia had special advantages in reacting to the West's industrial lead and special motivation for paying attention to this lead. Russia had been part of Europe's diplomatic network since about 1700. It saw itself as one of Europe's great powers, a participant in international conferences and military alliances. The country also had close cultural ties with western Europe, sharing in artistic styles and scientific developments—though Russian leadership had stepped back from cultural alignment because of the shock of the French Revolution in 1789 and subsequent political disorders in the West. Russian aristocrats and intellectuals routinely visited western Europe. Finally, Russia had prior experience in imitating Western technology and manufacturing: importation of Western metallurgy and shipbuilding had formed a major part of Peter the Great's reform program in the early eighteenth century.

Contacts of this sort explain why Russia began to receive an industrial outreach from the West within a few decades of the advent of the industrial revolution. British textile machinery was imported beginning in 1843. Ernst Knoop, a German immigrant to Britain who had clerked in a Manchester cotton factory, set himself up as export agent to the Russians. He also sponsored British workers who installed the machinery in Russia and told any Russian entrepreneur brash enough to ask not simply for British models but for alterations or adaptations: "That is not your affair; in England they know better than you." Despite the snobbism, a number of Russian entrepreneurs set up small factories to produce cotton, aware that even in Russia's small urban market they could make a substantial profit by underselling traditional manufactured cloth. Other factories were established directly by Britons.

Europeans and Americans were particularly active in responding to calls by the tsar's government for assistance in establishing railway and steamship lines. The first steamship appeared in Russia in 1815, and by 1820 a regular service ran on the Volga River. The first public railroad, joining St. Petersburg to the imperial residence in the suburbs, opened in 1837. In 1851 the first major line connected St. Petersburg and Moscow, along a remarkably straight route desired by Tsar Nicholas I himself. American engineers were brought in, again by the government, to set up a railroad industry so that Russians could build their own locomotives and cars. George Whistler, the father of the painter James McNeill Whistler (and thus husband of Whistler's mother), played an important role in the effort. He and some American workers helped train Russians in the needed crafts, frequently complaining about their slovenly habits but appreciating their willingness to learn.

Russian imports of machinery increased rapidly; they were over thirty times as great in 1860 as they had been in 1825. While in 1851 the nation manufactured only about half as many machines as it imported, by 1860 the equation was reversed, and the number of machine-building factories had quintupled (from 19 to 99).

The new cotton industry surged forward with most production organized in factories using wage labor.

These were important changes. They revealed that some Russians were alert to the business advantages of Western methods and that some Westerners saw the great profits to be made by setting up shop in a huge but largely agricultural country. The role of the government was vital: The tsars used tax money to offer substantial premiums to Western entrepreneurs, who liked the adventure of dealing with the Russians but liked their superior profit margins even more.

But Russia did not then industrialize. Modern industrial operations did not sufficiently dent established economic practices. The nation remained overwhelmingly agricultural. High percentage increases in manufacturing proceeded from such a low base that they had little general impact. Several structural barriers impeded a genuine industrial revolution. Russia's cities had never boasted a manufacturing tradition; there were few artisans skilled even in preindustrial methods. Only by the 1860s and 1870s had cities grown enough for an artisan core to take shape—in printing, for example—and even then large numbers of foreigners (particularly Germans) had to be imported. Even more serious was the system of serfdom that kept most Russians bound to agricultural estates. While some free laborers could be found, most rural Russians could not legally leave their land, and their obligation to devote extensive work service to their lords' estates reduced their incentive even for agricultural production. Peter the Great had managed to adapt serfdom to a preindustrial metallurgical industry by allowing landlords to sell villages and the labor therein for expansion of ironworks. But this mongrel system was not suitable for change on a grander scale, which is precisely what the industrial revolution entailed.

Furthermore, the West's industrial revolution, while it provided tangible examples for Russia to imitate, also produced pressures to develop more traditional sectors in lieu of structural change. The West's growing cities and rising prosperity claimed rising levels of Russian timber, hemp, tallow, and, increasingly, grain. These were export goods that could be produced without new technology and without altering the existing labor system. Indeed, many landlords boosted the work-service obligations of the serfs in order to generate more grain production for sale to the West. The obvious temptation was to lock in an older economy—to respond to new opportunity by incremental changes within the traditional system and to maintain serfdom and the rural preponderance rather than to risk fundamental internal transformation.

The proof of Russia's lag showed in foreign trade. It rose but rather modestly, posting a threefold increase between 1800 and 1860. Exports of raw materials approximately paid for the imports of some machinery, factory-made goods from abroad, and a substantial volume of luxury products for the aristocracy. And the regions that participated most in the growing trade were not the tiny industrial enclaves (in St. Petersburg, Moscow, and the iron-rich Urals) but the wheat-growing areas of southern Russia where even industrial pilot projects had yet to surface. Russian manufacturing exported nothing at all to the West, though it did find a few customers in Turkey, central Asia, and China.

The proof of Russia's lag showed even more dramatically in Russia's new military disadvantage. Peter the Great's main goal had been to keep Russian military production near enough to Western levels to remain competitive, with the huge Russian population added into the equation. This strategy now failed, for the West's industrial revolution changed the rules of the game. A war in 1854 pitting Russia against Britain and France led to Russia's defeat in its own backyard. The British and French objected to new Russian territorial gains (won at the expense of Turkey's Ottoman Empire) that brought Russia greater access to the Black Sea. The battleground was the Crimea. Yet British and French steamships connected their armies more reliably with supplies and reinforcements from home than did Russia's ground transportation system with its few railroads and mere 3,000 miles of first-class roads. And British and French industry could pour out more and higher-quality uniforms, guns, and munitions than traditional Russian manufacturing could hope to match. The Russians lost the Crimean War, surrendering their gains and swallowing their pride in 1856. Patchwork change had clearly proved insufficient to match the military, much less the economic, power the industrial revolution had generated in the West.

After a brief interlude, the Russians digested the implications of their defeat and launched a period of basic structural reforms. The linchpin was the abolition of serfdom in 1861. Peasants were not entirely freed, and rural discontent persisted, but many workers could now leave the land; the basis for a wage labor force was established. Other reforms focused on improving basic education and health, and while change in these areas was slow, it too set the basis for a genuine commitment to industrialization. A real industrial revolution lay in the future, however. By the 1870s Russia's contact with industrialization had deepened its economic gap vis-à-vis the West but had yielded a few interesting experiments with new methods and a growing realization of the need for further change.

Societies elsewhere in the world—those more removed from traditional ties to the West or more severely disadvantaged in the ties that did exist—saw even more tentative industrial pilot projects during the West's industrialization period. The Middle East and India tried some industrial imitation early on but largely failed—though not without generating some important economic change. Latin America also launched some revealingly limited technological change. Only eastern Asia and sub-Saharan Africa were largely untouched by any explicit industrial imitations until the late 1860s or beyond; they were too distant from European culture to venture a response so quickly.

Prior links with the West formed the key variable, as Russia's experience abundantly demonstrated. Societies that had some familiarity with Western merchants and some preindustrial awareness of the West's steady commercial gains mounted some early experiments in industrialization. Whether they benefited as a result compared with areas that did nothing before the late nineteenth century might be debated.

One industrial initiative in India developed around Calcutta, where British colonial rule had centered since the East India Company founded the city in 1690. A Hindu Brahman family, the Tagores, established close ties with many British administrators. Without becoming British, they sponsored a number of efforts to revivify India, including new colleges and research centers. Dwarkanath Tagore controlled tax collection in part of Bengal, and early in the nineteenth century he used part of his profit to found a bank. He also bought up a variety of commercial landholdings and traditional manufacturing operations. In 1834 he joined with British capitalists to establish a diversified company that boasted holdings in mines (including the first Indian coal mine), sugar refineries, and some new textile factories; the equipment was imported from Britain. Tagore's dominant idea was a British-Indian economic and cultural collaboration that would revitalize his country. He enjoyed a high reputation in Europe and for a short time made a success of his economic initiatives. Tagore died on a trip abroad, and his financial empire declined soon after.

This first taste of Indian industrialization was significant, but it brought few immediate results. The big news in India, even as Tagore launched his companies, was the rapid decline of traditional textiles under the bombardment of British factory competition; millions of Indian villagers were thrown out of work. Furthermore, relations between Britain and the Indian elite worsened after the mid-1830s as British officials sought a more active economic role and became more intolerant of Indian culture. One British official, admitting no knowledge of Indian scholarship, wrote that "all the historical information" and science available in Sanskrit was "less valuable than what may be found in the most paltry abridgements used at preparatory schools in England." With these attitudes, the kind of collaboration that might have aided Indian appropriation of British industry became impossible.

The next step in India's contact with the industrial revolution did not occur until the 1850s when the colonial government began to build a significant railroad network. The first passenger line opened in 1853. Some officials feared that Hindus might object to traveling on such smoke-filled monsters, but trains proved very popular and there ensued a period of rapid economic and social change. The principal result, however, was not industrial development but further extension of commercial agriculture (production of cotton and other goods for export) and intensification of British sales to India's interior. Coal mining did expand, but manufacturing continued to shrink. There was no hint of an industrial revolution in India.

Imitation in the Middle East was somewhat more elaborate, in part because most of this region, including parts of North Africa, retained independence from European colonialism. Muslims had long disdained Western culture and Christianity, and Muslim leaders, including the rulers of the great Ottoman Empire, had been very slow to recognize the West's growing dynamism after the fifteenth century. Some Western medicine was imported, but technology was ignored. Only in the eighteenth century did this attitude begin, haltingly, to change. The Ottoman government imported a printing press from Europe and began discussing Western-style technical training, primarily in relationship to the military.

In 1798 a French force briefly seized Egypt, providing a vivid symbol of Europe's growing technical superiority. Later an Ottoman governor, Muhammed Ali, seized Egypt from the imperial government and pursued an ambitious agenda of expansionism and modernization. Muhammed Ali sponsored many changes in Egyptian society in imitation of Western patterns, including a new tax system and new kinds of schooling. He also destroyed the traditional Egyptian elite. The government encouraged agricultural production by sponsoring major irrigation projects and began to import elements of the industrial revolution from the West in the 1830s. English machinery and technicians were brought in to build textile factories, sugar refineries, paper mills, and weapons shops. Muhammed Ali clearly contemplated a sweeping reform program in which industrialization would play a central role in making Egypt a powerhouse in the Middle East and an equal to the European powers. Many of his plans worked well, but the industrialization effort failed. Egyptian factories could not in the main compete with European imports, and the initial experiments either failed or stagnated. More durable changes involved the encouragement to the production of cash crops like sugar and cotton, which the government required in order to earn tax revenues to support its armies and its industrial imports. Growing concentration on cash crops also enriched a new group of Egyptian landlords and merchants. But the shift actually formalized Egypt's dependent position in the world economy, as European businesses and governments increasingly interfered with the internal economy. The Egyptian reaction to the West's industrial revolution, even more than the Russian response, was to generate massive economic redefinition without industrialization, a strategy that locked peasants into landlord control and made a manufacturing transformation at best a remote prospect.

Spurred by the West's example and by Muhammed Ali, the Ottoman government itself set up some factories after 1839, importing equipment from Europe to manufacture textiles, paper, and guns. Coal and iron mining were encouraged. The government established a postal system in 1834, a telegraph system in 1855, and steamships and the beginning of railway construction from 1866 onward. These changes increased the role of European traders and investors in the Ottoman economy and produced no overall industrial revolution. Again, the clearest result of improved transport and communication was a growing emphasis on the export of cash crops and minerals to pay for necessary manufactured imports from Europe. An industrial example had been set, and, as in Egypt, a growing though still tiny minority of Middle Easterners gained some factory experience, but no fundamental transformation occurred.

Latin American nations, newly independent after 1820, had strong historical ties with western Europe. Although cultural links to Spain and Portugal did little for industrialization—these areas lagged within Europe—the broader European connection was solid, and Western merchants, led by the British, expanded commercial ties. Because of economic disorder following the independence wars, little imitation was possible until about 1850; more pressing problems of political consolidation commanded the most attention. A steam-driven sugar mill was set up as early as 1815 in Brazil, however, and the number of engines, all imported, had risen to 64 by 1834. Coffee processors began acquiring steam equipment at this time also, and by 1852 the nation boasted 144 engines in all. These were interesting developments: They enhanced the operations Brazilians performed on some of their leading export crops, but they served largely to confirm Brazil's concentration on these sectors. The effort led neither to a more general industrial development focused on internal demand nor to a balanced set of innovations that would foster Brazilian industries in machine building and metallurgy. As was true elsewhere, the difference between important technical imitation and a real industrial revolution, even if partly imitated, remained clear. Most Brazilian workers and most sectors of the Brazilian economy did not move toward industrialization. Change was real but came mainly in the form of growing emphasis on the export crops.

While Cuba first built a rail line in 1838 (from Havana to Guines), Brazil and other Latin American nations began to sponsor railroad development in the 1850s using capital borrowed from European banks and equipment purchased from Europe. Brazil passed a law in 1852 granting financial incentives to any entrepreneur wishing to undertake railroad construction. Viscount Maua accepted the challenge, opening a ten-mile line in 1854. Twenty years later Brazil had 800 miles of track. Paraguay inaugurated steamship and rail lines after 1858; the nation also built Latin America's first iron foundry. The country was unique in the region in hiring British technicians with current tax revenues, thus avoiding dependence on foreign loans. This promising start was cut short by loss in a war with Argentina, Uruguay, and Brazil. Chile inaugurated its first rail line in 1852 after some previous development of steam-powered flour mills, distilleries, sawmills, and coal mines. Mexico lagged in rail construction, with only 400 miles in 1876. And many other Latin American nations envisaged only short lines connecting seaports to the interior, not nationwide networks. Overall, early rail development helped spur mineral and food exports—the cash-crop economy—while increasing reliance on foreign banks and technologies.

Developments of preliminary industrial trappings—a few factories, a few railroads—nowhere outside Europe converted whole economies to an industrialization process until late in the nineteenth century, though they provided some relevant experience on which later (mainly after 1870) and more intensive efforts could build. A few workers became factory hands and experienced some of the same upheaval as their Western counterparts in terms of new routines and pressures on work pace. Many sought to limit their factory experience, leaving for other work or for the countryside after a short time; transience was a problem for much the same reasons as in the West: the clash with traditional work and leisure values. Some technical and business expertise also developed. Governments took the lead in most attempts to imitate the West, which was another portent for the future; with some exceptions, local merchant groups had neither the capital nor the motivation to undertake such ambitious and uncertain projects. By the 1850s a number of governments were clearly beginning to realize that some policy response to the industrial revolution was absolutely essential, lest Western influence become still more overwhelming. On balance, however, the principal results of very limited imitation tended to heighten the economic imbalance with western Europe, a disparity that made it easier to focus on nonindustrial exports. This too was a heritage for the future.

Two major geographic areas essentially avoided significant contact with the industrial revolution until the late nineteenth century, ignoring or shunning even modest imitation. Sub-Saharan Africa faced great economic changes after 1820, mainly because of the effective ending of the Atlantic slave trade. This reduced tremendous pressures on Africa's labor force (though East African slave trade with the Middle East actually accelerated for a time), but it also cut the revenues available to West African merchants and governments. Some attempts were made to expand traditional industries, but there was no basis for major technical change, and no capital was available to venture new directions. African societies had long-standing experience with ironworking and other relevant technologies, and they had a substantial commercial tradition. Weakened governments and major economic dislocation, however, made quick response to Europe's transformation virtually impossible. Soon, the principal innovation in Africa involved Europe's industrially based imperial conquests, not industrialization.

East Asia also largely avoided reaction to the initial phase of the industrial revolution. China had a long history of technological innovation and indeed had been adding to its list into the late seventeenth century. Its hostility to outside influence, however, inhibited significant interaction with western Europe. The Chinese typically sought to blend technological change with traditional political and social structures; their past did not encourage any deliberate adoption of an explicitly revolutionary technology. Confucianism also prompted distaste for too much attention to commerce and merchant activity. Further, Chinese leadership grew more conservative during the eighteenth century, exhibiting less interest even in creative reworkings of traditional philosophy. China was also burdened with rapid population growth and growing peasant misery, which drained resources. Governments became less efficient. All this added up to a situation in which Chinese leadership sought to deal with growing evidence of Western industrialization mainly by avoiding it.

Britain, which acquired the port city of Hong Kong in the 1840s, set up some initial factories in its new territory. Several regional rulers in China established military industries in hopes that Chinese defenses could improve; a governor at Naking directed several gun factories and a machine factory by the 1850s. New arsenals to manufacture weaponry were created in a few other centers. Until the 1870s the only innovation envisaged was for military purposes; then the central government began to expand its initiatives somewhat. No railroad was constructed until 1876, when a Western company built a line without government authorization (the government's response was to tear up the line and let the remnants rust away); the first successful railroad was opened in 1882 to carry coal from the K'ai-ping mines to a port. No textiles were produced by machinery in China proper until 1890, though some sluggish planning efforts preceded this project. In effect, until almost the end of the nineteenth century, the industrial revolution passed China by. The same held true for much of Southeast Asia and, until the 1860s, for Japan.

Restructuring the International Economy

Direct contact with industrial organization and technology formed a significant facet of world history during the middle decades of the nineteenth century, but it was overshadowed by a more general reorientation in international economic relationships as the West began to display its industrial muscle. Already the world's premier commercial society, the West greatly increased its world role as a direct consequence of industrialization. Economic inequalities among major world societies accelerated, and some economies were durably redirected in response to Western pressure. The significance of international trade expanded as well, and several new institutions were created to facilitate this exchange.

The West's industrial revolution meant a flood of cheap manufactured goods directed toward world markets. Some societies could absorb new imports of textiles and metal products without facing massive dislocation. Russia, as we have seen, raised its imports, but its internal manufacturing sector, which included production of a wide array of goods in individual villages for local consumption, was sufficiently large that its overall manufacturing performance improved. Its relative economic position in the world declined as the country failed to keep up with Western gains, but its absolute levels held strong, aided by a modest amount of new technology in a few sectors.

The impact of Western imports in other cases was more disruptive. Latin American nations had gained their independence from Spain by 1820, but the attendant wars and internal strife inevitably weakened the domestic economy for a time. Simultaneously, the withdrawal of Spanish regulations had opened Latin American markets to massive imports of machine-made textiles from Britain. What had been a growing industry of manual production of textiles at home was virtually crushed. Tens of thousands of people, urban and rural, were thrown out of work. Urban women were particularly hard hit as a major source of supplementary income disappeared. Poverty and prostitution increased rapidly as a result. Similar disruption of the traditional manufacturing sector occurred in India, where Britain had, even before outright industrialization, manipulated tariff regulations to discourage the once-thriving Indian cotton industry. These were cases in which the crippling of manufacturing thrust important economies backward toward fuller concentration on agriculture and mining.

The combination of Western industrial growth and the resultant disruption of the internal economies of many other areas steadily increased the inequalities in international economic performance. In 1800 Mexico's per capita income was about a third of that of Great Britain and half of that of the United States. Because of growing Western competition and internal disarray following the wars of independence, Mexican per capita national income actually fell until 1860; at that point it stood at a mere 13 percent of British levels and 14 percent of the U.S. average. This was graphic illustration of the new balance sheet between industrializers and most of the nonindustrial regions.

Disruption and decline were not the whole story. The West's industrial revolution provided new economic opportunities for some regions outside the industrial orbit. A herding economy in the Mosul region of northeastern Turkey expanded rapidly in the midnineteenth century. Demand in the West for raw wool for its growing factories spurred a host of trade representatives to seek new sources of supply. Both the British and the French governments, through their local consular officials in this part of the Ottoman Empire, kept tabs on wool production, while Turkish merchants and urban authorities did the direct bargaining with the tribespeople. The British directly encouraged expansion of cotton production in Egypt because they sought a more reliable and cheaper source of supply than the southern United States offered, particularly after the disruptions of the American Civil War. And of course opportunities to sell food to urban western Europe increased. Russian grain exports responded, and other areas in east-central Europe, like Hungary, did the same. Latin American nations found new opportunities for export earnings by expanding their production of cash crops like coffee, which added to existing commercial agriculture in sugar and tobacco.

A commercialized export economy expanded steadily in a growing number of regions in Africa, Latin America, and Asia. Local merchants and landlords found substantial profits in their changing economy. They helped press a growing number of workers, in particular former peasants but also immigrants, to change their work habits in a fashion not entirely dissimilar to patterns developing in the West's factory centers. Latin American landlords, backed by liberal governments, pried land from traditional Indian or mestizo villagers in order to expand coffee or sugar production. They then attempted to alter the work habits of these new agricultural laborers, trying to reduce the time spent on festivals and drinking and urging more regular and efficient work routines and a new sense of time. Along with local labor, immigrant workers fueled this new commercial economy. Brazil and Argentina began to recruit growing numbers of Spaniards, Italians, and Portuguese. In Brazil the many immigrant workers directed to the coffee-growing regions helped to propel this sector to a commanding position in the world coffee trade by the 1880s—56 percent of the total market share. Workers from India and Southeast Asia were sent under long-term indenture contracts to work on commercial estates in the Caribbean region and elsewhere.

Changes of this sort were vitally important, and they brought important profit opportunities to several local groups, merchants and landowners in particular but also some other elements like the herders in Mosul. At the same time, however, these shifts increased vulnerabilities on the world market, and they most definitely failed to generate any sort of economic parity with the industrial West. The simple fact was that the goods exported to the West—agricultural and mineral products almost exclusively—were not as valuable as the manufactured products that the West exported. The terms of trade favored the West. Furthermore, Western capitalists controlled many operations directly. They ran the shipping and most of the international trading companies. With their greater capital resources, they bought many mines and estates outright. For example, Westerners, including entrepreneurs from the United States, owned most railroads, banks, and mines in Colombia and Chile by the late nineteenth century.

The fundamental imbalance showed in many ways. Cash-crop and mineral exports involved little new technology, except in the transport systems used to get them out of the country. These sectors were much more dependent than Western factories on very cheap labor, often kept in semiservitude by indenture contracts or company stores. The new working class being created around the world had some features in common with the worker of the industrial West, but it was far more miserable.

Local governments and businesses, seeking to develop their export opportunities and in some cases sincerely hoping to generate a more diversified economy, frequently went into debt. The construction of modern port and rail facilities in Latin America, though vital to expanding the export sector, cost more money than the exports easily paid for. The solution was to borrow from eager, capital-rich banks in western Europe and the United States; the result was a growing debt that made additional investment more difficult and that invited Western interference, including military threats on occasion, in basic economic policy.

Impoverished workers and growing foreign debt made it difficult to imagine a real industrial revolution, though by the late nineteenth century some Latin American leaders saw this as a valid goal. Latin America became a classic area of economic dependence, importing manufactured products and luxury goods from the West while trying desperately to stay afloat with low-cost exports.

How could an industrial revolution even be contemplated in nineteenth-century India? Even aside from the fact that India, unlike the Latin American nations, was still ruled from Europe—by an English government that had no interest in creating a new industrial rival—the result of Western industrialization had impoverished large stretches of the nation. Cotton manufacturing had collapsed by

1833 as millions of Indian women and men, domestic spinners and weavers, were thrown out of work by machines half a world away. The peasant economy became increasingly dependent, and it harbored unprecedented numbers of outright unemployed. In the 1850s the British turned from a concentration primarily on sales to India to a new, parallel interest in cheap supplies. The railroads were introduced in the 1850s not only to facilitate sales of British goods but also to encourage production of raw materials like jute and cotton. As commercial estates expanded with the aid of huge reserves of cheap labor, India became increasingly locked into a dependent position in the Western-dominated world economy.

Western industrialization further exacerbated the military imbalance of world power. Even earlier, Western armaments had assured predominance on the seas and had allowed Europeans to establish colonies in a number of ports and on islands like Java, Borneo, and the Philippines. With industrialization, Western forces gained even greater maritime potency by virtue of larger ships and bigger cannon; new advantages in land wars accrued as well. In the 1830s this growing military superiority, plus the insatiable thirst for new markets and sources of supply, began to usher in a new age of European expansion. To be sure, the Americas were now largely independent, though economic penetration continued nevertheless. But Africa, Asia, and the Pacific islands offered almost irresistible allure. It became obvious that Polynesian islands like Hawaii, discovered by Europeans in the eighteenth century, could be made over into additional sources of sugar and other goods; it was logical to take over the government as well. China, long proudly resistant to Europe's economic overtures, was forced open in the Opium Wars that began in 1839. European gunboats, backed by small forces of well-armed soldiers, did the trick. The carving of North Africa began. France seized Algeria beginning in the late 1820s. Britain and France disputed control of Egypt. A French industrial concern in 1869 completed construction of the vital Suez Canal, a major improvement in access to India and the rest of Asia, but it was the British who gained effective control in the 1870s. By this time also, European expeditions in Southeast Asia and particularly in sub-Saharan Africa were adding huge swaths of territory to Western empires old and new.

The industrial revolution directly prompted this last and greatest imperialist outburst from the West. Steamships enabled Europeans to sail upriver, giving them new entry to China and particularly to the previously unnavigable rivers of central Africa. Mass-produced repeating rifles provided new advantages in gunnery, and by the 1860s early versions of the machine gun offered even more deadly fire. When this basic muscle was added to the quest for secure markets and cheap supplies, the age of industrial imperialism was at hand. Completion of imperialist conquest and full economic exploitation of new holdings particularly in Africa came only after 1880, but the stage was clearly set as a direct result of the first phase of the industrial revolution. And the consequence of new imperialism, in turn, was further to heighten the economic and political imbalance in the world at large.

Structural imbalance intensified Western scorn for peoples who seemed incapable of mastering advanced technology and modern organization. A variety of factors fed growing racism, but a rooted belief that performance in economy and technology measured the worth of a society played a growing role.

Finally, the first decades of industrialization's entry onto the world stage brought the West's initial attempts to create an international infrastructure. Forming part of this structure were international trading companies and shipping lines, which were expanded by the technology of the steamship. After 1850 telegraph lines were laid across the Atlantic and then to other regions outside the West; this development was vital to the transmission of commercial as well as political information. Also in the 1850s and 1860s international conferences (effectively confined to the Western powers) began to discuss world postal arrangements and worked to standardize some agreements on patents and commercial law. The world postal union, established in 1878, greatly facilitated international mailings; international copyright rules on works of literature and art were set in 1886. The globe was shrinking because of industrial technology and new levels of world trade, and unprecedented arrangements to reduce dispute and ease communication both reflected and furthered this fact. Western control of the initial agreements was inevitable and assured their application in other parts of the world as well; some of the consequences in terms of spreading new ideas and technical knowledge ultimately led in less predictable directions.

The growing imbalance created by the West's exploitation of its industrial lead would not be permanent, though some of its results affected the global economy even a century later. The West's industrial monopoly could not be preserved, and its first modifications helped set up the second phase of the industrial revolution in world history.

PART TWO

The Second Phase, 1880–1950: The New International Cast

6

The Industrial Revolution
Changes Stripes

FOUR MAJOR developments defined the second phase of the industrial revolution in world history: industrialization outside the West; redefinition of the West's industrial economy; growing involvement of nonindustrial parts of the world; and intensification of international impact. This phase began to take shape in the late nineteenth century, though no firm markers divided it from previous trends. Several Western societies, including Germany and the United States, were still actively completing their basic revolutionary transformation, becoming more fully urban and committed to the factory system as their manufacturing power presented new challenges to Britain, the established industrial power. Large numbers of new workers, fresh from the countryside, still poured into German and, particularly, American factories, experiencing much of the same shock of adjustment to a new work life that earlier arrivals had faced a few decades before. Other trends continued: The West retained its international lead in industrialization, and the growth of large business organizations persisted.

Second-Phase Trends

Newer trends gained ground. Several major new players began to industrialize by the 1880s and were the first clearly non-Western societies to undergo an industrial revolution. Russia's industrial revolution had a massive impact on world diplomacy. Japan's revolution altered world diplomacy as well and ultimately had an even greater effect on the international balance of economic power. The focal point of the second phase of the industrial revolution involved the transformation of these two key nations. By 1950, when their revolutionary phases were essentially complete, neither had matched the West's ongoing industrial strength. But a

MAP 6.1 *The industrial revolution in Europe, 1870–1914.*

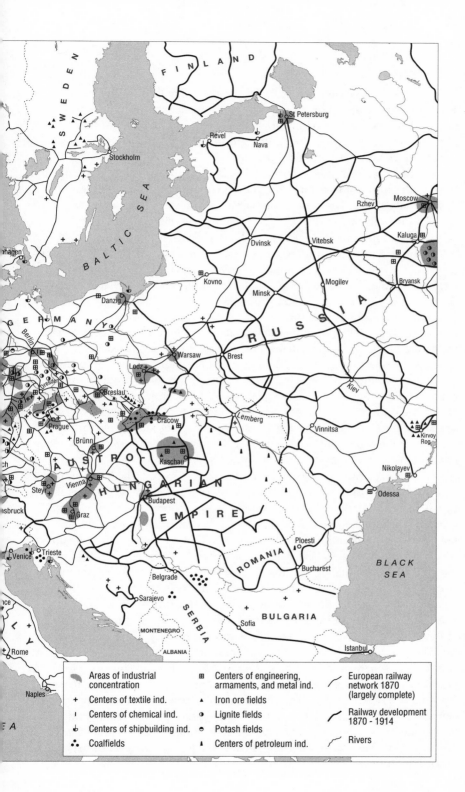

SWEDEN

FINLAND

St Petersburg

Stockholm

Revel

Nava

BALTIC SEA

Copenhagen

Dvinsk

Vitebsk

Rzhev

Moscow

Kaluga

GERMANY

Danzig

Kovno

Minsk

Mogilev

Bryansk

Berlin

Warsaw

Brest

RUSSIA

Lodz

Dresden

Breslau

Prague

Cracow

Lemberg

Kiev

Vinnitsa

Brünn

Kirvoy Rog

Kaschau

Nikolayev

AUSTRO-

Steyr

Vienna

HUNGARIAN

Budapest

Odessa

Innsbruck

Graz

EMPIRE

Trieste

Venice

Ploesti

ROMANIA

Bucharest

BLACK SEA

Belgrade

Rome

Sarajevo

SERBIA

Naples

MONTENEGRO

Sofia

BULGARIA

ALBANIA

Istanbul

Areas of industrial concentration	Centers of engineering, armaments, and metal ind.	European railway network 1870 (largely complete)
+ Centers of textile ind.	▲ Iron ore fields	Railway development 1870 - 1914
ı Centers of chemical ind.	◕ Lignite fields	
⚓ Centers of shipbuilding ind.	◒ Potash fields	Rivers
∴ Coalfields	◣ Centers of petroleum ind.	

key measure of these later industrial revolutions—like those of the United States and Germany before—was the capacity of the societies involved to grow more rapidly than the established industrial powers. The industrial revolution could allow newcomers to begin to catch up, and this feature marked many aspects of world history from 1880 to the present day.

Industrial revolutions in Japan and Russia constituted the most striking additions to the roster of transformed economies, but several British dominions industrialized as well. Canadian industrialization, which in fact had many features in common with the Russian process, began in the 1870s and by 1950 had propelled the country to a ranking among the world's ten leading industrial powers.

The industrialization of newcomers raises important questions. For example, why could some nations but not others begin to match the West at its own game? Or, how did these later industrial revolutions compare with earlier Western versions and with each other? Later industrial revolutions had many elements in common with the basic phenomenon in the West. They involved massive technological and organizational change and huge shifts in the experience of work and the nature of family life. But later industrial revolutions also revealed the effect of different chronology; the newcomers had to find the means to compensate for initial backwardness and to react to the relatively advanced industrial forms already established elsewhere. Finally, later industrializations outside the West reflected the different preindustrial cultures and institutions. They emerged from somewhat different strengths and weaknesses and took distinctive forms in the process. These challenging issues must be addressed in interpreting the second phase of the world's industrial revolution.

Other characteristics surfaced during the same decades. The West, in important ways, began to transform its own transformation. The late nineteenth century is sometimes referred to as a "second industrial revolution" in western Europe and the United States, and while the term is misleading—the changes were not nearly as profound as in initial industrialization, and many fundamental trends simply intensified—it invites inquiry into the recurrent shifts in direction the industrial revolution set in motion even when most of the basic features were already established. A changing industrial West also affected the rest of the world, including of course the areas now industrializing for the first time.

A third development involved a partial redefinition of how the industrial revolution affected areas not involved in the process directly. Here too many prior trends persisted. New levels of Western economic exploitation of resources in Africa mirrored many trends visible earlier in Asia and Latin America. There was, however, an increase of manufacturing, including factory production, in a growing number of world areas. The rise of manufacturing proved compatible with continued economic imbalance, as the West began to export certain kinds of factory production without encouraging full-scale industrial revolutions. The result, from China to Mexico, was not only major change but also a set of nagging, familiar limitations.

Finally, the global impact of the industrial revolution intensified, literally around the world. Further industrial development in the West, including the rise of new branches of chemical production and electrical equipment, additional industrial revolutions in Russia and Japan, and important if more diffuse economic change elsewhere under the spur of industrialization added up to a much greater potential change. The effects were widespread: New kinds of international economic crises emerged, most notably the great depression of the 1920s and 1930s. Industrialization of conflict emerged on an international scale in the world wars of 1914–1918 and 1939–1945. Industrial impact on the environment gained new visibility and prompted some new concern. The industrial revolution was entering a new world phase, often in troubling ways. The spread of industrialization did not equalize the societies of the world; important gaps separated new from more mature industrial economies and both from regions that still concentrated on providing food and raw materials to the international economy. Nevertheless, the process generated pervasive change worldwide.

Why Japan and Russia?

The engagement of two nations outside the West in the industrial process was the most striking new element in the world's industrial panoply by the late nineteenth century. Why were these two countries and not others able to participate? Neither Russia nor Japan shared the factors that had prompted the West's industrial revolution a half century earlier. Further, neither country had such obvious advantages in approaching industrialization that their lead over several other areas should be viewed as automatic. Japan, particularly, long isolated from much international trade and lacking crucial resources, notably coal, for an industrial economy, would have been on no observer's list in 1850 of countries most likely to succeed industrially. Thus, it is essential to undertake a new assessment from the standpoints of both causation and comparison.

Areas held as outright colonies were not likely candidates for full-fledged industrial revolutions in the late nineteenth and early twentieth centuries. Although significant factory industry existed in India by 1900, the dominant thrust of British colonial control emphasized maintenance of India as a source of cheap goods and a market for Britain's manufacturing. Colonial exploitation of Southeast Asia and Africa aimed even more single-mindedly at preserving the imbalance between hinterland and industrial homeland. Portugal, for example, began pressing its colony of Mozambique to produce cotton for developing Portuguese factories; this came at the expense of balanced agricultural practice and secure local food supplies and of any chance to expand an urban manufacturing base in this part of southern Africa. Widespread population growth in many colonial territories also provided such ready cheap labor that extensive mechanization could be avoided.

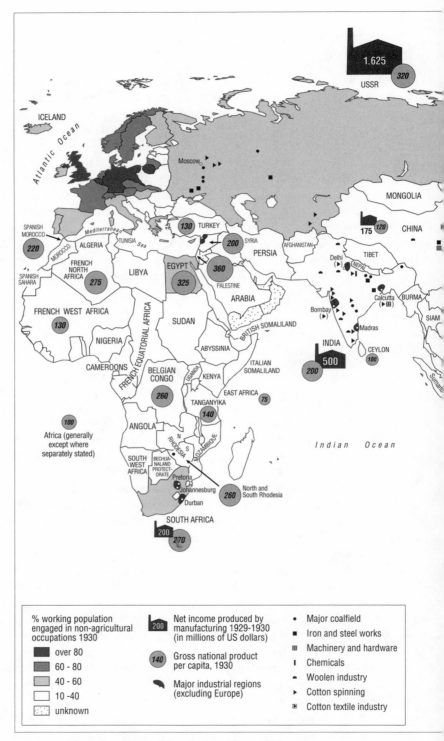

ICELAND

Atlantic Ocean

Moscow

MONGOLIA

SPANISH MOROCCO
220

Mediterranean Sea

MOROCCO

ALGERIA

TUNISIA

130 TURKEY

SYRIA **200**

PERSIA

AFGHANISTAN

1.625 **320**
USSR

175 **120** CHINA

TIBET

Delhi

NEPAL

SPANISH SAHARA

FRENCH NORTH AFRICA **275**

LIBYA

EGYPT **325** **360**

PALESTINE

ARABIA

Calcutta

BURMA

SIAM

FRENCH WEST AFRICA **130**

FRENCH EQUATORIAL AFRICA

SUDAN

Bombay

BRITISH SOMALILAND

Madras

INDIA

NIGERIA

ABYSSINIA

CEYLON **100**

CAMEROONS

BELGIAN CONGO **260**

UGANDA

KENYA

ITALIAN SOMALILAND

500

200

EAST AFRICA **75**

TANGANYIKA **140**

ANGOLA

100

Africa (generally except where separately stated)

RHODESIA
N
S

MOZAMBIQUE

Indian Ocean

Sumatra

SOUTH WEST AFRICA

BECHUA-NALAND PROTECT-ORATE

Pretoria
Johannesburg
Durban

260 North and South Rhodesia

SOUTH AFRICA

200 **270**

% working population engaged in non-agricultural occupations 1930

- over 80
- 60 - 80
- 40 - 60
- 10 -40
- unknown

200 Net income produced by manufacturing 1929-1930 (in millions of US dollars)

140 Gross national product per capita, 1930

Major industrial regions (excluding Europe)

- • Major coalfield
- ■ Iron and steel works
- ⊞ Machinery and hardware
- I Chemicals
- ◄ Woolen industry
- ► Cotton spinning
- ▣ Cotton textile industry

MAP 6.2   *The industrial revolution in the wider world by 1929.*

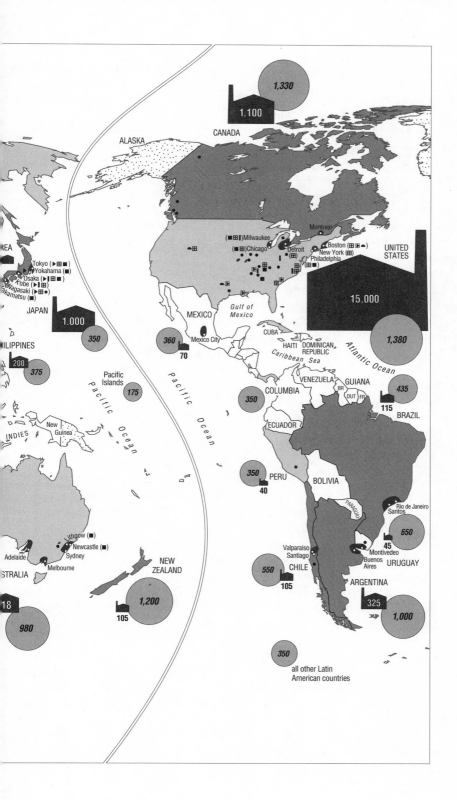

CANADA

1,330

1.100

ALASKA

UNITED
STATES

Montreal

(■⊞)Milwaukee
(■⊞)Chicago
Detroit
Boston (⊞▶•)
New York (⊞)
Philadelphia
(⊞■)

15.000

1,380

Atlantic Ocean

REA

Tokyo (▶•■)
Yokahama (■)
Osaka (▶I⊞■)
Kobe (▶I⊞)
Nagasaki (▶⊞•)
Takamatsu (■)

JAPAN

1.000

350

MEXICO

Gulf of
Mexico

CUBA

HAITI DOMINICAN
REPUBLIC

Caribbean Sea

ILIPPINES

200

375

Mexico City

360

70

175

Pacific
Islands

Pacific Ocean

COLUMBIA

VENEZUELA

GUIANA

BR

DUT FR

435

115

BRAZIL

INDIES

New
Guinea

Pacific
Ocean

350

ECUADOR

Pacific
Ocean

350

PERU

BOLIVIA

40

Rio de Janeiro
Santos

650

45

Lithgow (■)
Newcastle (■)
Adelaide
Sydney
Melbourne

STRALIA

18

980

NEW
ZEALAND

1,200

105

350

Valparaiso
Santiago

550

CHILE

105

Montivedeo
Buenos
Aires

PARAGUAY

URUGUAY

ARGENTINA

325

1,000

350

all other Latin
American countries

To reduce labor costs even further, European companies in Africa used essentially forced recruitment into labor gangs.

Latin America, though no longer literally colonial, was similarly dominated by the industrial West, including the United States. Heavy foreign indebtedness, lack of local capital and entrepreneurial drive, cheap labor, and a long tradition of production of specialty foods and raw materials for export to the West blocked most of Latin America from a full leap toward an industrial economy. Foreign ownership of key sectors, like the copper mines of Chile, further inhibited the emergence of a corresponding manufacturing sector. Significant change occurred, including expansion of some industry, but full industrialization was not yet possible.

China and the Ottoman Middle East, however, raise different analytical problems. These two societies were not held as colonies, though European seizures cut into the territory of both states. China, furthermore, had a long history of technological innovation, leading the world in developments such as printing and the use of coal in metallurgy up until the fifteenth century. Why did these well-established civilizations, both with dynamic economic traditions, fail to spearhead a second wave of industrial revolutions? Answers are difficult, but some of the ingredients are clear. Both areas, though China in particular, were beset by political weakness and ongoing population pressure during the nineteenth century, which inhibited their response. Both China and the Ottoman Empire remained suspicious of outside example and consequently, even while recognizing the West's growing industrial power, tended to concentrate on modest, piecemeal reforms. Both states, for example, sought to improve their military technology and organization without constructing an industrial foundation. Their economies changed but were increasingly penetrated by Western business interests. Outright industrialization was not initially sought and remained elusive even when its desirability was more clearly recognized.

What did Japan and Russia offer that made them more successful second-wave industrializers? Russia had extensive coal and iron holdings. Its prior contacts with the West could be put to good use: Many Russian leaders knew Western languages (particularly French), and while Westerners frequently thought of Russia as economically backward, they did include the nation in their frame of reference. Japan had an extensive merchant class, though it was based entirely on internal trade. It had developed an important urban culture and a productive, market-oriented agricultural sector. The Japanese population also boasted a high rate of literacy, thanks to Confucian-led programs in the seventeenth and eighteenth centuries. While Japanese education had to be rethought extensively in preparing directly for the industrial revolution, a relevant tradition and substantial skills were already available.

Japan and Russia also shared some very general characteristics that differentiated them from most other societies outside the West in the late nineteenth century. Neither was a colony, and neither had an economy that had become dominated by Western-directed commercial patterns. The Japanese had virtually no foreign trade at all, though a vital contact with Dutch merchants was preserved at the port of Nagasaki. Russia's commercial ties were more extensive; Western merchants controlled most of the trade with the West, and the terms of trade were potentially to Russia's disadvantage in their emphasis on cheap labor and unprocessed goods exported in return for finished products from western Europe. But Russia's internal economy was not massively skewed toward this trade, in contrast, for example, with parts of Latin America. In sum, Japan and Russia brought considerable economic independence to their encounters with the industrializing West.

Both countries also had reasonably strong governments. Russian tsars claimed vast authority, and they ran an active government with considerable confidence. Recurrent territorial expansion, particularly at Turkey's expense, revealed Russian vigor well into the nineteenth century. Administrative efficiency was on the rise (along with enhancement of a repressive political police). Japan's shogunate had introduced an active bureaucracy during the seventeenth and eighteenth centuries, preserving feudalism in name but supplementing it with a dynamic central state. The shogunate had lost some of its vitality by the early nineteenth century, and it lacked a consistently secure tax base, but its effectiveness was considerable even so. Compared with China's political deterioration—the ability of its imperial administration to command loyalty was plummeting by the midnineteenth century—Japan and Russia were both in good political shape. Not surprisingly, government directives in each instance helped set the industrialization process in motion.

Russia and Japan also knew from experience the salutary results of well-planned imitation of other societies. Russia, of course, had been selectively learning from the West for several centuries and even before that had borrowed from the Byzantine Empire. Japan had gained greatly from earlier imitation of China. It had renounced its willingness to copy in establishing an isolationist policy early in the seventeenth century (after a flurry of active interest in sixteenth-century Western merchants and missionaries), but it had a tradition its leaders could recall. Further, contact with Dutch merchants kept interest alive among a small group capable of pushing for a change in direction. The so-called Dutch school of trained translators began to press for more elaborate contacts with Western culture by the late eighteenth century, pointing particularly to Japan's inferiority in science and medicine. Confucian traditionalism was attacked. This debate did not by itself reorient Japanese culture, but it provided some precedent for later change. The basic point was clear: Both Russia and Japan knew that learning from outsiders could be profitable and need not overwhelm their own distinctive values.

For all their advantages, neither Russia nor Japan voluntarily decided upon an industrial revolution in the nineteenth century. As late as the 1850s both had regimes that would have preferred to maintain the status quo. But Western assertiveness abruptly removed that option. The British-French victory over Russia in the Crimean War convinced the tsarist regime, after only brief hesitation, that it had to sponsor bolder initiatives lest its independent foreign policy be hopelessly compromised and the country become captive to superior western economic and military strength. During the same years Japan faced an even more direct threat to its internal control. In 1853 an American fleet sailed into Edo Bay, near Tokyo, demanding that Japan open its markets to trade—or face bombardment. Commodore Perry's return in 1854 was bolstered by a visit from the British fleet. Japan had no choice but to open two additional ports to foreign trade. Britain, Russia, and Holland quickly won additional trading rights, and Western merchant enclaves were set up that operated under their own laws. Several shellings of Japanese forts by Western naval vessels drove the point home further. Japan's isolation had become impossible; the only issue was whether the country could master the terms of change.

Both Russia and Japan responded to the challenge by making explicit commitments to major reforms; quickly included were the early stages of industrialization. Their decision was unusual. Most of the rest of the world consisted of colonies that lacked power to decide or of nations like China not yet ready to make such a precedent-shattering choice. The decision to embark on industrialization in itself reflected the unusual position of Russia and Japan. Intent alone was not enough, to be sure, as many countries later discovered in the twentieth century. Both Russia and Japan faced immense strain and no small amount of internal disagreement in implementing their fundamental decision to meet the Western challenge by adopting key features of the Western economy. Nevertheless, conscious policy choice formed the first step. Japan and Russia soon took different paths as they followed up their choice—indeed, Japan tested its industrial achievement in outright war with Russia in 1904. Developments in the two countries conjoined, however, to break the West's industrial monopoly, and this in turn marked the emergence of a decisive new phase in the world's industrial history.

7

The Industrial Revolution in Russia

RUSSIA AND JAPAN, which began their industrial revolutions at least a half century behind most of the West, had to meet a number of special challenges. They had to acquire Western technical expertise. Outright invention was not necessary, but the process of imitation in societies not accustomed to technological change was at least as demanding. Both societies had to make reasonably explicit decisions about not only how to further but how to control the process of foreign imitation. These new industrializers had to provide capital—this had been true in the West as well, but for societies that had scanty preindustrial capital resources, trying to catch up imposed special burdens. Both societies had to provide motivation. Neither Russia nor Japan had a large preindustrial merchant class burning to set up factories; Russia had little merchant class at all, while Japan's was heavily tied into the feudal order. The two nations proved capable of producing vigorous entrepreneurs and managers, but this group relied more on government to launch the process in the first place. Government in turn, concerned about military issues and diplomatic position, gave the industrial revolution a distinctive twist. Certainly the state's ability to guarantee loans and to invest tax resources was crucial to early industrialization, given the distinctive conditions of Russia and Japan. In broad outline, industrializing as a latecomer required more explicit policy decision and a more careful shepherding than had been necessary in the West in the early nineteenth century. This was true in the two great industrial revolutions that took shape around 1900; it was true later for post-1950 industrializers as well.

Both Russia and Japan moved to industrialization in stages. A tentative experimental phase—which Russia had already experienced to an extent before 1870—included larger reforms that helped free up economic change. This preliminary period was followed by more rapid growth in a society still overwhelmingly agricultural. Russia and Japan had well-developed industrial sectors by the early twentieth century, but both lagged well behind the West. Both also needed some serious structural adjustments before they could move further, and these were introduced in the 1920s and 1930s as the specific characteristics of the Japanese and Russian versions of an industrial society were more clearly delineated.

Finally, both nations had to cope with extraordinarily rapid change because their industrial revolutions had to be combined with a wider set of reforms, all introduced not by spontaneous demand from within but by the West's outside threat. In this aspect too, latecomer industrialization displayed some features not present, at least in such intensity, in the West.

Yet Russia and Japan took very different industrial paths, and many of the differences survive to the present day. The diversity resulted from preindustrial traditions, including the structure of rural society, from varied kinds of contacts with the West, and from distinctions in the way the industrial revolution was initiated. Most obviously, Japan was able to industrialize without massive collective unrest, whereas Russia became the only society to date to experience full-fledged political and social revolution after the industrialization process was well under way. Correspondingly, Japan's industrial revolution followed a somewhat more consistent style than Russia's did, though there was substantial revision of Japanese policy in the 1920s. Russia tried two formats, one before its 1917 upheaval and one after; only in combination did they produce a genuine if unusual industrial economy in the nation.

Early Industrialization: Before the Revolution

The reform period in the 1860s that brought limited freedom for the serfs also produced a host of other political changes, some of which involved economic policy. Government budget procedures were regularized, and a state bank was created in 1866 to centralize credit and finance. New law codes adopted soon thereafter standardized commercial law and facilitated business operations. Government policy also encouraged more foreign investment.

Russia's reform era ended in 1881, after which highly conservative, even repressive policies went into effect in most quarters. The Ministry of Finance, however, maintained a commitment to change. The resultant tension was no small factor in the ultimately revolutionary impact of Russian industrialization, as Russia tried to combine industrial dynamics with a stagnant political context and even then had to contend with resistant conservatives who objected to the social danger of continued industrialization. Nevertheless, vigorous economic policies were sufficient to propel growth despite the political recalcitrance. The minister of finance during the 1890s, Serge Witte, was a genuine economic planner of a type that rarely had been seen in Russian bureaucracy at the time. Witte devoted his great talents to the stabilization of Russian finance. Among his goals for the country were acquisition of a considerable gold reserve, the rapid growth of railroads, and the promotion of heavy industry.

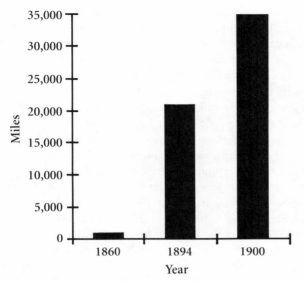

FIGURE 7.1 *Railroads in Russia, 1860–1900.*

Witte's background was as a railroad official, and he advocated rapid additions to the Russian network. Mileage doubled between 1895 and 1905, the additions including almost the whole of a line across Siberia that opened the vast resources of this region to industrial use. In 1860 Russia had boasted less than 700 miles of railroads, but by 1894 the total was already 21,000 miles, and by 1900 it had soared to over 36,000. Private companies, working under government concessions, did much of the work, but after 1880 state control increased. Most new lines were built and operated directly by the government. Some private lines were purchased; the rest were strictly supervised. The Russian railroad boom encouraged fuller utilization of Russia's considerable resources in coal and iron and of its extensive production of wool. The boom also directly induced increased output in heavy industry to create the rails and rolling stock and to provide the necessary fuel. As in the United States, railroad development became integral to the further advance of industry.

The Russian government assumed an unusually extensive role in investment banking. Private banks, virtually unknown before the reform period, did exist; the first corporate commercial bank was founded in 1864, and the number of institutions grew steadily thereafter. In addition, the government operated not only a state bank for commerce but also a number of other special credit institutions. Regularization of Russia's monetary system was another crucial government contribution. Russia's paper money had been nearly worthless in foreign exchange during the 1850s. Gradually the gold backing of Russian currency was increased, which made the ruble more stable and more open to international trade. Further, as part of improvements in commercial law, the government facilitated the formation of joint stock companies, or corporations. Only 80 corporations had existed in the whole of Russia before 1860. During the period 1861–1873 there were 3,547 new companies formed, and this trend accelerated in later decades. Finally, the government enacted high tariffs on industrial products, protecting nascent Russian industry and encouraging still further manufacturing.

The third key ingredient in Russia's early industrial revolution, along with increasingly focused government planning and railway development, involved foreign entrepreneurs, from whom Russia gained much-needed capital and technical knowledge. Yet the Russian government retained enough power over them to prevent the sort of undue exploitation that marked Western operations in many parts of Africa and Latin America. The line between foreign participation and foreign intrusion was a fine one, but on the whole Russia's industrialization process benefited from considerable openness in the early decades.

West European industrialists were quite aware of Russia's vast potential. The huge population, though largely impoverished, presented a tempting market to target. Still more obviously, the rich reserves of coal and iron begged for rapid exploitation. There were clear profits to be made, potentially at higher yield rates than in the more crowded industrial fields of western Europe. Foreign enthusiasm for Russia rivaled that for the United States, another huge nation heavily dependent on European capital. But the smaller business class in Russia made the foreign presence there even more noticeable and its role in guiding industrialization even greater.

Foreign capital was absolutely essential to Russian industry. It constituted at least 20 percent of all capital invested before the 1890s and then began to expand even further, accounting by 1914 for a full 47 percent of all corporate investment in the nation. Because the government was not actually pumping much funding directly into industry—even railroad construction commanded only about 5 percent of the total budget—the west European component effectively compensated both for Russia's poverty and for the state's commitment to wide-ranging military and bureaucratic programs that strained its resources. France, Belgium, Germany, and, after only a slight lag, Britain all developed extensive interests in Russian industry.

West European activities spread across Russia's industrial map. A number of French and Belgian metallurgical firms set up Russian branches. A French steel maker, Eugène Verdié, established a steel company in Russian Poland in 1877 as an extension of his French firm and then, with a St. Petersburg ironmaster of Scottish origin, formed a Russian company in order to supply 30,000 tons of steel rails to the Russian government. Another branch of the same operation provided metal to a navy shipyard. A variety of Belgian firms, including the Cockerills, operated in specialty steels, encouraged in part by their desire to penetrate the Russian market and break through the nation's high tariffs. The two great German electrical firms dominated the same industry in Russia through wholly owned subsidiaries, though the Westinghouse company of Pittsburgh, Pennsylvania, operated as well through a French subsidiary. German companies were also active in textiles, sometimes in partnership with Russians or Poles. French and Belgians joined the textiles parade as well; the Artificial Silk Company of Myszkov, for example, was founded with a link to Brussels in 1911 and claimed an improved process for treating cellulose and producing rayon. Western subsidiaries in public utilities, construction products, medicinal drugs, explosives, and even mirrors helped widen the range of Russian industrialization. Not only Western companies establishing branches but also individual entrepreneurs setting up Russian operations on their own played a vital role in this expansion process. For example, a Frenchman named Goujon, a longtime resident of Moscow, formed a company to produce wire in 1872, remaining its boss until 1909 even with additional Western and Russian investment; Goujon was described as "one of the oldest and best known Frenchmen in Russia, which he understands completely."

Encouraged both by the government and by Russian and foreign promoters, European engineers poured into Russia to investigate market conditions and resources. Some interest was directly linked to Russia's growing military expenditures—a French firm studied existing Russian shipyards in 1911 both to size up potential competition and to determine if a technical modernization was feasible for purposes of filling a recent government order for nine new torpedo boats. The zeal for Russian operations stemmed not only from awareness of markets and resources but also from the correct assumption that Western business had a crucial technological edge over Russian competition. By the same token, of course, the growing foreign presence rapidly increased Russian technology levels, a critical component in the country's industrial revolution. In general Western engineers assumed that advanced equipment could be transferred to Russia without major modification, a notion that placed some obvious burdens on Russian labor by subjecting it to novel machinery and radically new work settings. In many cases a handful of skilled workers from the West helped launch a new technology in Russia.

Not surprisingly, failures and disputes in Russia were common, and some foreigners pulled out after extensive problems with their work force or clashes with local property owners deriving from unfamiliarity with Russian property law. Foreign managers were themselves not always of top quality, and mistakes in equipment installation or business calculations were frequent. A French cotton manufacturer described a pattern in a 1903 report to his firm:

> The workers showed themselves hostile to all progress, and never succeeded in reaching normal production. We vainly tried to introduce piece work to stimulate their ardor; yet this only increased their dissatisfaction. We returned badly disillusioned, if not completely disheartened. We decided that the only solution was to send teams of experienced foreign workers to train Russian workers and stimulate production.
>
> Events decreed otherwise. Shortly after our return a strike followed persistent agitation and after three weeks rioting broke out. The mills were stormed three times by

the rioters. ... The entire French and Belgian personnel fled for their lives, and left the government to protect the mills. ...

After such an adventure there was no question of using foreigners to reform our top management; we needed Russians for our top personnel at any price, and above all a Russian managing director. ... We have chosen Morganov, a Russian engineer who has been well recommended. Let us hope he has what we desire—that he combines honesty and unwavering energy with technical skill.

In fact the company did prosper modestly, expanding on the basis of reinvestment of profits. Its decision to turn to an increasingly Russian staff was part of a general trend after 1900 toward reliance on local management. This trend was furthered by a growing number of contests with government officials. Russian bureaucrats, keenly aware of the need to keep powerful foreign interests under control, frequently blocked company merger plans or demanded that discontented workers be granted concessions for the sake of public order. Foreign investments continued until 1914, and government encouragement persisted as well—hence the steadily increasing percentage of capital investment provided from abroad. The process not only brought money and technology to Russia but also contributed to the expansion of a pool of Russian managers and technical experts.

A number of individual Russians exploited new industrial opportunities from the 1860s onward. Certain groups, like the Old Believers, a religious minority that had clung to older Orthodox traditions and gained state disfavor in the eighteenth century, provided disproportionate numbers of entrepreneurs. As in western Europe earlier, minority status was often a spur to seeking achievement in this new field. A surprising number of former peasants launched industrial operations; some even got started before their emancipation in 1861. This group was particularly important in setting up small textile operations in spinning, weaving, and cloth printing.

Russian industrial growth increased steadily and then had its first extraordinary spurt in the 1890s. A worldwide recession early in the twentieth century slowed development, but growth resumed at a rapid pace from 1908 until the outbreak of World War I.

Exploitation of Russia's iron and coal fields began slowly in the 1850s and was pioneered by individual Western industrialists. Coal deposits in the Donets district of south Russia had been discovered late in the eighteenth century, but there was no extensive mining until after 1850—the effective beginning of a modern coal-mining industry in the nation. Oil was discovered in the Caucasus around 1870, and a growing petroleum industry took shape soon thereafter: By 1900 Russia was second in world production of petroleum, supplying about one-fourth the international total. Heavy industry in general grew rapidly. During the 1890s the number of industrial companies grew by a full 216 percent. Oil production rose 132 percent; pig iron 190 percent; coal 131 percent; manufactured iron 116 percent; and cotton manufactures 76 percent. Overall industrial growth rates held at 6 percent per year during the late 1880s, soared to 8 percent during the 1890s, and then resumed a 6 percent level after 1908.

International comparisons show a similar Russian story. Russia's overall industrial growth rate between 1860 and 1913 matched that of the United States (though it started from a lower base). Under this measure, the country expanded almost twice as fast as Germany in the same years, over three times as fast as France, and over four times as fast as Britain—though again the starting point was much lower. In a host of industries, Russia had become the fourth or fifth largest producer by the early twentieth century; it ranked fourth, for example, in steel output. To be sure, these achievements were somewhat misleading, given the unusual size of Russia's population—per capita industrial production was less impressive, and it included some technologically backward sectors as well as relatively advanced heavy industry. Even textiles, however, showed the usual symptoms of industrialization: increasing mechanization, greater use of cotton (and Russia increased its homegrown cotton supplies accordingly by encouraging production in central Asia), and falling average prices for manufactured goods.

By 1914 there was no question that Russia had passed through a first industrialization phase. It had concentrated particularly on heavy industry because of resources, foreign interest, and the government's military needs. This emphasis helped generate a substantial number of large factories and encouraged relative neglect of the consumer-goods sector despite the growth in textiles and other light industry. Technology development had also been impressive, in part because of the input from abroad. Expansion of the number of trained Russian engineers had helped maintain the pace of change; the availability of skilled workers grew though probably lagged somewhat. Russia's previous lack of an extensive artisanal tradition limited available manufacturing skills. The factory labor force expanded rapidly. Skilled workers accumulated in St. Petersburg and Moscow, and there were old hands in metallurgy in the Urals region. The rapidly growing Donets basin, however, seemed chronically short of workers of any sort and of skilled operatives in particular. Some foreign companies compensated by importing the most up-to-date equipment that could be operated by semiskilled workers, but the problem of matching a labor force to industrialization—a considerable hurdle in any industrial revolution—was perhaps greater than average in Russia. There was progress in this nevertheless. The number of experienced miners and metallurgists more than doubled in the Donets area in the decade after 1904. The emergence of St. Petersburg and Moscow as multifaceted manufacturing centers that combined factories and smaller crafts was another sign of Russia's move toward the type of industrial economy common in the West. Overall, rapid urbanization rates paralleled the spurts of industrial growth around 1900 and resembled patterns in Germany or Britain a half century or more before.

Russian involvement in World War I, however, strained industrial capacity. Russia was attempting to fight an established industrial power—Germany—by using advantages in numbers to compensate for less abundant war material. The war not only interrupted industrial growth but also ripped the social fabric, bringing political revolution and, after this further dislocation, a radically altered framework for a resumption of industrialization.

Social Impacts: Industrialization and Revolution

Russia is the only nation to have experienced massive political revolution after starting a successful industrialization effort. Russia's working class played major roles both in the revolution of 1905 and then in the great uprising of 1917, in which workers' councils, or soviets, formed the backbone of the revolutionary effort. Russian workers became unusually successful at expressing moral outrage. Despite substantial internal differences common to most industrial working groups—urban artisans, workers in heavy industry, more isolated coal miners, and less skilled and often largely female labor forces in textile factories—a sense of class consciousness emerged at least by the early twentieth century. Workers in many Western countries had felt some of the grievances the Russian workers articulated; a few comparable outpourings formed a labor ingredient in the revolutions of 1848 in France and Germany. But industrial workers as part of a sustained, successful revolutionary effort constituted a Russian first, and the phenomenon has never wholly recurred.

The rapidly growing Russian working class faced many material problems. Child labor was widely used and abused in some cotton factories. The emancipation of the serfs, combined with substantial population growth, unleashed a flood of potential urban workers, and wages in many early factories were quite low in consequence. Moscow industrialists, slower to mechanize than their colleagues in St. Petersburg but able to draw from a densely populated rural hinterland, compensated for their shortcomings through cheap labor. Factories in the Urals, where a traditional heavy industry had already attracted many workers, paid low wages. To be sure, places that had to recruit new workers, like St. Petersburg or the growing Donets area, offered high pay at least to a skilled minority. Even in these regions, however, conditions were worsened by employer imposition of company stores or shoddy worker barracks. Housing conditions in factory centers were typically crowded, and a stark iron bedstead with straw mattress was the only furnishing. Housing in the rapidly growing cities deteriorated as construction failed to keep pace, and foul sanitary conditions added to worker woes. Many employers reduced pay by arbitrary fines. Sanitary conditions were dreadful; textile factories were dusty, chemical works filled with noxious smells. Hours of work were long, ranging up to fourteen a day. Family life was often disrupted. Many male workers left families back in the villages as they wandered in search of temporary factory work. Considerable use of adult women in textiles and other industries cut into family time. Sexual habits loosened. Workers with some experience in the factories began to engage more commonly in sexual intercourse before marriage, and working-class attitudes toward sexuality—though particularly for men—relaxed traditional peasant standards. Finally, there was the new work regime itself to come to terms with. Russian peasant labor had not been joyous, but the pace and regimen of the factories came as a tremendous shock.

Workers reacted to their new environment in many ways. Job changing and leaving factory centers to return to the countryside were endemic. Many companies "worried about the long absence of workers for four or five months in the summer." Drinking, already a popular pastime among the Russian peasant masses, often increased among a group that had few other regular leisure outlets.

The unusual foreign involvement in Russian industrialization played some role in stimulating grievances beyond the levels prevailing earlier in the industrializing West. The privileges of foreign workers often drew attack. In 1900, after a mutual name-calling incident, 200 workers burned all the buildings and possessions of 60 thoroughly frightened Belgian workers in a glass factory. Western managers were an obvious target for some labor leaders who associated foreignness with exploitation.

The speed of Russia's industrial development placed many former peasants in large and technically sophisticated factories to work without the benefit of any intermediate stage of smaller plants and less demanding equipment. In 1900, when Germany had only 14 percent of its manufacturing labor force in factories with over 500 people, Russia had 34 percent—and nearly a quarter of all Russian workers labored in factories with over 1,000 people. Opportunities for disorientation and alienation in these settings were particularly great for workers who came from the highly, even excessively personalized context of village life. To be sure, earlier Russian factories had created a minority of workers with substantial industrial experience, and a second or even third generation of factory hands existed by 1900. But the confrontation with novelty might have been unusually great and helped to propel even badly paid transient workers toward a broader class consciousness.

The speed factor affected craft workers as well. Growing factories and cities meant needs for new numbers of urban bakers, construction workers, and printers. Some of these groups, such as printers in St. Petersburg, briefly displayed some of the preindustrial cohesion characteristic of artisans earlier in the West, in part because some of them had been recruited from Germany. Journeymen and masters gathered for joint ceremonies such as feasts and gift giving and expressed thanks for the employers' "paternal concern"; employers responded in kind by invoking their "love for their younger brothers." This collegial atmosphere lasted into the 1880s, but it was soon shattered by the growing size of printing establishments, more complex equipment, and a definite class consciousness on the part of the employers—including those bedecked in fraternal affection just a decade before. By 1905 workers were attacking their employers' "arbitrary authority," and erstwhile fraternalists were responding "I am the boss, and I can dismiss workers from my shop if I don't like them." This transition from familial atmosphere to sharp employer-worker division had occurred in western Europe also but over a longer period of time and without the sheer newness of the craft itself adding to the confusion. Not surprisingly, the St. Petersburg printers, briefly a moderate voice among Russian workers, helped fuel the radicalism of the revolutionary era.

Worker protest also reflected the unrest of the Russian countryside. New workers brought in peasant grievances against landlords and the state, while the heady experience of urban life and association with other workers helped enliven isolated villages when workers returned. In no other large industrial revolution were peasants still so aggrieved as in Russia (the only comparable case was Catalonia, in Spain, which was drawing from peasant migrants in the south at precisely the same point in time). Unquestionably, grievances of the related sections of the Russian populace fed each other.

Furthermore, Russian workers had a more abundant array of ideological inspirations than Western workers had enjoyed in a comparably disruptive phase of industrialization. As Russia imported factory techniques, its discontented intellectuals also imported Western socialist ideas, and a largely homegrown anarchist movement added ideological fuel from another source. Urban workers gained rapid access to radical doctrines and leaders. Indeed, they could learn socialism at precisely the same time Western workers were learning it—in the 1880s and 1890s. But Western workers by then were in a more advanced industrial stage, able to see some improvements at least in material conditions. They absorbed socialism but on the whole discounted its literal revolutionary content. Russian workers were more likely to buy the whole package.

Finally, Russian workers felt keenly their isolation from urban society and from the state. This added to their resentment and also built their sense of mutual cohesion. Workers in the cities were addressed condescendingly by their social "betters," treated in fact as peasants when many of them were quite proud of having cast off that former life. The government was remote and repressive. A few factory laws were passed, one of them as early as 1845 limiting child labor, but they were largely unenforced. Workers knew the government best as the repressor of strikes and unions, both of which were firmly illegal. As workers, particularly in St. Petersburg and Moscow, learned new ideas and horizons from the radical intellectuals, they gained a sharp sense of their powerlessness.

These factors operated in combination. They reflected conditions common to early industrialization, the rigidity of Russian politics and social hierarchy, and the larger agitations of Russian society. The amalgam differentiated Russian workers from their counterparts in earlier Western industrialization and from workers in Japan with whom they shared many problems but not the same cultural context. When further mixed with growing peasant and liberal protest, the combination produced a major worker revolution.

Organizations among industrial workers began in the 1870s, though there had been important strikes even before then. Unions in Odessa and St. Petersburg were broken up by the police. A great textile strike occurred in 1878, and strikes began to pepper the industrial landscape. Many resulted in arrests and trials, but these in turn publicized the hardships of factory life and spread a message of liberation. The government issued a new factory law in 1866 to protect against unsafe conditions, but it also reaffirmed the prohibition on worker organizations and increased the penalties for striking. Employer pressure brought a softening of the factory law in 1890, but workers were gaining new ground. By the 1890s Lenin and other Marxist leaders were spreading socialist doctrines in the cities. New strike waves occurred in 1896 and 1897. The Social Democratic Workers Party, headed by Lenin, was formed in 1898. The economic slump after 1900 caused widespread unemployment and new unrest, including strikes in many centers.

From this context emerged the general strike of 1905, triggered by Russia's loss to Japan in war. Soviets were established in many factory centers. Workers briefly won the vote and the legality of strikes for economic (but not political) goals. Employer resistance stiffened, however, creating growing class antagonism. The government banned the Marxist party, jailing or exiling many leaders. Workers were briefly cowed, but a new and more determined strike wave resumed in 1912. Several strikes led to brutal confrontations with police and many arrests and injuries. When the hardships of World War I added still greater incentive, workers were ready to rebel in 1917. Again the soviets formed, and this time they served as the basis for the new communist regime headed by Lenin, which overturned the short-lived middle-class government that had initially replaced the tsar. The world's most genuine working-class revolution had triumphed.

The Industrial Revolution Under Communism

The Russian Revolution and subsequent civil war, following on the heels of World War I, dealt a blow to the country's economy. Manufacturing output declined, and many workers left the cities to scour the countryside for food. Lenin's government probably compounded the difficulties by nationalizing all the great factories and soon nationalizing small business as well. Management was disaffected, and production faltered further. The communist regime also renounced all foreign debts, seizing the factories that had been built in part by foreign capital. This provided the new Soviet Union with substantial industrial assets, but in the short run it both antagonized foreign investors and further disrupted established management.

During the early 1920s Lenin modified his policies through the New Economic Program, which gave some leeway to private business while maintaining government management of the big factories. Lenin and his colleagues were committed to extending the industrial revolution. Marxist doctrine assumed an industrialized economy capable of abundant production; it attacked capitalism but not industry or technology. Further, Soviet leaders, isolated from the rest of the world, saw the need for industry to assure the nation's defense.

In pursuing further industrialization, the communist state expanded several themes that had already developed in Russia's first industrial decades. It relied still more extensively on state guidance and control. It emphasized heavy industry, a sector in which the Soviet Union had a resource advantage and considerable on-going momentum and that had a particularly close relationship to military strength. Industrialization under Soviet communism also maintained the emphasis on big factories and management hierarchies, though the managers were largely new faces. Private ownership was banned in industry, but a managerial class gradually assembled that was closely linked to the Communist Party. Issues of recruiting and supervising workers, though affected by propaganda praising the working class and by prohibitions on strikes and independent unions, continued to demand considerable attention.

The communist version of an industrial society also placed great emphasis on women's work. In the 1920s Soviet society began to display some of the same family adjustments that had occurred earlier in the West. The new focus on schooling led to withdrawal of children from the labor force, and families reacted by cutting their birthrate, either through birth control or abortion. Lower birthrates meant protecting the family standard of living (now that children were an expense rather than an income source) and lavishing concern on children as individuals. These same elements had developed in the Western response to industrialization, and the result was the same as well: rapid slowing of overall population growth. But the Western pattern of withdrawing married women from the labor force did not widely apply. The need for additional workers was too great, particularly because mechanization was only selectively introduced. Many women did jobs performed in Western society either by unskilled men or by machines, such as street cleaning or hauling work. Communist leaders proudly made a virtue of women's work, arguing that Soviet society avoided imposing the domestic inferiority on women characteristic of the industrial West.

The new regime also explicitly departed from a number of prior industrial policies, even aside from the vast expansion of government control or the new rhetoric surrounding women's work. It reduced dependence on foreigners. Lenin imported some engineers and skilled workers from the United States and western Europe, and he was eager to introduce up-to-date technologies and organizational schemes like the assembly line. But foreign expertise was now clearly supplementary to an impressive Soviet effort. Recruitment of talented managers from the peasantry and working class and rapid expansion of the educational system, including technical training, provided necessary skills internally. The Soviet economy was substantially cut off from the rest of the world. It exported little and imported little. This was the first case in which industrialization was completed in such isolation, though of course it could be argued that prerevolutionary Russia's earlier start, under extensive foreign guidance, also permitted this pattern. Finally, while the new regime emphasized big factories, it was far more attentive to worker demands and interests than had been the case before. Worker protest was forbidden again, and the working class was enrolled in unions led by party members. Strikes were considered an attack on the state. But government knew its practical and ideological roots in the working class, and it listened informally to potential grievances. Elaborate welfare measures to provide medical care, old-age pensions, and leisure facilities, began increasingly to supplement industrial life; these were provided by the communist state.

Industrial production reached prewar levels by about 1926, an impressive achievement given the earlier disorder and the removal of most foreign experts and many previous Russian business leaders. Urban living standards improved as well. New communist managers gained increasing competence in running factories and other enterprises. Then in 1927 Stalin came to power and effectively ended a long debate over the proper structure for the Soviet economy. The Communist Party congress in 1927 approved the first five-year plan, a scheme designed to go beyond mere economic recovery to build state-run industrial growth and fuller self-sufficiency vis-à-vis the outside world.

The five-year plans—the first one was proclaimed completed in 1932, ahead of schedule, and it was followed by other plans prepared by the State Planning Commission (Gosplan)—emphasized heavy industries, big factories, and technological modernization. Vast state funds were poured into new plants; in the period 1933–1935 over half of all state construction money was devoted to industry, and of this 78 percent went to heavy industry as opposed to consumer-goods sectors. Agriculture was collectivized, which led to great brutality against the wealthier peasants but increased the mechanization of agriculture and freed growing numbers of peasants for work in the factories. The labor force expanded rapidly once again, which meant among other things a new set of problems of incorporating former peasants into big, impersonal factory settings. Work efficiency remained inconsistent, and there was an endemic shortage of skilled operatives. Because the focus was on heavy industrial technology, other manufacturing operations depended on large numbers of workers using less advanced equipment, and even some of the big industrial factories used larger numbers of workers in relation to output than was true in the West or Japan.

Resources were allocated by state boards and independently of market forces. Conscious policy, not profits or direct competition, was intended to guide this industrialization process. This approach sometimes reduced waste and redundancy. It allowed the state and not consumer demand to set the tone for the economy. It also produced serious imbalances even within the favored industrial sectors. Not all state operations were effective. Planning impeded easy delivery of goods. The state itself sometimes tried shortcuts in order to pour money into heavy industry. Railroad development, for example, lagged, which created transportation bottlenecks across the giant nation.

The most obvious drawback of the new approach to industrialization involved worker motivation. Deliberate neglect of consumer goods meant that workers were confronted with few attractive options for purchase. Even food production often broke down, for collective farms did not assure rapid agricultural growth. Subsequent five-year plans trumpeted increased attention to consumer goods, but the stress on heavy industry continued, and scarcities of food, clothing, and housing made life in the cities extremely difficult. Working wives, particularly, had to spend much of their free time in long shopping lines, in what became a daily reminder of the limitations of Soviet industrial life. On the brighter side, workers had considerable security. They were assured of full employment, and the Soviet Union's massive industrial growth during the 1930s contrasted vividly with the depression-filled miseries of economies in the West. Not only educational levels but also opportunities for mobility increased. Health and life expectancy improved also, a basic measure of standard-of-living gains.

The communist regime spared no pains to create a sense of dignity for the working class and to reverse its previous sense of being scorned and isolated. Art and drama glorified the heroic worker. Special programs also were created to deal with some of the characteristic goals of an industrializing economy. The government, taking a page from capitalist factories, introduced a series of incentive schemes in the 1930s to try to stimulate harder work. Stakhanovite workers were given bonuses and hero-of-labor pins. Aleksei Stakhanov, a miner in the Donets basin, developed a new method of extracting coal in 1935, which allowed him greatly to exceed the established rates of output. Within a few weeks his example was given tremendous publicity by the government and was emulated by workers in a variety of trades—partly from patriotic devotion, partly to win higher wages.

The system had a dark side. The Soviet regime imprisoned millions of people for a variety of political offenses as part of its enforcement of rigid political orthodoxy, including the ban on open labor dissent. Many of these prisoners were used in forced labor, essentially as slaves, particularly for big construction projects like dams and canals and in some isolated mines. Exactly how extensive forced labor was remains controversial, and it was not the primary ingredient of industrial success, but it played some role.

By the standards the government most cherished, the new industrial system worked. Output expanded rapidly. In 1928, as the first five-year plan began, the Soviet Union stood fifth in the world in manufacturing output. In scarcely more than twenty years and despite the tremendous toll exacted by World War II, it moved to second place, behind only the United States. Coal production of 35 million tons in 1928 escalated to 109 million tons in 1935. Pig iron production almost quadrupled, and steel production tripled. Chemical and machine-building industries, poorly developed before, came into their own. By 1936 the Soviet Union produced more tractors than any other nation in the world. New regional centers that developed, particularly in Siberia, were important both in mining and metallurgy. Electrification proceeded rapidly. In fifteenth place internationally in the generation of electric power in 1913, the nation moved to third place by 1935. Le-

Harvesting grain by a "northern" combine at the "Tshorvonny Kollektivist" farm in Russia. (Courtesy of AP/Wide World Photos. Reprinted by permission.)

nin had said, "Electrification plus Soviet power equals communism," and the mechanical power came with a vengeance.

Although Soviet production figures were sometimes inflated, the massive industrial growth of the 1930s was one of the great surges in the history of the industrial revolution anywhere. The quality of goods was sometimes dubious, and particularly in the neglected consumer sector items were not only hard to find but frequently shoddily made. A whole host of problems lurked within the Soviet industrial system, and the world did not become fully aware of them until the late 1980s. Yet the achievements at the time were breathtaking. The industrial labor force tripled, to about 6.5 million workers. Gigantic industrial complexes were built from scratch in resource-rich centers like Magnitogorsk in the Urals and Kuznetsk in western Siberia. Magnitogorsk acquired an industrial population of a quarter million in just a few years, a reminder that industrial revolutions still had the same power to entice people to relocate that they had demonstrated in the days of Manchester or the Ruhr. Over 1,500 new Soviet factories were built during the 1930s.

As opposed to the government's unreliable claims of 20 percent annual industrial growth, Soviet industrial output seems to have expanded between 12 percent and 14 percent per year during the 1930s, unquestionably one of the best sustained records in the world's industrial history. To accomplish this essentially alone—the

Soviets had only modest outside technical expertise and almost no outside financing—simply magnified the achievement. By the 1950s, when the Soviet economy recovered from World War II and resumed impressive growth and when a full half of the population was urbanized, the Soviet Union had completed one of the few full industrial revolutions in world history and certainly one of the most unconventional.

8

The Industrial Revolution in Japan

JAPAN's industrial revolution began to take shape in the 1870s. As in Germany and Russia, railroad building both symbolized and caused a more general pattern of rapid industrial growth. The story of early Japanese railroads also suggests some of the patterns involved in larger industrialization, including the immense constraints of early initiatives.

The Meiji government launched a major railroad development plan in 1870, only two years after the regime had consolidated its hold and abolished feudalism. Railroads were considered necessary for the overall economic unification of Japan and as a basis for further modernization. The state initially hoped to rely on private capital, guaranteeing a dividend rate of seven percent on any capital invested and asking the Mitsui firm to raise funds for a line between Osaka and Kyoto. But when few capitalists stepped forward, and the company did not materialize, the government acted directly, establishing an important precedent for state involvement in the industrialization process as a whole. Between 1870 and 1874 railroad building accounted for nearly a third of all state investments in modern industry. Foreign loans added to the mix. An initial line between Tokyo and Yokohama, completed by 1872, was built with a million-pound loan from the British Oriental Bank. The government initially hoped to use U.S. contractors, but British pressure forced ultimate reliance on the Oriental Bank (after a further delay in which Americans successfully revoked an interim British deal).

Whatever the birth pains, government lines proved to be immediately profitable, and after 1874 subsidies were sufficient to attract private investment. By 1892 Japan had a total of 1,870 miles of track, 550 miles of it government-owned and 1,320 in private hands. An early private company formed by a group of nobles had problems completing plans but opened a line between Tokyo and Aomori in 1881; capitalized with 20 million yen, their company was the largest enterprise in Japan. The government guaranteed 10 percent dividends and employed 256 engineers (under the Ministry of Industry) to provide necessary technical expertise. After

113

the success of this first company, other firms formed, and private railway invest-ment increased fiftyfold between 1881 and 1891. Japanese heavy industry was un-able to supply equipment until after 1900, which meant continued dependence on imports from Europe. In 1907, however, the Kawasaki shipyard began to produce the first locomotives and coaches in Japan's brief industrial history.

The government also pioneered in developing new mines for iron, lead, copper, gold, silver, and coal. Private mines existed, but only the state enterprises—there were six by 1881—operated on a large scale with modern imported machinery. The government invested heavily in the technical modernization process. It put 2.4 million yen into the Kamaishi iron mines, but the effort failed and the mines were put out of operation and ultimately (in 1887) sold to a private investor for a mere 12,600 yen. A copper mine also sputtered along and finally was sold for a fifth of what the government had invested. The Miike coal mines, however, were successful and turned a good profit upon sale—six times the state's outlay.

Other mines developed through Western investment. A feudal lord (daimyo) cofounded a mine with the British firm Thomas Glover. The agreement was that Glover would provide the money to open the mine and run it for seven years, pay-ing a royalty on any coal produced; the mine would be returned to the lord there-after. The Meiji government soon intervened, taking over the mine and selling it to a businessman, Goto Shojiro. Goto made another deal with the British firm to acquire capital, pledging that Glover would have exclusive sales rights on the coal—as "monopoly sales agent for the coal in East Asia." Profits would be di-vided equally between the two partners. But the mine failed, and Goto went bank-rupt; Japanese courts distributed his assets among Japanese creditors but awarded very little to Glover, which sold its share in the mine to the Mitsubishi shipping company in 1877. Western investment in this and in other instances, helped launch Japanese industry but under strict controls and with many setbacks. The contrast to the more open situation in Russia was obvious.

Shipping and shipbuilding early attracted government attention. Japan was an obvious candidate for maritime activity, despite over two centuries of govern-mental restrictions on seagoing ventures. The focus on shipping proved a crucial move in helping the Japanese escape Western control of commerce. The Mitsubishi company began operations after a complex evolution from a semifeudal armaments arrangement. A feudal samurai, Iwasaki Yataro (1834–1885), managed armaments procurements for a regional feudal lord, buying for-eign weapons and ships; he proved efficient in reorganizing older feudal enter-prises and procuring funds for arms purchases. After the Meiji regime was estab-lished, his firm became an independent company, though it was still supposed to help the feudal lords and provide jobs for samurai. Iwasaki converted the com-pany into his personal property in 1873, renaming it Mitsubishi. He developed a loyal staff of former samurai—much of his success stemmed from the high mo-rale and group solidarity among these lieutenants. Mitsubishi competed directly with a government shipping line, the Nippon Postal Steamship Company, which carried passengers, rice, and other freight along the coast. Mitsubishi's ships were more modern and its bureaucracy was less cumbersome. Iwasaki's firm soon drove the Nippon Company out of business and became a major government carrier. In 1874–1875 the government bought eleven iron steamers for military transport, loaning (ultimately giving) all of them to Iwasaki; major government subsidies also poured in. The condition was that Mitsubishi engage in direct competition with foreign lines, opening a regular route between Japan and China where the Americans and British had established domination. By 1877 Iwasaki had badly beaten the Pacific Mail Company and an English steam company.

By this time Mitsubishi had acquired massive assets—6.3 million yen, of which 3.3 million lay in the value of the ships. It was time to extend operations. Iwasaki bought into a maritime insurance company in 1878 and broadened out into foreign-exchange banking. A new challenge arose in the form of a rival shipping company established in 1883 with capital from the government. Iwasaki was cordially detested by this point for his dominant position in shipping, his outrageous profits, and his overbearing personality. The new company helped drive down coastal passenger fares by over 1,000 percent. But the government did not want to risk either company's collapse, and its mediation, plus a secret deal Iwasaki arranged just before his death, led to an amalgamation into a massive new company that had 112 million yen capital and was controlled de facto by Mitsubishi. By this time the huge conglomerate had also established a stake in coal mining and shipbuilding, borrowing the Nagasaki shipyard from the government in 1877 and buying it outright in 1887. Big business entered early into Japan's industrial scene.

The Japanese government also stimulated the textile industry. In 1877, when only three modern cotton-spinning mills were operating in Japan, the Meiji government owned two of them. This sector also required large amounts of capital, and the government was one of the only available sources. But the Japanese state played only a modest role in light industries. It supported no construction of textile equipment, for example, relying entirely on imports for the few modern factories that existed. By 1910 the government was sponsoring the construction of the world's largest battleship, the *Satsuma*, but had yet to develop an overall plan to modernize textile production.

Some historians have argued that the Japanese government sensibly focused on investments that inherently involved large scale and technological complexity and, further, that limited resources dictated leaving other areas to private hands even at the cost of much slower technological change. Others have contended that the government focused on heavy industry simply because of its direct bearing on military production, essential not only for defense but for imperialist adventures—which Japan began to experiment with as early as the 1870s in an expedition against Taiwan and undertook more seriously in the 1890s with a successful war against China. Whatever its mix of motives, the state played a vital role in early Japanese industrialization, as even a few impressions of the period clearly demonstrate.

Government involvement in early industry far exceeded that of Russia before the 1917 revolution—correspondingly, foreign investors were much more successfully limited. Government operations blended readily with private business, however, and the boundary lines were far fuzzier than in the Western or Russian traditions. Private use of government assets had certainly occurred in the West—as in the huge public land grants to American railroads—but the Japanese moved investment funds and business management back and forth in a distinctive fashion. Within big private firms, a modified feudal tradition built intense group loyalty, which coexisted with intense individual profit-seeking on the part of individuals like Iwasaki. This was another way in which a vigorous preindustrial culture fed into successful but distinctive industrial management.

The Context for Industrialization

Japan was in many ways an unlikely candidate for a quick industrial response to the new economic challenge of western Europe and the United States. The nation, long isolated, faced many problems trying to comprehend the West even as it began to realize that some imitation of Western ways was essential (among them, of course, an industrial revolution). Japanese visitors to the United States commented, for example, on the bizarre lack of veneration for leadership; most Americans in the 1860s seemed to have no idea of what had happened to George Washington's descendants. Political parties baffled them—how could groups dispute so bitterly yet manage to sit in the same legislative chamber? To be sure, these same visitors early saw the centrality of Western technology. They proudly noted that Japan learned how to build a steamship very quickly. They also realized the importance of science in Western education and began fairly rapidly to incorporate this in Japanese training, jettisoning Confucian traditionalism though not the larger Confucian emphasis on group harmony and devotion to society.

Not surprisingly, as in Russia, a number of Japanese continued to oppose even the limited Westernization that occurred. A number of feudal lords hoped to restore isolation in the 1860s rather than industrialize; they lost, and on balance antiindustrial sentiment was lower in Japan than in Russia. But a broader concern about the direction of change complicated aspects of the industrialization process.

Japan was also poor in relevant natural resources. It had some coal and copper and traces of other minerals, but it quickly recognized the need to trade not simply for complex equipment from the industrialized nations but for the raw materials that were the sinews of industry. Textile fibers appropriate for mechanization, notably cotton, also had to be imported. In short, understanding the resource problems that guided Japanese industrialization almost from the start is an aid to understanding several facets of the process: why the government subsidized mining ventures so quickly—but also why several failed; why there was an early and lasting attempt to develop a large export sector; and why Japan engaged in early imperialist expansion to acquire territory that could provide secure, cheap supplies of needed materials.

Japan also faced the burdens of established Western competition. This is one reason both Japan and Russia urged extensive government involvement in the industrialization effort as a way to compensate for backwardness and to provide guidance and capital designed to speed the process of change lest catching up become impossible. Japan, however, faced foreign constraints far greater that those of Russia. It could not impose high tariffs on industrial imports. British and American pressure, backed by military threats, forced largely open markets; only in 1911 did Japan regain control over its tariff policy. Western businesses operated in parts of Japan under Western, not Japanese, commercial law. In this context the Japanese government had to work even harder than its Russian counterpart to achieve the same result—adequate national control over the economy and adequate national monitoring of the necessary borrowing from Western experts and financiers. Japan managed to prevail: Western investments were limited to a far greater extent than in Russia. Government subsidies and guarantees on investment earnings made up part of the difference. Japan also early established a policy of encouraging Japanese business to "buy Japanese" rather than to import from abroad. Some imports were technically imperative, but where there were options, the government pushed cultural pride in Japanese distinctiveness and cultural traditions of social solidarity to prevent overreliance on foreign economies. This was another distinctive feature inserted in the industrial economy that continued to affect policy into the late twentieth century.

Japan's industrial achievement against formidable obstacles was unquestionably impressive. The energy and focused policy that pushed the nation toward the top of the world's industrial leadership in the late twentieth century were absolutely essential in getting the industrialization process launched in the first place. Every available asset, from prior culture to high levels of education to the sweat of Japanese workers, had to be brought to bear. At the same time, Japanese industrialization inevitably advanced slowly at first because of the special impediments Japan faced.

The Early Stages

Japan's early commitment to industrialization came in the 1860s. In contrast to Russia, Japan altered political as well as social structures, though without revolution, thus reducing some of the tensions industrialization created when inserted into a traditional political fabric. The abolition of feudalism did not eliminate the powerful nobility, however, and finding outlets for samurai energies continued to be a preoccupation. Many samurai were able to adapt their values to successful industrial management, and the way was left open for other kinds of leaders, notably successful businessmen, to join elements in the former nobility in forming a new elite. The Russian dilemma—seeking industrialization while trying to preserve the political dominance of the tsar and nobility—was thus avoided.

Initial Meiji reforms brought additional gains. With abolition of feudalism came freedom of occupations. Farmers were able to trade directly. Earlier monopolies on regional trade were eliminated, which meant open access to urban markets and abolition of tax barriers on roads. A fully national economy emerged for the first time. Most traditional merchant houses—and preindustrial Japan had developed a large merchant class and big trading companies—were tied to the finances of feudal lords and proved unable to make the transition to a new economy. Many business failures occurred. But new commercial ventures proliferated, bringing a host of new small businesses and a few potential giants to the fore. What was happening by the 1870s, even before much outright industrialization, was a liberation, an unshackling of the Japanese economy. The resultant dynamism fed easily into new industrial ventures.

Agriculture changed as well. Taxes on peasants were reduced slightly; farmers gained clear title to the land, which enable them to buy and sell land. Rural society was increasingly divided between market-oriented landowners and tenants and laborers. The owners, including progressive landlords, began to introduce fertilizers and farm equipment. The government provided technical assistance, setting up a faculty of agriculture at the Tokyo Imperial University. Production soared. Rice output more than doubled between 1880 and 1930. At the same time, the Japanese government quickly copied some Western public health measures. The result, along with greater food supplies, was a rapid population increase, from about 30 million in 1868 to 45 million in 1900 (and on to 73 million in 1940). Because the numbers of people needed on the land did not increase, given more productive agricultural methods, vast new labor supplies were available for factory and other urban jobs.

This was the context in the 1870s in which the government began to sponsor pilot industries. The Ministry of Industry was established in 1870 under Ito Hirobumi and quickly became one of the leading agencies of the state. The government expanded arsenals and shipyards, built telegraph lines, and of course made a start on railroads and new mining. The railroad network was absolutely vital, for Japanese commerce previously had depended on very expensive coastal shipping. In 1868 it cost as much to ship goods fifty miles inland as to transport them to Europe. Railroads gave Japan an internal circulatory system, opening up previously isolated areas both to sales and to purchases. The state also set up a few model factories in textiles, cement, glass, and machine tools. These early factories generated little output, but they helped train Japanese technical experts and labor. New roads and ports, more suitable commercial laws, and a new banking system helped round out the government-sponsored infrastructure.

The first truly industrial phase of growth began in the 1880s. Big businesses emerged, the forerunners of the great industrial combines known as *zaibatsu*.

Would-be industrial giants faced obvious problems in finding capital. A few won some loans from Western banks. Still more, like the Mitsubishi founder, gained capital from political connections, serving government shipping and military needs. Other new entrepreneurs were mavericks, rising from the growing group of commercial farmers and winning success through business acumen. Shibuzawa Eiichi (1840–1931) was born into a peasant family that produced indigo. He became a merchant and won a government post in the Finance Ministry by backing the right side in Japan's 1860s conflicts that led to the establishment of the Meiji regime. In 1873 he made the so-called heavenly descent from government to private business. He founded the First Bank and began to develop an uncanny knack for using his depositors' money to launch new industry. His initial success was the Osaka Cotton Spinning Mill, created as a corporation in 1880. It was a big mill, for Shibuzawa had decided that smaller mills were uneconomical. Huge profits resulted, and it was easy to find investment funds for additional plants. Between 1896 and 1913 the yarn output of the company rose tenfold. The company turned to cloth production after 1900, here experiencing a 100-fold growth, from 22 million square yards in 1900 to 2.7 billion in 1936.

With operations of this sort established, there was a rapidly growing, industrialized textile sector by 1890. Textile growth also gave Japanese industrialization a more rounded quality than existed in the contemporaneous process in Russia. Consumer goods drew considerable attention in Japan, despite the government's urgent interest in shipbuilding and other industries more directly relevant to military strength. During the 1890s modern industries were established in construction goods—cement, bricks, glass—and in food processing (including beer), match production, and chemicals. These industries drew a variety of new Japanese entrepreneurs who operated within the solid context for growth the government had established.

By the 1890s a vast increase in education was beginning to pay off in terms of the technical expertise available in Japan and also the quality of the factory labor force. In 1890 primary schools had 64 percent of boys and 31 percent of girls in attendance, figures that rose to 96 percent and 90 percent by 1905 as primary education became virtually universal. Increasing numbers of primary school graduates, in turn, went on to middle and higher education. These developments steadily increased Japan's ability to assimilate the latest Western technologies. The nation was not yet producing new inventions of its own (as opposed to making appropriate adaptations of Western devices), and virtually all of the technology used in industries like textiles was foreign. But Japan's capacity to absorb innovations from elsewhere was becoming legendary.

Study trips abroad, often government-sponsored and launched even before the Meiji regime, continued, providing the information flow on which the leading Japanese industries depended to stay up-to-date. By 1900 many Western companies had also established engineering staffs in Japan to promote their product sales. A British company, for example, sold virtually all of the textile-spinning equipment used in Japan until 1925, and it had personnel on hand to explain its use. Arrangements within Japan also facilitated information exchange. There were lags, to be sure, and small companies in particular found it difficult to keep up with their bigger rivals. The government, of course, actively assisted in providing technical expertise to all branches of modern industry. Associations formed among Japanese companies also helped. Given the cooperative spirit in Japanese culture, cartels that reduced internal competition formed even more rapidly than in Germany. Boren, the Cotton-Spinners Trade Association, issued technical publications and exchanged engineers among companies to keep knowledge current. Very few companies established monopolies on technology, and when cooperation did not suffice, experts were hired away from other firms.

A second major industrial spurt took shape after 1905 and extended until 1918. The boom centered on light industries, but there was growth in shipping, coal, chemicals, and electric power as well. It was at this point also that Japan installed a significant metallurgical sector, developing the ability to produce its own locomotives and other heavy equipment besides ships. By 1921 machinery, just 3 percent of total Japanese manufacturing output in 1880, had soared to 14 percent. Generation of electric power, virtually nonexistent before 1910, rose sevenfold between 1910 and 1920. Whereas Japan's first industrialization period in the 1880s and 1890s had featured the displacement of human and water power by steam engines, in this second growth period electrification replaced steam engines. These successive developments—first the widespread adoption of steam power, then the rapid conversion to electricity—occurred much more rapidly in Japan than in other industrial countries, including Russia as well as the West.

If Japan's industrial revolution displayed unusual vigor along with some unusual characteristics, it was a gradual process, not an overnight conversion. Japan's economy, well into the twentieth century, was by no means fully industrialized. Like the West a half century earlier, Japan continued to depend on a large agricultural sector and on a host of small operations. Factory workers formed only a small percentage of the total labor force. Japan also had an unusually large number of small businesses along with the more visible giants. In 1900 Japan's agricultural population was still 67 percent of the total (down from 80 percent in 1870). Thereafter the percentage fell rapidly—more rapidly than in most Western industrializers, including the United States, and much more rapidly than in the agriculture-dominated Soviet Union. By 1920 Japan's rural population was only 51 percent of the total. More surprising were the numbers of small businesses; Japan ranked well above all industrial nations in the percentage of small business into the 1930s.

The importance of small business, in turn, reflected more than Japan's late start in the industrial revolution—a late start that made it virtually inevitable that traditional branches would retain vitality for some time. Substantial consumer needs for processed foods and other goods normally produced by small units sustained modest establishments. But Japan's early industrial decades also featured an unusual reliance on exports, not of factory goods but of goods produced in small shops with relatively modest equipment. In this regard, Japan's economy long bore some resemblance to that of other nations that depended on earnings from sales to the industrial West: Japan needed a cash specialty, and it needed a low-wage labor force that could make this specialty pay off.

The overall problem was obvious. Despite rapid industrial growth, Japan depended heavily on machine and raw-materials imports from the West. This meant a heavy dependence on international trade, which in turn meant the need to earn foreign exchange. In this respect, too, Japan's situation differed considerably from that of Russia. The Japanese worked hard on the problem by trying to limit imports to basic industrial necessities. They developed internal production to replace imports relatively quickly. And they rapidly extended international shipping (and shipbuilding) operations to prevent loss of earnings to foreign traders—a key move that already distinguished early industrial Japan from many nonindustrial areas.

But still, there had to be goods to sell abroad to win the needed foreign earnings. The answer, early on, was silk, a traditional Japanese industry that with government assistance was quickly modernized. During the 1870s the state introduced mechanical reeling, developed in Europe, which allowed a higher output of silk production per worker. Silk looms were not expensive (small businesses thus dominated the sector), and technological demands were not high, but the rewards were considerable. Mechanized silk production enabled Japan to capture export markets from China, which still relied on manual methods. Silk output rose from 2.3 million pounds around 1870 to 16 million in 1900 and to 93 million in 1929. A full two-thirds of this production was exported, which gave Japan vitally needed foreign exchange. The labor force in textiles expanded rapidly as a result, doubling between 1909 and 1930 and vastly overshadowing the number of workers in machine building and heavy industry.

Japan's industrial advance between the 1870s and the 1920s was startlingly swift. The notion had parlayed industrial growth into imperial expansion with its successful wars against China and Russia. It had roused concern in the West—leaders like Germany's emperor were warning of a "yellow peril." Lacking several obvious ingredients for an industrial revolution, Japan had compensated by means of government direction—converting prior habits like group solidarity into industrial assets and fostering an active export sector. Inevitably, the same thrust brought tensions and vulnerabilities to Japanese society. Rapid industrialization had many familiar consequences, but it also had several special features resulting from the speed and the precise emphases wrapped up in the Japanese surge.

Social Impacts

Many results of Japan's industrial revolution followed convention. Work was redefined. Preindustrial Japan had featured an urban artisanry with rich traditions. Artisans enjoyed substantial skill and considerable penchant for leisure—"wine,

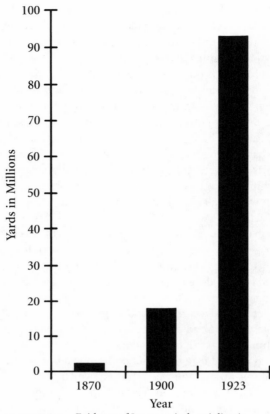

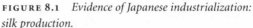

FIGURE 8.1   *Evidence of Japanese industrialization:*
silk production.

women, and gambling" were entertainments characteristic of this group when resources permitted. Individual crafts had important rituals and guild organizations. The rise of factories, many of them government-run at first, cut into these
traditions. High wages were offered to skilled workers, whose attraction was essential, but the work was far more strictly regulated than in the past. Rigid timeta-
bles for starting and stopping work and for taking breaks were imposed. Japanese
management strove to create a new definition of work habits. In return, some
benefits were offered early on, including compensation for job injuries; such government involvement made Japanese programs more systematic at an earlier date
than had been true in the West. Private factories, however, established lower
wages than those in government enterprises.

Some skilled workers early developed a sense of pride and status that perhaps
cushioned the adjustments to more rigorous working conditions. On the one
hand, because of a culture that urged people to revere government officials, the
important role of government pilot projects helped commit some workers to an

attitude of humility and docility in return for certain kinds of preferential treatment. On the other, as factories spread, conditions tended to deteriorate for the
skilled workers, in part because better education provided larger numbers and
training was speeded up—another familiar theme. Many skilled factory workers
began changing jobs with some frequency, seeking temporarily better deals from
employers. This transiency enhanced employer nervousness about forming a stable corps of skilled operatives, but it did not improve living conditions, which
were often difficult in the factory centers. Workers had to borrow or pawn their
furnishings periodically just to get by—another echo from earlier industrial revolutions.

Leisure decreased notably, in part because of low wages, in part because work
days increased to twelve hours or more in addition to commuting time. Going to
public baths, drinking sake, and occasionally visiting brothels or gambling establishments constituted the recreation of many skilled workers. As one contemporary noted: "They returned home, and after eating and drinking they read about
half the paper, and if they took a bath it was past ten. If they didn't get up the next
morning, they would be late to work; they could barely rest their bodies." Middle-
class critics, as in Europe earlier, lambasted wasteful habits, but in fact outlets for
leisure declined even as work became more arduous. Workers found protest organization difficult. Although some observers claimed to find close comradery
among factory workers—"because each has experienced difficulties of his own
and thus has become considerate of others"—in fact early unions were small. An
ironworkers union in 1899 boasted only 3,000 members.

Coal miners suffered unusually poor conditions. Most were drifters from the
villages, and they had low status in society's eyes and their own. Many employers
hired subcontractors, who had an interest in getting as much work for as little pay
as possible and who supervised the miners literally twenty-four hours a day. Some
miners ran away. Others were beaten by thugs the employers hired. Labor turnover was high; in 1906 one survey showed that 45 percent of the coal miners had
been on the job less than a year. Few unions developed.

Japanese industrialization was also marked by its unusual reliance on women
workers. This was the result of the prominence of textiles and uneven levels of
mechanization, along with the drumming need for low wages in order to assure
export sales. In 1909 Japan's factory labor force was 62 percent female compared
with 43 percent in France at a comparable stage of industrialization (in 1866). In
the extent of dependence on women factory workers, Japan surpassed the American South, Italy, and even India. Most of these women worked in small shops.
They were young and usually unmarried. Many were imported from distant farm
villages, where a father or brother signed them into what often amounted to industrial servitude. They had very low social status. Most were housed in dormitories entirely under their supervisors' control. They worked at least twelve hours a
day, sometimes much more. After electrification in the 1920s, which illuminated
the factories at night, hours often went up further. Factories had full say over

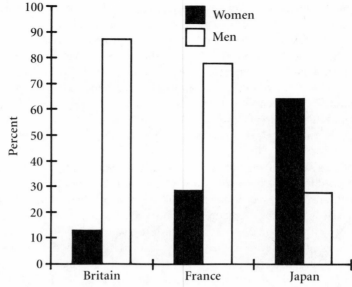

FIGURE 8.2   *Men and women in the labor force in Britain, France, and Japan, late nineteenth century.*

when and how wages were paid, and workers were often cheated. Managers argued that women wasted their money, so their wages were saved up by the factories; in fact they worried that if wages were paid out, the women would run away. Ill health was rampant, not only because of low pay but also because of dusty conditions in the plants. An 1897 report revealed that 84 percent of all the young women working in the cotton industry were either sick or suffering from injuries. Virtually no leisure activities were possible. Many workers developed irregular sexual liaisons, and some became prostitutes.

These problems of women workers (and of low-paid workers generally) were not unique to Japanese industrialization. The sheer numbers, however, were startling, for women formed the majority of the factory labor force. Most intended to work only a short time, and transience was very high. Almost half of all cotton textile workers in 1897 had served a year or less, and the figure grew worse with time. Japan's female labor force was more unstable than that of other industrial countries. Indeed, an unusual number of women simply ran away.

The toll of forming an industrial labor force showed in Japanese family life around 1900. The industrial revolution had a familiar impact in forcing families gradually to separate home and work. Many metal workers left their wives at home, though because of low pay the latter often had to do some cheap craft production in the household. Workers moved about frequently, which disrupted family life still more directly. So too did the confusion surrounding women workers. While many women hoped to return to village life and a traditional marriage, their lowered status and their removal from key local traditions often made this difficult. For a time Japan had the highest divorce rate in the world, and it centered on the lower classes. In a society with strong traditions of family life, this instability was profoundly troubling, not least to those directly involved.

Formal labor protest, however, was infrequent. Because workers were strangers to each other and changed jobs often, organizing potential was reduced. Women thought more of escaping factory life than of protesting to improve it. Employers showed some talent in treating skilled workers separately, such as enrolling them in benefit societies that provided funds in case of illness or accident. The government also moved quickly to suppress any signs of unrest. A socialist party was formed by some Christian idealists in 1901, but the government immediately banned it. Other socialist movements arose in the 1920s, but most were quickly crushed by the police. Workers did not have the vote until the 1920s in any event, which further limited their protest potential.

Nevertheless, strikes were not unknown. In 1914 the male workers in a Tokyo cotton factory voted a strike after half their number had been dismissed and pay cut 40 percent in reaction to a decline in sales. The company rescinded its measures in response to the general walkout, but women workers continued their protest, demanding shorter hours and better food. A union was formed, and although its charter proclaimed goals of mutual aid and "progress for the company," the company fired the twelve union leaders and the police arrested the leader of a mass meeting. The workers' resolve crumbled, and the union disbanded. Shipyard workers struck several times early in the twentieth century, often appealing for social respect and self-improvement in addition to making other demands; commonly heard was a call for more dignified titles of address. Again, however, organizational efforts failed. The Public Order Police Law, though it did not ban unions outright, gave government wide policing powers against leaders, and this played a major role in failure.

The lack of significant labor unrest or organization during the early phases of Japanese industrialization bore some similarities to earlier conditions in the West. While the different contexts had some of the same factors, including the participants' sheer newness to the industrial scene, Japan's relative tranquillity was nevertheless surprising. It contrasted even more obviously with the revolutionary mood in early industrial Russia. The stern repression by a government controlled by a confident oligarchy of former aristocrats and new entrepreneurs was responsible for some of Japan's distinctiveness. There was less dispute or uncertainty at the top than in Russia or many Western countries, and state control was more strict. Lack of a consistent background of peasant unrest prior to industrialization certainly differentiated Japan from Russia. Major rural agitation had taken place in eighteenth-century Japan, but it had lessened by the midnineteenth century, and thus new workers brought little protest baggage with them to the factories. Perhaps some larger traditions of obedience played a role. Certainly the high percentage of women in the labor force in a strongly patriarchal society in which women exercised no public leadership functions reduced labor's collective capacity. The absence of protest did not result from workers' easy adjustment to industrial life, for the signs of strain were numerous. Rather, it forced workers to handle their discontents individually. Transience and family instability showed the tensions endemic to the industrial revolution and yet perhaps made protest all the more difficult.

The Industrial Economy Matures: 1920s–1950s

Many features of Japan's industrial revolution persisted into later decades, including the balance between light and heavy industry, the importance of government involvement, strong but group-oriented management, and the lack of consistent or vigorous labor protest. Yet something of a turning point occurred between 1920 and the mid-1930s that altered several key policies and furthered Japan's industrial drive.

The most obvious trigger for change came first in the form of a pronounced economic stagnation during much of the 1920s and then the catastrophic impact of worldwide depression early in the 1930s. Japanese leaders, in essence, had to widen their definitions of industrialization or risk the nation's collapse. Japan's economy slumped after World War I, as did most industrial economies in the West. Recovery was hampered, however, by the rise of massive competition Japan's silk industry faced as a result of the development of artificial fibers like nylon and rayon by Western chemical companies. Silk retained prestige, but for women's stockings and a host of other consumer products the cost and difficulty of silk began to seem a drawback. Exports to the West declined, which not only threatened employment levels in Japan but also limited earnings of foreign currency. Agricultural problems also surfaced, and Tokyo was flattened by a massive earthquake in 1923, which led to costly reconstruction that strained the economy. Several banks failed in 1927.

The worldwide depression hit, signaled by the U.S. stock market crash in 1929. The West's luxury market collapsed along with the stock exchange, which cut further into sales of silk. Between 1929 and 1931 the value of Japanese exports fell by 50 percent. Workers' real income dropped by a third, and there were over 3 million unemployed. Compounding the depression were poor harvests in several regions, which led to widespread rural begging and near-starvation.

By 1932, however, recovery was under way. The Japanese government increased military purchases, which supported shipbuilding and heavy industry. Exports rose also as Japan stepped up its sales to other parts of Asia and reduced its dependence on Western markets. These two developments were linked to Japan's renewed involvement in war: The nation attempted new conquests in China and pushed for greater influence throughout eastern and Southeast Asia. The result was unquestionably useful to the home economy. Not only did the nation bounce back from the depression far more quickly than the industrial West, but it also moved to a new stage of industrialization as mechanization accelerated and a larger metallurgical sector emerged.

During the 1930s production of iron and steel and chemicals doubled. Japan for the first time gained the capacity to build its own machine tools, scientific instruments, and electric power stations; imports of manufactured products declined rapidly. The expansion of shipbuilding gave Japan by 1937 the third largest merchant fleet in the world and by far the newest. Cotton manufacturing outstripped wool, though textiles began to decline among all factory sectors. The quality of Japanese goods also rose. Japan still exported only a small amount of the world's manufacturing total—about 4 percent in 1936. It still had to focus on a variety of novelty items, including cheap souvenirs for sales in the United States and western Europe, in its desperate quest for foreign earnings to pay for imports of fuel and other materials. But it could now compete in quality manufactured products as well.

The maturation of the industrial economy was reflected in the composition of the labor force. New male workers poured in from the farms to take jobs in metallurgy, machinery, and mining. The number of workers in metals and machine building rose sevenfold between 1930 and 1940, a phenomenal increase, even as the total manufacturing labor force more than doubled.

These industrial changes also moved big business to greater prominence, for it dominated the most rapidly growing sectors. The political power of the *zaibatsu* expanded accordingly. The experience of the working class was increasingly shaped by big-business policies. Large factories introduced assembly-line methods and other scientific management procedures imitated from the United States—just as the Soviet Union was doing in the same years.

The transition involved more than new industrial balance and big business. Attitudes toward the labor force were revised, and Japanese industrialization developed a more distinctive social orientation—a characteristic that has been largely preserved to the present day.

The policies of the elite had begun to shift in several related areas even before the 1930s boom. Concerned about social instability, the government in 1919 began to promote more active patriotic loyalty among Japanese citizens, workers included. Themes of duty, national glory, and loyalty to the emperor gained ground steadily. This set a context for relatively modest levels of labor unrest—despite recurrent political crises—and for a new devotion to work and productivity. More directly important were new policies adopted by the big industrial firms. These companies paid better wages than average anyway, in part because they needed more male skilled workers. They also began to increase their welfare facilities. Further, in the 1920s they launched a distinctive Japanese policy known initially as *fukaiko-shugi*, or no dismissal (now called *shushin koyo*, or lifetime employment). Under these policies, workers hired by large factories on a regular basis would not be dismissed. They might suffer pay cuts in a recession, but basic job security was assured. Furthermore, bonuses and wage increases were tied to seniority, as was the lump sum paid out on retirement. Japanese industry was bent on tying a growing minority of the labor force to the firm as a way to reduce the job changing and transience associated with the first industrial decades.

Many factories supplemented these new policies with rituals designed to promote group solidarity. Some conducted calisthenics for all workers before the working day began. Others promoted group singing or other cooperative measures. Some of these routines recalled older Japanese paternalism and group loyalty, though the policies themselves were new. Japan was certainly inventing a new set of industrial traditions that tied many workers more firmly to their company and might well have improved morale. The contrast with the more individualistic and conflict-ridden industrial atmosphere of the West was striking. Many workers, to be sure, were excluded from these security arrangements, and thus manufacturers had much flexibility in augmenting or reducing their labor force and altering pay levels. Emphasis on company loyalty, however, prompted many workers to develop a new commitment to hard work. Hours of work did decline, and leisure interests expanded. Many companies set up libraries, game rooms, and sports facilities to associate leisure with the firm and to preempt separate labor organizations. Regular workers joined company organizations at a rate of nearly 100 percent—in sharp contrast to separate unions that gained only modestly, winning at most 8 percent adherence. Hard work seemed a logical complement to devotion to the firm, and many Japanese workers and white-collar employees, either because of an internalized work ethic or management-manipulated peer pressure, continued to accept much longer working weeks than their counterparts in the West.

Changes in both industry and policy reduced the percentage of women in the labor force. Growing prosperity and a desire to regain more personal stability prompted the Japanese increasingly to emphasize the importance of women's domestic functions. Through industrial policies, firms with women workers increasingly tried to improve their status. Courses on sewing, etiquette, flower arranging, and tea ceremonies were designed to improve later marriageability—while also drawing a more reliable, less transient labor force in the short run. Japanese workers themselves pressed for more commitment to family life, accepting work by women for a period before marriage but assuming their primary commitment to household and children thereafter. Even in the 1950s, when white-collar employment for women increased in the West, the Japanese commitment to lower work rates for women persisted. In this, as in other respects, Japan seemed on a somewhat different industrial trajectory from that of the West or the Soviet Union.

By the 1930s most workers were benefiting from the industrial revolution in a material sense. Standards of living improved. Diets became more varied, as did leisure opportunities. However, real wages did not catch up to Western levels, and

Japanese culture as encouraged by employers and the government tended to divert workers from a full commitment to an individualistic consumer ethic. Relatively long work hours and a high savings rate reflected somewhat cautious personal values.

Japan's industrial surge was set back by the losses in World War II. The standard of living dropped well below 1930s levels, recovering only by 1953. American occupation forces pushed for a break up of the old *zaibatsu* on grounds that their power inhibited Japanese democracy and promoted militarism. A more democratic political structure encouraged the growth of labor unions, which pressed for better working conditions. They also attempted, with some success, to improve the status of blue-collar workers. Workers' wives, for example, were now to be called by the same term as those of white-collar employees rather than the less polite term previously used.

After a brief adjustment, however, most of the trends visible previously in Japanese industrialization resurfaced. Unions largely supported the lifetime security policies and other measures that tied workers to their firms. The government abandoned policies aimed at reducing big business and returned to active support for large firms having close mutual links and intimate ties with government. Growth rates quickly resumed as well, and Japan by the 1950s was demonstrating (as it had done in the periods 1905–1919 and 1931–1940) more rapid expansion of productivity and manufacturing output than almost all other industrialized nations.

Clearly, Japan's industrial revolution by midcentury had been successful in implanting a solid industrial economy on what had been an isolated, largely agricultural nation such a short time before. The same revolution had built distinctive organizational policies and worker habits that proved deeply ingrained in Japan's ongoing development. Finally, the revolution not only had resulted from but had seemed regularly to generate an unusual dynamism.

9

New Developments in Western Societies: Redefinitions of the Industrial Economy

CHANGES in the industrial economies of western Europe and the United States were not as decisive as those surrounding the advent of industrialization in Russia and Japan between the 1880s and the 1950s. To speak of a "second industrial revolution" in the West is misleading, for it downplays the unique significance of the basic conversion from an agricultural to an industrial economy. Instead, a number of developments simply completed the elemental revolution in countries like the United States and Germany (only Britain had in any real sense fully converted to an industrial economy before the 1880s). It was only about 1900 that Germany became half urbanized (the marker Britain had achieved in 1850); the United States and France reached this crude measurement of extensive industrialization by 1920. Rapid growth of the industrial labor force through immigration ended in the United States only during the 1920s, and even then rural movement, including the great migration of African Americans from the South, continued to provide newcomers to the basic experience of factory work. Thus, the overlap between the essential industrial revolution and new trends surfacing in the early twentieth century was considerable.

Nevertheless, several important innovations transformed the Western industrial scene between 1880 and 1950. Earlier trends intensified to the point of unrecognizability; the pace of work, for example, accelerated well beyond anything imagined during the industrial revolution itself. Furthermore, several outgrowths of initial industrialization were rethought to produce a substantially different version of the larger industrial experience.

Obviously, the process of industrialization in the West guaranteed further change even after the initial phase had ended. Geographical balances continued to shift within the industrial West. Britain's relative decline persisted in the second major phase of the industrial revolution as Germany and particularly the United States gained ground. British iron resources were less appropriate for steel making than when iron had predominated, and technical training and organizational coordination within big business lagged. Devastating losses in both world wars further hampered Britain's standing. British industrialization proceeded, however. There was no retreat, and the British even pioneered in some new product development, establishing the first version of the television industry in the late 1930s. But the laurels of overall leadership passed elsewhere.

The industrial revolution also continued to fan out from earlier Western centers. Northern Italy and Catalonia in northeastern Spain began to industrialize rapidly in the late nineteenth century. Catalonian factories emphasized textiles as industrialists combined relatively advanced technology with somewhat cheaper labor—in competition with earlier industrializers such as Britain. Industrialization also began to spread to the American South; the industries that grew were those in which new techniques and cheaper labor drew businesses from earlier factory centers such as New England.

Two crucial developments in the industrial West overshadowed the geographical refinements. Both effectively continued the dynamic the initial industrial revolution had already established, but both involved new specifics and new intensities. Both, finally, had obvious international repercussions in strengthening the West's economic potential in the world and setting more arduous competitive standards for new industrializers like Russia and Japan.

Machines and the Drive for Organizational Change

The two developments were, simply, new versions of the industrial revolution's basic essentials: technology and organization. A new round of technological innovation had in some senses begun with the Bessemer process for steelmaking in the 1850s, and there followed in the 1870s other new furnace designs that made a wider range of iron ores readily usable. Also in the late nineteenth century came the introduction of new engines that supplemented and ultimately overshadowed the steam engine: Electric turbines generated energy from coal, hydroelectric power, and petroleum; internal-combustion engines generated power from petroleum.

Both new engine types had a number of implications for the further development of industrial economies. They competed with older industrial forms: By the early twentieth century coal-mining districts were beginning to suffer because less coal was needed for power given the rise of internal combustion and petroleum. Along with the eclipse of earlier factory textile centers caused by competition from new areas, this decline in the coal industry offered the first example of the industrial revolution's capacity to destroy prior achievements. Just as the revolution had displaced earlier domestic manufacturing, so too did subsequent developments force the gradual, painful deindustrialization of some prior industrial centers. Even before 1900 some of the less efficient mining districts in France were losing jobs. By the 1920s the industrial north in Britain, based on steam and textiles, was suffering, and here as in many instances workers found it difficult to respond rapidly, which created durable regional pools of unemployment.

The new machines also made possible the dissemination of powered equipment to a wide range of production sectors, for electric motors and gasoline engines did not require concentration in a factory. The manufacture of clothing, previously a household or craft occupation, began to move into sweatshops, thanks to the use of electrically powered sewing machines. A host of crafts faced direct technological innovation for the first time. Commercial bakeries introduced mechanical kneading machines. Construction work was transformed by the use of mechanical saws and gasoline-powered cranes and by new materials like preformed concrete. Canning machines and refrigeration changed the food-processing industries. Technology spread beyond manufacturing, particularly with the use of gasoline-powered tractors, harvesters, and other devices on the farm. Even housework was altered by the introduction of washing machines and vacuum cleaners in the 1920s. Almost every type of work could now, in a technological sense, be industrialized. This meant that hundreds of thousands of people, many of whom had already come to terms with the initial industrial revolution, had to adjust to further shifts in methods—some more fundamental than anything that had come before.

Ongoing technological change did more than create new excitement and uncertainty. It tended to homogenize the experience of work. Artisans, particularly, became more like factory workers even when, as in the construction industry, their jobs did not literally move into a factory setting. Skill remained important, but it was no longer likely to be purely traditional, and because of the mechanization of many operations, it was more likely to be easily learned. At the same time, unskilled jobs declined. Sheer physical strength counted for less than before, since there were machines to do the lifting and hauling. Semiskilled work, already the category most characteristic of the industrialized labor force, increasingly predominated.

Renewed technological change also increased the pace and specialization of many important sectors of production. Shoe manufacturing shifted from craft to factory, thanks to the sewing machine. Textile workers saw their machines steadily expand in size and pace. Machine builders, including shipbuilders, witnessed an even greater transformation around 1900 as automatic drilling and riveting machines displaced older skill categories and thus enabled semi-skilled workers (including some women) to take over key operations.

The technological changes of the postrevolutionary industrial economy focused on a steady proliferation of new product lines. Even before 1900 the chemicals industry had begun to develop a host of novel products, including new kinds

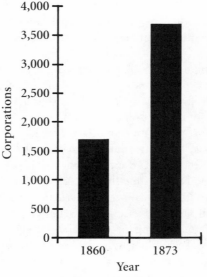

FIGURE 9.1   *Corporations in western Europe, 1860–1873.*

of explosives and dyes. As this process continued after World War I, there were such achievements as the production of artificial fibers like the nylon and rayon that provided disturbing competition for Japan's silk exports. Electrical equipment was another area of product development, and there appeared not only a steady stream of new household appliances but unprecedented consumer items like the radio.

Finally, in the early twentieth century technological development became wedded to the other basic facet of the industrial revolution, the growing size and sophistication of organizational structure. Major industrial corporations began explicitly to sponsor research and development, seeking additional gains in mechanization and per worker productivity and in product diversification. German industry led the way, even before 1900, and benefited from some close links with university-based chemicals research. New medicinal drugs and chemical fertilizers were among the diverse results of this self-conscious organizational thrust toward innovation. Shortly after 1900 major firms in the United States began tentative experiments with regular research staffs.

Growing organizational sophistication involved more than technology, however. The assembly line became both symbol and reality of the increasing application of systematic organization to the workplace. Pioneered in the United States, particularly by automobile manufacturer Henry Ford after 1910, the assembly line crystallized earlier efforts to measure and routinize work. With the assembly line, semiskilled workers using electrically powered equipment repeated simple opera-

Workers inspect automobiles coming down an early assembly line at the Ford Motor Company. The growing automobile industry contributed to economic prosperity in the United States during the 1920s. (Courtesy of the Henry Ford Museum and Greenfield Village. Reprinted by permission.)

tions such as riveting bolts as an engine block or chassis moved by them on a conveyer belt. The goal was, as Ford's engineers put it, to make workers as much like machines as possible—to remove any need for thought or reflection. These developments not only intensified the industrial experience in places like the United States or France, where work had already been substantially transformed; they also were built into the very process of industrial revolution in newcomers like Russia, where the effort to incorporate advanced organizational features from the West ran particularly strong after the 1917 revolution.

With larger and more sophisticated organization came the spread of giant corporations—a trend already intrinsic to industrial economies by the 1880s but extended steadily thereafter. Hundreds of new corporations formed each year in countries like France and the United States. Some of them were small, but by selling shares to the public, they acquired considerable resources for expansion. Huge firms strengthened their hold in heavy industry and chemicals. Newer industrial sectors, such as the burgeoning automobile industry, initially opened the way for small-scale industrialists. Car companies proliferated throughout western Europe and the United States between 1900 and 1914. Competition drove many under, however. New technologies, including the assembly line, increased the costs of operation, which favored larger units. Many companies were bought up or merged with the growing giants. By the 1920s big business was well on its way to predominance in this industrial branch as well.

Increasingly also, big business now meant international links. Major industrial companies had set up sales operations internationally even before the 1880s; British textile firms, for example, had agents in Latin America. Some companies had also spun off manufacturing operations; French textile firms had sponsored subsidiaries in New England and Latin America by the midnineteenth century, and American firms had set up international subsidiaries by the 1870s. With further growth and increasing interest in international investment, these trends accelerated after 1880. German chemical companies established branches in the United States to exploit its market with their growing array of products. American car manufacturers were returning the favor by the 1920s. Multinational business was beginning to come into its own.

Both technological and organizational changes rapidly increased the size of the average work unit. Small businesses still had a chance in retailing and in new branches of industry, but their role measurably declined after about 1900. Even many small firms—like the automobile repair shops that sprang up widely in the 1920s and that seemed reminiscent of a craft atmosphere—were effectively controlled by the large manufacturing operations on which they depended for supplies or orders. Formal, rationalized organization increasingly became the norm. Team play rather than freewheeling entrepreneurship began to be emphasized: This trend even reached into boys' games—American football gained in school popularity because it simultaneously enhanced masculinity and taught the importance of cooperation. For many workers, the growth of big business meant the need to deal with increasingly impersonal organization and with generalized work rules. U.S. corporations in the 1920s began to sponsor personnel research conducted by trained industrial psychologists; the goal was to find ways to manipulate the work environment to raise output and reduce friction. Soon music was being played over loudspeakers in many settings because its impact was discovered to increase productivity. And foremen were being taught that if they prompted an aggrieved worker to repeat a complaint several times, the worker would ultimately become embarrassed and often reluctant to press the grievance further.

These developments, extending fairly steadily through the decades after 1880, continued the rapid alteration of economic structure and working life. The industrial revolution clearly did not yield to a period of tranquillity. Many workers, rightly or wrongly, argued that the changes they faced were greater than those the initial factory workers had encountered. By the 1890s British workers were claiming that an earlier ability to sneak naps in the corner, unnoticed by a foreman, had yielded to a much more intense pace. Complaints about nervous exhaustion increased. A German worker lamented that because of the concentration required on a fast-paced assembly line, "my eyes burn so that I can hardly sleep." Americans in the 1880s discovered a new disease, neurasthenia, which they claimed afflicted middle-class businessmen who drove themselves too hard; this was the first of a host of ailments that gained popularity in industrial America—ranging to stress and "burnout" in the late twentieth century—and that could highlight the disparity between industrial pace and human capacity. Even with the industrial revolution well established, the intensification of it and the commitment to persistent change continued to have recurrently unsettling effects. The fundamental trends were not novel, but their changing incarnations often seemed startling as industrial economies matured.

The Service Sector

The ramifications of the ongoing redefinition of technology and organization opened up several new facets of the industrial experience. In these cases more than simple intensification was involved; significant new trends were being added to the mix.

During the industrial revolution proper, the growth of the factory labor force provided the most dynamic change in social composition. The numbers of urban workers and miners expanded faster than those of any other social group. This situation began to change as the industrial economy matured from the 1880s onward. The factory labor force continued to expand, but its rate of growth was surpassed by a new service sector.

The service sector was fueled by the expansion of commerce and the growth of business and government bureaucracy—a handmaiden to expanding levels of organization. Accelerating industrial output necessitated new sales outlets, and the department store, already introduced during the industrial revolution, was an obvious response. Larger stores needed larger sales forces, and sales clerks began to come into their own. Growing banks needed tellers. Hotels for business travelers or vacationers needed staff. A growing white-collar work force serviced a variety of commercial establishments and leisure facilities.

Large organizations needed secretaries, file clerks, and low-level managers. Technology also spurred new opportunities; the occupation of telephone operator joined the list of available jobs in the late nineteenth century. The steady growth of government functions brought proliferation not only of clerks but of schoolteachers, factory inspectors, and police officers. These jobs varied in status somewhat, but people holding them shared with other lower-middle-class workers a dependence on wage earnings, the intent to avoid outright manual labor, and a lack of high professional standing. Growing hospitals, whether public or private, produced another set of employees in addition to professional doctors: Nurses and medical technicians formed a growing service sector of their own.

The sheer rate of growth was staggering. Britain had 7,000 female secretaries in 1881, 22,200 in 1891, and 90,000 in 1901. By 1900 the British lower middle class included a full 20 percent of the total population, double its relative size a mere thirty years before.

In many respects the growth of the service sector constituted a slightly novel twist on the emergence of industrial work more generally. White-collar personnel operated under the supervision of others. Department-store supervisors could bully just as hard as their factory counterparts. One German store manager in the 1920s even installed a steam jet in the toilets, timed to go off every two minutes, so that the clerks could not linger out of sight. Efforts to speed the pace formed part of many white-collar operations. New technology added its own contribution. By the 1880s the skill levels of many clerks were being altered—some said reduced— by the advent of typewriters; handwriting no longer counted for so much. Cash registers reduced the arithmetic requirements for sales personnel and speeded the work. Schoolteachers during the early twentieth century faced little new technology, but they directly encountered the general trends toward organizational control. City school boards in the United States imposed standardized curriculums and texts throughout the schools and thus reduced teacher autonomy as part of the same rationalization effort that dominated big business in the period.

If the growth of the service sector exemplified important trends in industrial work, it also added undeniable complexity to the labor force. Service work attracted far more women than factory work did. The rise of the service sector did not yet reverse the limitations on women's jobs that the industrial revolution had imposed in the West, but it did begin to modify them. Women quickly dominated the typewriter, partly because male clerks were too proud to learn the new techniques. Women also gained ground in occupations like librarianship and social work, service-sector jobs par excellence. The basic life course of most women remained about the same: Only a minority of women worked after marriage, and only a handful of women worked instead of marrying. But the respectability of work for women was rising. Young middle-class women increasingly held a job for a time before marriage and in this were like their working-class sisters. By the same token, men working in the service sector were far more accustomed to the presence of women than were most of their factory-worker counterparts. The stage was being set for some larger redefinitions of women's role in the labor force after the substantial withdrawal that had accompanied initial industrialization.

Furthermore, male and female white-collar workers did not think of themselves as part of a larger industrial labor force. They felt separate from blue-collar workers. They touted their ability to wear middle-class clothing to work, rather than the dirty outfits of the factory. They liked to think more in terms of potential mobility than most blue-collar workers did, though they sometimes exaggerated their real opportunities. Employers, for their part, deliberately treated white-collar employees separately. They paid them a monthly rather than hourly wage and gave them different (usually somewhat better) benefit packages. One of the first private pension schemes was introduced in the United States in the 1870s by the American Express travel firm for its white-collar personnel.

Even some of the drawbacks of white-collar work kept the group separate. White-collar workers were pushed to control their emotions in the interests of in- gratiating themselves with customers or managers. Secretarial manuals urged: "The secretary should never forget that in order to please people, he needs to ex- ert himself." Sales personnel were told to learn the "satisfaction of controlling [your] temper, the satisfaction of returning kindness for an insult." Department- store clerks were taught middle-class ways, regardless of their origins, so that they could deal with their best clientele. A level of emotional control and even self-ma- nipulation was involved in many facets of service work that industrial labor could largely ignore.

Certainly the bulk of service-sector workers proudly proclaimed their member- ship in a wider middle class, not the working class. They either shunned unions and strikes or at least organized separately. Even many workers agreed that eleva- tion into the white-collar ranks was a step upward; thus the growth of white-col- lar work, whatever its real constraints, seemed to add to mobility potential. This was an important new development in the social implications of an advancing in- dustrial economy.

Leisure and the Consumer Economy

A second feature of the redefinition of the industrial economy had even more sweeping implications: Mass affluence and leisure time increased, and these fac- tors substantially modified the work-dominated tone of the industrial revolution proper. Work became more intense, and many of the West's leaders continued to tout the importance of a vigorous work ethic. But for most people the waking hours now consisted of a definite division between work time and other time, and for many there was some margin of income above subsistence to help define what that "other" time involved.

Reductions in the work day were painfully won. Many workers had to strike or use political muscle to win days of fewer than twelve hours. By 1900, however, ten- hour days were becoming more common, and some well-organized groups, like coal miners, in scattered areas even attained eight-hour legislation. Campaigns to reduce hours won wider success in the early 1920s, again through a combination of legislation and strike demands. An increasing number of employers were also coming to realize that shorter days might produce better, more sustained work— intensity traded for time with no damage to output. Further hours reductions oc- curred in the 1930s in response to widespread unemployment during the depres- sion. In addition to the trend toward an eight-hour day, weekends were gradually extended to include Saturday off or at least Saturday afternoon. Brief annual vaca- tions were granted—as early as the 1880s Lancashire textile workers won an occasional day off to take a train to the beach where (not knowing how to swim) they sat, presumably contentedly, in their Sunday best.

Simultaneously, standards of living rose. By 1900 most people in the industrial West were predictably earning over subsistence level, though a distressing minority still suffered greatly. Earnings went up further in the 1920s except for workers in some of the declining sectors like coal mining.

These developments set the stage for a redefinition of the relationship between leisure and industrial life. Leisure opportunities, fiercely reduced during the industrial revolution, began to explode. Popular theater emerged—called music hall in Britain and vaudeville in the United States, the mixture of song and comedy helped lead directly to the new motion picture industry after 1900. Professional sports teams drew huge crowds to soccer and rugby in Europe, to football and baseball in the maverick United States. The new leisure had a number of features. It organized masses of people for rather standardized, commercial fare. It provided escape from the daily routine, but in some versions (notably sports) it also replicated features of industrial work such as rules, speed consciousness, and specialization. Much of the new leisure also depended on industrial technology, from the tram lines that took the urban masses to huge concrete and metal stadiums to the vulcanized rubber balls that were mass produced from the 1840s onward. Clearly, a revolution in leisure was under way, but it came a bit later than the industrial revolution itself.

Wider consumer values were not new; they had surfaced in the eighteenth century around the new interests in stylish clothing that had helped trigger the industrial revolution. By the late nineteenth century, however, consumerism could be more widely indulged throughout the West. New products like bicycles—an 1880s fad—and the automobile represented more expensive consumer items than had ever before been sold widely. Interests in soaps and cosmetics reflected new compulsions surrounding personal hygiene and appearance. For some people, consumerism involved more than money to spend. It came to express deep personal impulses and identities in a society where work conveyed less meaning than was traditionally the case. A growing advertising industry—another service-sector outcropping—worked to encourage and channel impulse—to make people care deeply about the things they could acquire or aspire to acquire.

Class Warfare

Along with the rise of the service sector and new leisure and consumerism in Western society, levels of popular protest increased greatly from the late nineteenth century into the 1950s. There were fits and starts in this development, but the trend was obvious. More and more workers gained the ability to protest through strikes, unions, and political parties. American workers showed less interest in socialism than did their European counterparts, but they participated

"Memorial Day Massacre" near the Republic Steel Corporation plant, South Chicago, May 30, 1937. (Courtesy of AP/Wide World Photos. Reprinted by permission.)

strongly in the same kinds of industrial campaigns. These were peak decades of factory conflict.

Strike rates rose almost every decade until the late 1950s, interrupted only by wars and depression. Increasing numbers of factory workers gained the ability to strike periodically. Unskilled workers, like dockers in Britain, gained the capacity in the 1880s to strike powerfully for the first time. Many strikes focused on improving wages and hours, no small goals in themselves; workers showed an increasing ability to phrase progressive demands, asking for conditions—like a shorter working day—that they were convinced they deserved but that had not existed before. More sweeping objectives were voiced in some major strike movements that disputed employers' rights unilaterally to set conditions of work. A rash of these strikes over workers' control occurred in western Europe and the United States right after World War I; most failed.

New levels of unionization matched the surge of strikes and involved even larger numbers of workers. Craft workers continued to organize, and as factory labor joined the trend, new industrial unions emerged that stressed the power of numbers rather than special skills. Large national confederations grouped the unions, making them more politically potent and counterbalancing to an extent the growth of big-business power. The French General Labor Confederation was formed in 1895. The American Federation of Labor started a bit earlier, while the more aggressive, industrially based Congress of Industrial Organizations was launched in the 1930s. Finally, in most European countries, massive votes, largely though not exclusively from the working class, impelled socialist (and, after 1918, communist) parties to great prominence.

For many workers, a new commitment to socialism meant far more than a passing political preference. A German worker, not a fanatic, put it this way shortly before 1900: "You know, I never read a social democratic book and rarely a newspaper. ... All that does not amount to much. We really do not want to become like the rich and refined people. There will always have to be rich and poor. ... But we want a better and more just organization at the factory and in the state. I openly express what I think about that, even though it might not be legal." Others could be more intense: "We are driven like dumb cattle in our folly until the flesh is off our bones, and the marrow out of them." Deep-seated resentment was heard too: "The consciousness of dependence on the employer embitters me. A gesture of the director is enough to make my blood boil."

The surge of working-class protest reflected new capabilities. Most Western governments had introduced democracy by the 1880s and reduced the legal limitations on strikes and unions. These changes, plus growing experience in industrial life, made more protest feasible. Workers were not necessarily angrier than they had been during the industrial revolution—indeed, they may have accepted more aspects of industrial life—but they could now do something about their discontent, and they had plenty of discontent left. Furthermore, additional work changes by 1900 triggered unrest that found outlet in the unions and protest votes. More impersonal employers, new pressures on the pace of work, loss of accustomed skills (even factory skills), and technological threats to job security—all these fueled an unprecedented outburst.

To be sure, there was no outright revolution. The contrast with the pressures early industrialization generated in Russia remained important. A number of sectors in Western society were content or at least hostile to the workers' cause. Workers themselves were more typically bent on shorter hours or higher pay than on fundamental restructuring. Many seemed more intent on bettering their position within industrial society than in challenging industrial structures directly. Nevertheless, during the maturing of the West's industrialization, the class warfare implicit in the industrial revolution emerged to color not only factory life but the political process itself.

Redefining the Scope of Industrialization

The extension of the industrial economy in the West, plus some of the specific changes that took shape after the 1880s, linked industrialization to a variety of other developments. During this period the implications of the industrial revolution for war were fully realized. World War I broke out in part because of the social tensions building in industrial life. It cannot be said that leaders in countries like Britain and Germany saw war as desirable, but they at least viewed it as a potential distraction for the aggressive working class. Military buildups and, particularly, the naval arms race that more directly engulfed Britain, Germany, and France related to the growing capacity in heavy industry and the power of big businesses to induce governments to buy their wares. Germany's Navy League consisted of a mixture of aristocrats, who saw military glory as a compensation for the decline in their economic status, and armaments manufacturers, both bent on a big spending program. Part of the war's causation, then, stemmed from stresses in the industrial economy. The conflict itself showed the power of industrial technology in gruesome starkness: Poison gas, long-range artillery, submarines, and aerial bombardments were the reverse side of technological wizardry. They killed far more troops than had ever before died in combat, and they blurred the distinction between soldiers and civilians in many areas. Industrial organization helped governments devise plans to ration goods and labor and to propagandize the citizenry. Total war, a twentieth-century creation, was industrial war, and World War II next served to document its further advancement.

Spreading industrialization in the West also began to create new kinds of environmental issues. Early factories spewed out smoke and were often condemned for their ugliness. Railroad lines had provoked realistic fears about fires and noise. Many disputes had developed over the damming of streams for water power. The industrial revolution proper, however, had not generated an explicit environmental concern. Even after 1900 most reformist attention focused on issues of worker and consumer safety. New regulations, common in the West's industrial states, called for more protective devices around machines and in the mines. They curtailed unhygienic practices in food processing; they introduced some regulation over the production of medicinal drugs.

Water quality drew attention as well. The sheer growth of cities, which often had unprocessed sewage running into local rivers, and the growth of the chemical industry with its cost-saving impulse to dump industrial waste products into the same rivers produced noticeable health hazards by the end of the nineteenth century. Government regulations gradually worked against this tide, though the effort to keep pace with industrial and urban growth often seemed hopeless. Pollution rates perhaps increased more slowly in the second quarter of the twentieth century, but the basic problem remained. Air quality was another obvious concern. Heavy industrial centers like Pittsburgh, Pennsylvania, generated such intense smoke by the 1920s that midday could be no different than dusk. Realization of the health hazards involved came slowly from a public that depended on this same industry for jobs; a Pittsburgh legend lasting into the 1930s held that smoke was beneficial in keeping down the germs. Any industrial setback, like the 1930s depression, retarded pollution-control efforts, for employment was paramount.

Looking toward Second Avenue and the Jones and Laughlin Steel Corporation, Pittsburgh, circa 1950. (Courtesy of the Carnegie Library of Pittsburgh. Reprinted by permission.)

"We like to see smoke," said one politico in 1939 as the city eliminated its Bureau of Smoke Regulation: "It means prosperity." Nevertheless, concern did grow in Pittsburgh and other industrial areas during the first half of the twentieth century, though the environmental problems generated by expanding industry grew faster.

The West as New Model

The aftermath of the West's industrial revolution had revolutionary qualities of its own. Some basic early industrial trends were reversed—for example, there was an expansion of leisure. A fierce concentration on production gave way to new interest in consumption and to a new need to provide for a growing output that frequently seemed to outstrip demand. Other trends magnified developments inherent in the industrial revolution itself: Class conflict was a case in point, while environmental problems and renewed organizational innovation directly extended industrial-revolution themes and increased their visibility.

Recurrent upheaval in the industrial West enhanced the industrial revolution's impact on the course of modern history. While it would be wrong simply to argue that the world wars resulted from the industrial revolution, it would be folly to ignore industrialization's vast influence. The same ongoing dynamism and disruption obviously affected the wider impact of the industrial revolution on the world. The West continued to innovate sufficiently to maintain its industrial lead over the rest of the world—though it diminished in relationship to Japan and Russia—and this lead persisted despite devastating internal warfare. New productive capacity and problems of generating adequate internal demand, even given the rise of consumerism, increased the pressure to find markets and supplies elsewhere. Definitely, this theme of the industrial revolution echoed throughout the twentieth century.

Finally, the West's new features—its consumerism and mass leisure, its industrial unrest, its further innovations in technology and organization—obviously set potential models for other societies involved in some effort to industrialize. Many Russians, for example, ultimately wondered how successful their industrial society would be if it did not match the consumer standards the West had generated by the midtwentieth century. Ongoing changes in established industrial societies, in sum, despite their many limitations and drawbacks, continued to affect the definition of what the industrial revolution was all about. This was true in the West and in the rest of the world.

10

The Industrial Revolution in International Context

EVEN in 1950 most people in the world lived in societies that were not, at least as yet, engaged in a full industrial revolution. The industrial revolution was still geographically concentrated in Europe (now including east-central regions like Poland and Czechoslovakia plus parts of Spain and Italy), Russia, Japan, and much of North America. Most of Asia and virtually all of Africa and Latin America were not yet industrialized. However, the spread and intensification of the industrial revolution inevitably had far greater world impact than during the revolution's earlier decades. Shipping increased in volume as international trade climbed, while the airplane and radio speeded communication worldwide.

Within this context, several regional reactions to the industrial revolution took shape. First, there was heightened exploitation of nonindustrial areas by the grasping industrial economies. Africa was more fully drawn into the process of supplying foods and raw materials to slake the seemingly unquenchable thirst of industrial Europe. Japan began exploiting raw-materials areas in Southeast Asia. Europe but particularly the United States increased the use of Latin America as a source of cheap supplies. Indeed, North-South trading began to gain ground with great rapidity as large sections of the Northern Hemisphere industrialized and used areas in the Southern Hemisphere for supplies and materials. Western Europe used Africa as its primary reserve, the United States used Latin America, and, more tentatively, Japan began carving out a zone in eastern Asia.

Second, concomitant with the growing industrial reliance on raw-materials suppliers (and the dependence of the latter on investments and manufactured goods from the industrialized states) was an important extension of manufacturing, including factory production, in centers that were not yet industrialized in any full sense. Many of these centers produced relatively cheap factory goods for sale to the industrial West. They experienced considerable economic change, in-

147

cluding shifts in work patterns and in technology, but they did not escape considerable inferiority to the industrialized states. Unlike Japan, they did not gain ground in relative terms. Rather, their manufacturing resembled the outpouring of raw materials from the least industrial regions in tying their economies to world trade on unfavorable terms. Parts of the Middle East, port regions in China, and some Latin American countries such as Mexico experienced this kind of manufacturing expansion.

A third development involved the emergence of significant but discrete industrial sectors within a still largely agricultural economy; these produced goods mainly for internal use. India, for example, developed an impressive metallurgical industry, though it did not affect the bulk of the economy or generate a full industrial revolution.

Finally, several societies within the British Commonwealth developed extensive industry along with the sophisticated commercial production of food or minerals for sale to the West and Japan. Canada, in particular, became a significant industrial power. Canada, Australia, and New Zealand were industrialized in a distinctive fashion because of the continued importance of the nonmanufacturing sector, but their populations enjoyed essentially industrial living standards and experienced essentially industrial work habits. Even the United States, an industrial giant also dependent on significant exports from commercial agriculture, fell in this last category to some extent.

Thus, along with the growing international impact of the industrial revolution, different regional responses generated an increasingly complex world economic map. The simple division—between those involved and those not involved in an industrial revolution—was inadequate to describe the variety of reactions that industrialization now spawned.

The Expansion of Commercial Exploitation

Industrialized areas needed growing amounts of food and raw materials from other parts of the world. Expanding transportation and new technologies in mining and other resource extractions encouraged growing incursions into otherwise nonindustrial economies. Labor was rearranged to generate the necessary output. In crucial cases such as Africa, new and increasingly effective colonial administrations provided a political framework for economic change. Even in the independent nations of Latin America, Western businesses often acquired direct ownership and management of crucial enterprises, no longer relying on local leadership to manage laborers and produce the necessary export goods. For example, U.S. minerals firms owned and operated copper mines in Chile, while another concern, the United Fruit Company, ran plantations in many Central American nations. The fundamental spur was the spiraling volume of output required. Although recessions frequently cut into this international economy, the industrial markets of Europe and the United States consumed more and more tropical products, like bananas and coffee, and raw materials. Their need stimulated their increasingly direct role in nonindustrial economies.

Several tactics were devised to respond to new export opportunities, including outright compulsion. In the European colonies, peasants were subject to taxes that could only be paid in export goods or through wages earned by working on European estates. Forced labor occurred, particularly in the Belgian Congo in Africa, where villagers were flogged, mutilated, or even killed if they failed to meet production quotas. Other devices included company stores—used, for example, in the hemp-producing areas of eastern Mexico, where rope was made for export sale; workers could be tied to a company by their debts and forced to work long hours for low pay in consequence. In this case, Mexican landlords imposed on a largely Indian labor force, supplementing their debt control with outright cheating—"cooking the books" so that debts could never be paid off—and flogging. As one English observer noted in 1909, the Indian hemp worker "will never escape the cruel master who under law as at present administered in the Yucatan has as complete a disposal of his body as of one of the pigs which root around in the hacienda yard." Finally, in some parts of the Caribbean and Southeast Asia, plus Pacific islands like Hawaii rapidly being converted to cash-crop production, additional workers were imported from other areas (such as India, China, and the Philippines) to help keep wages low.

The search for cheap, easily controlled labor was not the only goal. Western managers and many local landlords tried also to compel workers in the export sectors to labor harder and more efficiently. They taught them new farming techniques designed to increase crop yields. And of course they prodded them to specialize in market crops rather than to produce the traditional array of subsistence foods. Cotton, cocoa, peanuts, palm oil, tropical fruits, rubber, and hemp, along with increased amounts of already popular items like coffee, tea, and sugar—these were the agricultural growth sectors in Africa, Latin America, and Southeast Asia, and they consumed a steadily increasing amount of land (most of it previously devoted to food products for local use) and a growing percentage of the rural labor force.

Along with cash-crop agriculture, mining sectors grew rapidly in much of the nonindustrial world during the late nineteenth and early twentieth centuries. Roads and railways were built primarily to facilitate the movement of minerals and farm produce from the interior of the nonindustrial areas to ports, where they were then shipped to Europe and the United States. In the mines themselves, advanced technology was introduced—for example, dynamite to loosen rock and of course rails to transport ore to the surface. As were rails and modern port equipment, mining technology was imported from the Western industrial nations, though there was little stimulus to local manufacturing. At the extreme, the dependent economies clearly reaped little advantage: They produced cheap goods for foreign companies, traded largely through foreign firms that took a healthy

Workers repair track in 1950 on Liberia's first railroad. This line connected the port of Monrovia with the rich iron ore deposits in the Bomi hills. (Courtesy of the United Nations. Reprinted by permission.)

profit for their services, imported expensive modern equipment that yielded another set of profits for the industrial West, and finally had to borrow from industrial areas to fund the whole arrangement—thus paying interest to the West on top of everything else.

These patterns of export expansion applied to many parts of the world in the second phase of the industrial revolution. Increasing use of rubber spurred the development of the export economy and Western-owned plantations in Malaysia. Other parts of Southeast Asia were drawn into production of a variety of cash crops. American and British estates grew sugar and pineapples in Hawaii.

Some of the smaller, newly independent nations of eastern Europe were also drawn into a pattern of increasing commercial production based on exports to the industrial West. Romania, for example, steadily expanded its agricultural exports to western Europe during the late nineteenth century. Initially, this expansion depended on the labor obligations of serfdom. Then, when serfdom was abolished in 1864, landlords pressed peasant laborers to step up their export production without, however, significantly changing their work habits or technology. To maintain this export agriculture, new techniques had to be introduced by about 1900. Landlords began to adopt steam-driven tractors and other machines, which boosted crop yields but also displaced many traditional rural workers. This process led to a fierce peasant revolt in 1907. At this point, Romania's agricultural exports, supplemented by some wood and petroleum sales, exceeded total imports. Both had sextupled since 1865 because Romania was fully engaged in the international market. Imports, however, became increasingly vital, for the mechanization needed to sustain modern agriculture depended on products made in Britain, France, and in particular Germany. After World War I, land reform gave greater voice to peasants who reduced export production by returning to more traditional farming methods. But standards of living also fell, and Romania's dependence on German industrial exports actually increased. The country seemed trapped in a subordinate economy.

The most dramatic economic change occurred in Africa, which now became Europe's southern economic backyard, just as Latin America increasingly served that role for the United States. European-owned mining firms produced gold, diamonds, copper, and other vital minerals in various parts of southern and central Africa, pulling in huge labor contingents in the process. African work and family patterns were disrupted as men were coerced or cajoled into long stints in mining areas, occasionally bringing back some cash earnings to their native villages and the families they had left behind. Both South Africa and the Congo drew workers not only from the immediate vicinity of the mining centers but also from adjoining colonies within a wide radius. Earnings from migratory workers employed in South African mines formed one of the foundations of the economy of southern Mozambique, a Portuguese colony, from about 1900 well into the late twentieth century.

European pressure also generated the familiar pattern of cash-crop dominance. Several areas in western Africa saw the advent or expansion of plantations producing coffee and sugar. The most widespread European interest, however, lay in developing African cotton exports that would reduce European dependence on the more expensive exports from the southern United States. Some African farmers voluntarily decided to shift toward cotton production, realizing that it could earn them enough money to buy other foods and some cheap imported manufactured products such as bicycles as well. Where self-interest did not work, however, European colonial administrators frequently employed compulsion.

This pattern emerged clearly in colonial Mozambique, particularly after 1926. Portugal, desperately trying to increase its own industrialization because it lagged behind most of western Europe, pressed peasant farmers to shift to cotton production. For a time officials relied on market incentives, hoping that peasants would seek to make money by specializing in cash-crop production. With a new authoritarian government in 1926, this policy changed to outright compulsion. A Colonial Cotton Board was established with powers to require peasants to plant a certain number of fields in cotton and to work a certain number of weeks each month to generate the targeted output. Loyal chiefs and police were used to back up these directives, while Christian missionaries preached a dual message of hard, efficient work and acceptance of cash-crop agriculture. Nearly 80,000 peasants in northern Mozambique had been forced into this system by 1937, and 645,000 were involved by 1941. A large number were women, particularly in portions of the colony where able-bodied men worked in South African mines. Peasants who refused to participate were whipped or imprisoned; outright terror cemented this system.

The peasants had every reason to prefer their older agriculture. Growing cotton paid little. It was a difficult crop in Mozambique's conditions and took both land and time away from producing food for survival. Peasants were also required to hand-carry their cotton to market, another burden on physical strength and time. One woman recalled the system from the peasant perspective in talking with an interviewer: "Cotton cultivation was very demanding on us. They [overseers or police] decided our fields were not sufficiently clean, they grabbed us when we were eating lunch and forced us to go back to weed. We planted, weeded, harvested and carried our cotton to market even when our husbands were gone. And when we were ill we were still forced to go to our cotton fields."

The index to peasant hardship in this system was the standard of living. While a few loyal chiefs and overseers earned good money, sometimes buying bicycles or cars and indulging in purchases of art, most of the farmers were impoverished. Diets deteriorated because of meager earnings combined with lack of time to grow traditional foods. Reliance on manioc increased, for the plant required little care; in some regions it came to constitute up to 80 percent of all food intake, even though it offered limited nutritional value and exacerbated health problems. It was small wonder that many peasants fled, while others sought ways to circumvent the cotton-production system.

The Mozambique case was particularly dire; not all cash-crop and mining systems produced such hardship. The Western-induced imposition of new agricultural patterns, plus the growth of mining, invariably distorted standard work routines, spreading some aspects of the industrial work system literally around the world. But these were not accompanied by some of the compensations (reduced hours and higher earnings) industrialization brought to factory workers.

While Latin America, Africa, and Southeast Asia were the principal scenes of evolving commercial dependency, other locations opened up in the twentieth century. Oil was discovered in the Middle East early in the century. In 1912 the Turkish Petroleum Company was founded by German, Dutch, and British capitalists to exploit oil reserves in Iraq. This company underwent several subsequent transformations, merging into a single Iraqi Petroleum Company in 1939 that unified oil explorations and production in several parts of the region. The bulk of the profits went to Western investors until 1952. Oil was discovered in the Persian Gulf in 1932, again by Western companies. In Saudi Arabia the American Standard Oil Company won exploration concessions during the 1930s; massive production developed after World War II.

In all these instances, Western companies provided the technology and technicians for oil production, including of course rail lines, roads, ports, and pipelines. They drew thousands of local Arab workers into the process as unskilled labor, in some cases importing workers from other areas where, as in the desert kingdoms, the local population was sparse. The bulk of the profits redounded to the Western concerns, though local officials who granted the concessions were able to earn handsome rewards. Finally, the system kept oil prices low because it inhibited any major buildup of capital in the oil-rich regions and prevented widespread improvement in standards of living. While petroleum was a particularly valuable product for the West and for Japan because they were increasingly converting to internal-combustion engines and transformers, much of the Middle East was drawn into an essentially Western-dominated economy as a result of oil production. Not until the 1970s did Middle Eastern governments gain sufficient control to dictate substantial price increases, and with this came some larger prospects of economic development.

The final regional expansion of the dependent-economy system revolved around Japan. The industrial West led in the exploitation and transformation of Africa, Latin America, the Middle East, and much of southern Asia. Russia's industrialization did not depend on extensive raw-materials imports from other regions, as the Russians essentially converted territories within the Soviet Union, particularly in central Asia, to some of these same functions—producing oil, cotton, and other products. Japan, however, began to feel the need for an economic hinterland by the twentieth century, and this theme guided its exploitation of Korea after it took over the peninsula in 1910. Korean peasants were compelled to concentrate on rice production for export to Japan, an emphasis that forced them to eat an inferior grain, millet, in order to generate the required cash-crop levels in rice. Other Korean resources were harnessed to the Japanese industrial economy, and railroads and mines were built in what was by now a familiar pattern. As Japanese conquests expanded in eastern Asia during the 1930s, a larger "Asian co-prosperity" scheme was trumpeted that involved Japanese use of crops and minerals from other Asian regions (including rubber from Malaysia and oil from Indonesia) in return for infrastructure development by and factory imports from Japan.

Historians and economists have debated the impact of this growing range of commercial expansion throughout most of the nonindustrial world. Some have argued that the results of increasing export specialization provided a sensible opportunity for nonindustrial regions to develop comparative advantages—that the new work skills and habits, railroads and ports, modern communication systems, and other technology introduced held great merit for use later in wider, independent development. In this view, then, the 1880–1950 period was a stage in a larger industrial process. Other theorists, however, have argued that the expansion of the cash-crop and mining thrust served simply to increase the dependency of key regions, impoverish many of the workers involved, and leave the profits and the

key technical knowledge resident in the West or Japan. Outright foreign ownership increased, and all the essential industrial goods—including modern ships
and rails—continued to come from the outside world. Clearly, some individuals
in Africa, Latin America, and the Middle East profited hugely. Even individual
farmers, as in parts of Mozambique, learned to take advantage of market special-
izations, organizing larger farms with paid labor. At the same time, many people
suffered from change, and many of the regions involved did not make a smooth
transition from this phase of expansion under outside industrial dominance to an
industrialization process outright. Different regions experienced the export-
driven commercial phase in distinctive ways, which further complicates any generalization. What is clear is that industrialization in some parts of the world was
now having intensive international effects, changing basic economic patterns in a
host of regions still remote from any involvement in industrialization itself. Even
as regional economic variety persisted and in some ways increased, the force of
change became universal.

Factory Expansion

Several regions experienced significant factory development from the late nineteenth century onward, but this expansion had a strong orientation to the export
sector. Factory growth occurred, in other words, but in selected branches of production and without bringing a full industrialization experience. The results were
in some ways more promising than in the cash-crop and mining regions in that a
wider array of technologies was brought to bear, but considerable dependency on
the industrialized regions persisted.

The Turkish portion of the Ottoman Empire was one region that generated increasing factory production for export in the late nineteenth century. Growing
prosperity in western Europe and the United States meant rising demand for
Turkish carpets—no middle-class home seemed to be without these beautiful
craft products. Western merchants, along with some Turks, organized expanded
hand production from the 1870s onward, drawing in thousands of new workers.
This helped provide some employment for workers displaced from traditional
textile industries, by then driven under by imports of machine-made Western
cloth. Carpet exports approximately doubled between the 1870s and the 1890s.
Given growing demand, methods of production began to change somewhat.
Chemical dyes, developed in the West, began to replace customary root and berry
dyes used for the rich colors of Turkish carpets. American consumers, in particular, liked the new bright colors better than the traditional ones. But the transition
gave Western merchant houses more control over the carpet industry because
many Turkish workers were unfamiliar with the dyeing procedures. In the 1890s
export opportunities and Western commercial pressures led to further change:
the introduction of factories to make carpets, alongside the more traditional do-

mestic manufacturing system. Several of the factories were set up by Turkish entrepreneurs. With the new system came increased work specialization and pressure to step up the work pace, not only in the new factories but also in home production because home workers had to compete with machines in order to survive. Steam-powered wool-spinning machines (imported from western Europe) were established in a number of towns in western and central Turkey. Factory workers, mostly women, were low-paid, but they could produce more than the hand workers. The development of rug factories was also stimulated by the establishment of railroads into the Turkish interior; these were sponsored by the Ottoman government with Western investment and technical assistance. Rails made it easier to supply the rug-making towns and to transport their expanding product to seaports for shipment to the West.

Rug workers, even those new to the trade, were profoundly upset by the changes in their conditions, including their loss of control over artistic design and the growing separation between work and home. Like Western workers before them, they sometimes responded by acts of Luddism. In 1908, for example, a crowd of women and children attacked three spinning factories in one rug-making center, Usak, carrying off great quantities of stored wool and destroying the engine rooms. But the factories were quickly rebuilt and were operating full tilt within three years.

The industrialization of Turkish carpet manufacturing shared features both with early industrialization in the West or Japan and with the growth of commercial production in dependent economies like those of Africa or southeastern Europe. It was, as a result, not quite like either of these patterns. Unlike in Africa, the growth of some factory industry in Turkey brought experience with machines other than those inherent in railroads and more modern mines. The rugs produced, while dependent on cheap labor, had considerable value; indeed, their price tended to go up because of Western demand and the fact that no Western country had the necessary craft tradition to replicate the more artistic features of Turkish carpets. Turkish merchants and workers gained genuine industrial experience, though (like their Western counterparts many decades before) they often resisted the process. Nevertheless, the establishment of carpet factories did not generate a larger industrial revolution in Turkey. The industry was dominated by Western demand and Western commercial control; it did not feed a broad expansion of the internal economy. Because key technology remained a Western specialty, it was necessary to import machinery, which created a new dependency. Finally, the factory sector was isolated in a much larger, traditional peasant and artisan economy. Even after Turkey gained independence and a vigorously reform-minded government eager to promote wider industrialization in the 1920s and 1930s took the helm, the overall Turkish economy lagged.

The experience of China at the end of the nineteenth century and in the early decades of the twentieth century was somewhat similar. A growing factory sector developed that provided important new work and commercial experience, but

Western interests controlled the process extensively. As in Turkey, this sector was not large or autonomous enough to trigger a wider industrial revolution. Political chaos and foreign attacks (problems Turkey faced also, in the 1920s) further limited China's industrial potential through the 1940s.

After about 1860 Western merchants operated freely throughout China. They even ran the government's custom service, which regulated foreign trade. Several major Chinese ports were acquired by treaty and run directly by Western states. In these places Western merchants established new banks and stores as well as factories, and local Chinese began to copy the economic practices of the dominant European commercial group.

Shanghai became the model of this new China, developing modern industry but under substantial Western control. British, French, and U.S. interests were paramount in the city, setting up businesses, hotels, and social clubs. They ran the local government and began to stimulate rapid economic change. Major banks were established. Modern printing presses made Shanghai the national center of book publishing. Western nations also established shipyards for repair purposes—not only for the oceangoing fleet but for river steamers that foreign companies operated within China. After 1895 other manufacturing was permitted. Foreign textile factories and flour mills competed with Chinese industrialists. Large numbers of poor workers were recruited as Shanghai came to symbolize for many Chinese both the enormous economic potential and the great social cost of Western capitalism.

At the end of the 1890s other treaty ports developed in somewhat similar fashion, and Western companies also set up additional railroads. (In a similar pattern, Russia sponsored railroads in Manchuria.) The result was considerable commercial and industrial growth, with many Chinese businesses gaining experience in new technology. By no means was this an entirely Western show, but Western influence predominated, and the basic equipment for the new factories largely came from the West. The new Chinese factories were either in light industries producing processed food and clothing for sale in China or were designed to manufacture export items (like silk cloth or decorative items) for the West. The overall result constituted major change but not full industrialization—partly because the massive Chinese interior did not participate, partly because foreign capital and technical expertise remained so essential.

China's 1911 revolution brought a new regime eager both to spur further economic advance and to limit Western influence, but the government's weakness limited any real change of direction. Resentments grew, however. Between 1925 and 1927 Chinese consumers and workers staged a massive boycott of British goods and businesses, severely damaging Britain's role in China even in the treaty port of Hong Kong. Britain prudently withdrew from several areas (though it retained Hong Kong), and the tension subsided. Continued unrest in China, government instability, and then Japanese invasion in the 1930s prevented any major new strides in industrial development. China's role in the world economy became slightly less subordinate, but internal industrialization if anything receded amid massive disruption.

A final case of important new industrial development was Mexico, but it too experienced extensive foreign control and faced limitations that prevented easy movement into an outright industrial revolution. Mexico had lagged economically through most of the nineteenth century. Public services were poorly organized, and few railroads were built. On some of the rail lines that did exist, mules rather than locomotives pulled the cars. A new dictator, Porfirio Díaz, took power in 1876, and the Mexican economy began a significant spurt. Per capita income rose by 30 percent between 1877 and 1910, even as the population expanded by 75 percent.

Industrial production increased by an average of 3 percent per year under the Porfirian regime. The number of manufacturing companies rose sevenfold. They included the nation's first major steel producer and a massive new brewery (Cervecería Cuauhtemoc, named after the last Aztec ruler). Established by a Mexican of German descent, José Schneider, the brewery had such rapid growth in production that it had to set up a bottle factory as well. The new steel company, in Monterrey, expanded its production of steel rails and beams during the first decade of the twentieth century. Other factories produced chemicals, construction supplies, tobacco, and textiles.

Mexico's industrial economy depended heavily on exports. The government sponsored rapid railroad development, taking over much Indian village land and recruiting thousands of impoverished laborers. Foreigners, particularly from the United States, invested heavily and provided much of the necessary technical expertise. The growth of railroads, combined with government sponsorship of new commercial codes and other organizational measures, encouraged growing foreign investment in mines and estate agriculture, both designed to produce goods for export. Silver continued to be a major export, but it was now joined by cotton, wool, canned foods, cigars, and a variety of raw materials including petroleum. Many factories, in turn, like the food-processing and rope-making operations, primarily served the Western-dominated export economy. Reliance on foreign capital pervaded virtually all sectors, from many of the cattle and sheep ranches to some of the leading mines, oil wells, and factories. Imports, correspondingly, increasingly focused on vital machinery. Mexico supplied a growing amount of its consumer needs—in this sense, some freedom from foreign industry was achieved—but it did not generate an advanced technology sector. By 1910 expensive equipment accounted for 57 percent of all imports.

The government, staffed by a number of economic experts, was quite conscious of the nation's economic patterns. It looked to foreigners not only for capital but for the business spirit that, in its judgment, Mexicans lacked. It assumed that this stage of development would yield to a wider-ranging, Mexican-dominated process. The policies in the short run did yield a favorable balance-of-payments situation: Mexican exports exceeded imports, and the overall growth rates were the highest in Mexican history—before or for many decades afterward. A large urban working class developed, many discontented not only over poor working conditions but also over their inferior position to foreign technicians. Several violent outbreaks occurred, often producing army attacks on unarmed workers. In 1907, for example, textile workers struck against a twelve-hour work day, low wages, and a dominant company store that workers were required to patronize. Strikers burned the company store, but troops responded by firing point-blank into the crowd, killing hundreds.

Worker discontent combined with nationalist resentment and grievances by smaller businesses that feared industrial growth and, particularly, increasing foreign business dominance. As Porfirio Díaz aged, a revolution broke out that unseated the regime and ushered in over a decade of political disorder. Political stability returned in the 1920s under one-party rule, and with it came renewed attempts to develop the Mexican economy, though some limitations were applied to foreign investment and ownership. The earlier momentum was not regained, however, and Mexico's industrial position slipped during the middle decades of the twentieth century.

The cases of Turkey, China, and Mexico were notably similar. They all involved significant factory development that occurred under extensive foreign control, and the results in each were insufficient to bring about a full industrial revolution. In all three cases the changes that did occur helped generate new kinds of unrest, including labor protest, that in combination with other developments (such as Turkey's loss in World War I) generated major political upheaval. This disruption delayed further industrialization. In contrast to the Soviet Union, where earlier industrialization had proceeded more rapidly and was able to revive soon after the 1917 revolution, industrial development in postrevolutionary Mexico and China actually declined for a while as political disputes seized center stage. New leadership in several instances reduced foreign economic interference, but this undermined part of the foundation for the industrial development that had occurred. The result, at least for a time, was a new level of uncertainty in societies where traditional economic forms had been modified but a fully industrial economy remained out of reach.

Industrial Sectors: Change amid Tradition

Several societies were able to develop particular industrial sectors, primarily for domestic use, that introduced substantial economic change without full industrialization. In several cases the result also reduced dependence on Western imports. Mexico's establishment of a significant steel industry was a case in point, though the larger contours of the Mexican economy diluted the impact of this step by involving the nation so extensively in foreign ownership.

Iran, under a new government in the 1920s, constituted a clearer example of sectoral industrialization. The government did more than organize a larger railroad network, though this was an important step in developing internal markets. It sponsored several manufacturing projects because local business leadership was lacking. It set up factories to produce cotton and woolen goods, refined sugar, and processed foods and plants to manufacture glass, paper, matches, and cigarettes. All these industries were for domestic consumption only and were deliberately designed to replace imports from the West. Oil was discovered in 1908 and was exploited by a British-controlled company; refineries were built in 1915. The government did not win extensive profits from this arrangement, but unlike its Arab neighbors it did not develop extensive dependence on oil revenues. The regime's principal focus was to construct a small but vigorous modern industrial sector in an otherwise backward economy. The government used advisers from Britain, Russia, and particularly Germany, seeking to balance these nations in order to avoid subordination to any one. The goals were more political than economic. The Iranian regime was determined to maintain independence and also to extend its control over the population at home; hence railroads were built more for security purposes—the movement of troops—than for industrial development. Little attention was given to peasant agriculture. Iran emerged with an elite urban economy complete with merchants and professionals who adopted many Western styles. It did avoid submersion in the larger world economy, but it did not industrialize in any general sense.

India constituted another case of sectoral development, though one entailing a more complex series of circumstances. British-sponsored railroad development proceeded rapidly in India from the 1850s onward. Designed mainly for military and export purposes, rails stimulated the internal economy as well. Some textile factories were established in the late nineteenth century, even in cotton; the machinery was imported from Britain. Most of the textile products were cheap goods, and many were exported to other parts of Asia; ironically, the bulk of India's internal market continued to be supplied by British factories. Growing nationalism, however, stimulated a boycott of British-made goods in 1905. Imported saris and other cloth were ritually burned. Overall import levels fell more than 25 percent by 1908, while many merchants replaced "made in Britain" with "made in Germany" labels to elude the boycott. Indian machine-made textiles boomed in this environment, and other factory industries started up in consumer goods such as sugar, matches, glass, and shoes. As in Iran and several other areas, limited industrialization reduced dependence on imports, even though the bulk of the economy remained in the hands of traditionalist peasants.

India also developed an important steel sector in West Bengal. A Bombay industrialist, Jamshed N. Tata, had begun his career in cotton mills, including some extensive factories. His sons, without government backing but with funding from well-placed Indian nationalists, moved into metallurgy, creating a major center of production during World War I. By 1939 the Tata Iron and Steel Company was the largest single steel complex in the British Empire. Tragically, India's economy overall not only failed to industrialize but deteriorated outright. Massive population growth in the 1920s and 1930s was not matched by increases in food production, and thus living standards deteriorated. Cities grew, but less because of factory gains than of a torrent of unemployed people from the countryside. Yet a significant industrial change occurred, giving India some hold in modern manufacturing and some breathing room vis-à-vis Britain's 200-year-old commercial dominance.

Brazil was a final major nation to develop an important modern industrial sector. The country had long been a center of cash-crop production, and this continued well into the twentieth century. By the early part of the century, however, local industrialists were beginning to establish factories capable of satisfying domestic consumer demand in the area of light industry—processed foods, textiles, and the like. (This was also true in Argentina and Chile.) The import thralldom to Western industrial economies was correspondingly reduced. Brazilian factories featured the characteristic low-wage labor, including many women and children. Half of all workers in the industrial center of São Paulo in 1920 were under 18. Safety and housing conditions were miserable, and fines and beatings punished workers for mistakes. Many strikes and unions surged against employer control. Industrialization remained limited, however, and Brazil like other Latin nations continued to depend on Western imports for heavy machinery. The depression severely damaged Brazil's economy by cutting coffee exports. In this context a new military regime launched a more aggressive industrialization policy designed to reduce reliance on cash crops. The national coffee board used surplus beans to fuel railroad locomotives, while the government supported Brazilian manufacturers with high tariffs, generous loans, and police-enforced labor peace. Early in World War II the government granted the United States military bases in Brazil in return for American construction of Brazil's first giant steel-making complex. By 1945 Brazil's industrial economy, centered particularly around São Paulo, was booming rapidly. Here, as in West Bengal, a genuine industrial center had taken shape in an economy in which earlier patterns of agriculture and cash-crop exports maintained important strength.

Economies of the British Dominions

Between 1880 and 1950 a distinct pattern appeared in four areas having particular attachments to Great Britain: Canada, Australia, New Zealand, and South Africa. The first three of these countries were largely settled by Europeans, who displaced earlier native inhabitants. South Africa had an important white minority. All four countries interacted as near-equals with Great Britain economically and politically and received substantial investments and commercial preferences. All four developed significant factory industry in major cities, like Toronto, Sydney, and

Johannesburg. Large factories grew up during the early twentieth century. What marked the four as a special category among industrial nations was their continued reliance on extensive production of foods and minerals sold at relatively favorable rates—well above the cash-crop levels of West Africa or Brazil—that assured an essentially industrial standard of living for the bulk of the population (or, in South Africa's case, the bulk of the white population). By the same token, all four nations became major players in the world's industrial economy, particularly in relationship to western Europe and the United States.

Like the United States and Russia, Canada in its industrial development depended heavily on the expansion of its railroad system. It also relied substantially on outside investment, initially primarily from Britain. Major railroad building began in the 1870s, and the completion of the Canadian Pacific Railway in 1905 opened the rich western prairie provinces to the international economy. Exploitation of mineral and forest resources and abundant wheat production were major factors for world trade. Canada exported food widely to Europe. It also exported wood products, including paper pulp, particularly to the United States. Blessed with abundant mineral deposits, including the world's largest holdings of nickel and asbestos, Canadian mines yielded a growing output. Foreign investors offered extensive capital, installing the most up-to-date mining equipment, which in turn assured rising production levels even with a relatively small labor force. Canadian development around 1900 was also marked by rapid immigration, particularly from eastern Europe; 2.7 million immigrants entered Canada between 1903 and 1914.

Canada's initial industrialization focused on processing mineral and agricultural wealth. Canadian paper manufacturing and food processing were booming in the late nineteenth century, undergirding substantial annual growth rates. After World War I, U.S. investments in Canada increased. Concentrated initially in the mines and transportation system, American capital expanded into manufacturing in the 1920s. Canadian automobile production, for example, became an extension of U.S. corporations. These developments produced a genuine industrial economy but one that had particularly close ties to the larger industrial operations of western Europe and especially the United States. By the 1950s Canadians were exporting approximately a third of their annual economic product in all fields and importing a third of all consumption needs (mainly manufactured goods). Foreign trade levels were three times as high per capita as those of the United States. This pattern also tied Canada particularly closely to the fate of other industrial nations. The economy suffered massively during the 1930s depression—exports fell by over 65 percent—and then boomed again during World War II when Canadian farms and factories helped supply the war effort against Nazi Germany.

Industrialization in Australia and New Zealand displayed similar combinations of extensive factory industry but pronounced reliance on agricultural and mineral exports, all leavened by massive foreign investment. New Zealand in the late nineteenth century began to serve as Britain's garden, providing massive agricultural exports, in particular mutton and wool, to the erstwhile mother country. Factory industries developed mainly for national needs in consumer goods—clothing, processed foods, and the like. By the 1950s a quarter of the New Zealand population worked in factory industry. Only a seventh worked in agriculture, but the value of agricultural products considerably exceeded that in manufacturing, and 80 percent of the nation's exports were agricultural. Australia generated some larger-scale industry. A major steel mill was established in 1915 and still constituted Australia's largest single company in the 1950s, by which time 28 percent of the labor force worked in manufacturing. Nevertheless, the Australian economy continued to depend heavily on farming and ranching. These activities produced over half the nation's income in the first half of the twentieth century; sheep grazing alone yielded 35 percent of the total. British investment spurred mining and factory industry, and investment from the United States increased during and after World War II. Australia boasted substantial factory production in textiles, steel, and automobiles, though these were almost entirely for domestic consumption.

South Africa, finally, entered the Western industrial economy on the basis of its unparalleled diamond and gold reserves as well as other minerals and some export agriculture. South Africa utilized masses of African workers, in that sense fitting the more general colonial African economy. But huge South African companies that developed the diamond and gold trade were important players in the international economy, and in their wake substantial local factory industry sprang up during the first half of the twentieth century, producing both consumer goods and some heavy industrial products.

The industrialization of the major British dominions depended on unusual agricultural and/or mineral wealth that provided investment opportunities for Western capital and that generated earnings to support a wider-ranging industrialization for national needs in the manufacturing area. Relatively small populations (or in South Africa, a relatively small white minority) won high living standards, as both mining and agriculture were conducted with up-to-date machinery that made productivity high. (South Africa, of course, supplemented this with masses of low-paid black workers.) Iron mines in Australia, nickel mines in Canada, and the vast, mechanized wheat fields of Saskatchewan all integrated agriculture and mineral extraction into the larger industrialization process. By the same token, the value of the export products enabled the dominions to be incorporated as roughly equal participants in international industrial trade, in contrast to most raw-materials producers in other parts of the world.

At the Brink of Global Change

Even aside from the substantial industrial development of Canada, Australia, New Zealand, and South Africa, the world impact of the industrial revolution literally transformed the international economy between 1880 and 1950. Radically altered were habits of work for millions of workers, male and female, in Asia, Latin America, and Africa. A significant working class and a working-class movement developed in port cities and export industries in many centers.

At the same time, outside Japan, Russia, and the British dominions, no full industrial revolutions emerged. Western competition and exploitation impeded full conversion to an industrial economy. So, often, did internal divisions and political disputes. In many areas Western demand for goods significantly reduced economic independence. Even many factory centers were established under substantial Western control. Dependence on sales to the West (and in a few cases to Japan) and on Western capital and entrepreneurship limited the possibilities for autonomous economic growth. For many regions the depression of 1929 served as a tragic measurement of world reliance on Western markets, because as opportunities for raw-materials exports plummeted, there followed starker misery than in the West itself. Indeed, several cash-crop areas had entered a depression even before 1929 because of the persistent tendency toward overproduction and falling export prices. Even areas that had launched some factory industry proved highly vulnerable if they depended on Western businesses or Western markets—in contrast to Japan, which managed, because of a wider-ranging industrial growth, to overcome its loss of silk markets during the 1920s and 1930s. Significant industrial growth actually increased dependence on the West if the essential heavy equipment had to be imported—as was true in Mexico. Change, in sum, was almost universal, but it did not all point to a standard direction of industrialization.

Yet the emergence of significant industrial sectors in several areas—those designed mainly for internal consumption rather than export—did reduce Western industrial dominance in consumer goods and, in certain instances, metallurgy. Political policies were a means to support this process—Iran and Brazil took this course—but it did not necessarily generate a full industrial revolution. Diversity, then, as well as change dominated the international economic scene outside the industrialized centers. A common industrial world was nowhere in sight, yet the industrialization of the world was proceeding inexorably.

PART THREE

The Third Phase, 1950s–1990s:
The Industrialization of the World

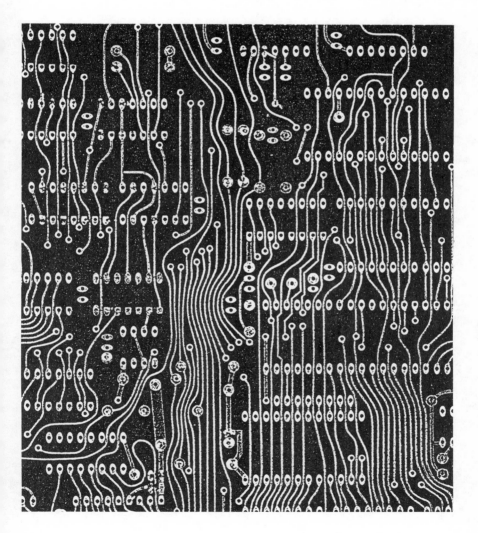

11

The Industrial Revolution in the Past Half Century

THE ADVANCE of industrialization was not high on the world's agenda after World War II. Europe's industrial economy was in shambles. The Soviet Union seized experts and material from its new satellites in Eastern Europe to try to rebuild. American aid assisted the recovery process in Western Europe, and American occupation forces directed political and economic reforms in Japan. For a brief time, however, only the economy of the United States seemed poised for further industrial growth. Many experts judged that Western Europe would become permanently dependent on American economic leadership. Simply rebuilding war-shattered economies seemed challenge enough. Outside the industrial world, political, not directly economic, issues predominated as a surge of independence movements led to rapid decolonization. Economic inequalities formed a backdrop to these struggles, and newly independent states quickly turned to hopes for economic development. But the initial priorities lay elsewhere.

Yet in fairly short order, the postwar world ushered in a third phase of international history—a phase societies are still grappling with in the 1990s. Key political events helped trigger important new developments. Decolonization did not magically generate industrial revolutions in the new states, and vast economic inequalities persisted, even deepened, among various regions of the world. Several major new governments, however, free from direct colonial control, launched new economic programs that expanded their manufacturing sectors. The Cold War between the Soviet Union and the United States had a massive impact on industrial activities in these two superpowers; it also helped stimulate industrialization in a few nations particularly drawn into Cold War rivalries. Western Europe reacted to the shock of World War II and the ensuing Cold War by seeking to reduce economic and political nationalism and by committing governments to industrial planning; this was the framework for the surprising economic resurgence of the region as Western Europe regained its position as one of the most advanced industrial areas of the world. Finally, the sheer momentum of previous industrialization helped spread new types of manufacturing and prepared a new round of technological change.

The world's third phase of the industrial revolution had four primary facets. First, there were some new industrial revolutions. These were fewer in number than in previous phases, but they were significant. They contributed to a new set of shifts in the world's industrial geography, and they showed that the process kindled 200 years previously in Britain had not burned itself out. Second, there were important industrial evolutions in several other societies, including giants such as India and China. Indeed, a gradual conversion to an industrial economy seemed to have become more characteristic than industrial revolutions outright. This process, too, built on patterns that had begun to emerge in the previous industrial phase. Third, established industrial societies moved toward a new set of technologies that had a new set of social implications. Some observers talked of a "third," or postindustrial, revolution in trying to convey the magnitude of these new developments. As before, continued advances in industrial economies set new challenges for the rest of the world, making it difficult to catch up even when modern manufacturing expanded. These same advances challenged different regions within the established industrial zones: Some made the turn to what was commonly called "high technology" quite readily; others faltered. Finally—and this facet is related strongly to the preceding three categories of change—industrialization had a more decisive impact on the international framework than ever before. Communications accelerated; commercial contacts moved to new levels; industrial units operated on a worldwide basis. The industrial revolution, which had already changed the nature and extent of international contacts, now burst beyond the bounds of nations and even whole civilizations.

New Members for the Industrial Club

The most dramatic new industrial revolutions took shape from the 1960s onward and occurred in medium-sized nations and city-states on the Pacific Rim. The industrialization of South Korea propelled this nation to unprecedented economic levels, making it a growing force in industrial exports of such goods as automobiles, electrical appliances, and ships. This area, historically isolated from the world economy, previously in the twentieth century had undergone a brutal, economically exploitative occupation by Japan and had then been divided between U.S.- and Soviet-dominated zones (South and North) after 1945. Taiwan (the Republic of China after Nationalist forces established their government there in 1948 following their loss to communist forces on the mainland) was a second site of Pacific Rim industrialization. The city-states of Hong Kong and Singapore rounded out the membership of the Pacific Rim's industrial club—along with Japan, of course, as senior member. In another part of the world, the new state of

Israel established an industrial economy, which included a strong commercial agricultural sector. And South Africa emerged further as the only clearly industrial economy on that vast continent.

These centers of new industrialization were not large, for literal industrial revolutions, in the sense of sudden breakthroughs to the new kind of economy, were becoming rarer. The rising industrial centers combined some distinctive features in their growing industrial success that were lacking in most other nonindustrial areas of the world. All the new industrial revolutions depended on careful government backing. Pacific Rim states, most of them operating under authoritarian strongman governments, meticulously planned industrial development, implicitly imitating many of the policies that had developed previously in Japan. These governments also limited political dissent, as did the racially repressive regime in South Africa. None of the economies was state-run: These countries encouraged free enterprise, but the planning role was crucial. All of the new industrial economies also benefited from strong contacts with the West. South Korea emerged from a war with the communist North early in the 1950s with massive U.S. support. American economic aid and military spending did not alone account for South Korea's industrialization, but they provided an important initial spur. Taiwan was another Asian Cold War center, as the United States long opposed the new communist regime on the mainland. Again, substantial economic aid and military spending—a U.S. fleet operated from Taiwan—helped launch an industrialization process. By the time the United States recognized the People's Republic of China in the 1970s and reduced its commitment to Taiwan, the island's industrial revolution was self-sustaining. Singapore and Hong Kong gained advantages into the 1960s from heavy British military and economic investment. Israel drew hundreds of thousands of European Jews, who brought with them devastating memories of the holocaust but also established industrial skills. Israel also won extensive foreign aid and investment, particularly from the United States. South Africa, finally, used its holdings of key resources like diamonds and gold to win substantial earnings and considerable investments from Western economies; here, considerable industrialization had occurred even before 1950.

Government focus and special economic relationships with the West did not alone occasion the new industrial revolutions. As before, causation was complex, and a host of factors had to combine to produce economic transformation. But these features helped account for the distinctiveness of these regions, for areas that lacked them were able to make marked industrial progress without—at least by the 1990s—generating an industrial revolution outright.

Industrial Evolutions

The measure of an industrial revolution in this period, as earlier in the twentieth century, was an ability to begin rapidly to catch up with the economic levels of the

established industrial areas—to change and grow more rapidly than these areas
had changed and grown. This was the stage Japan and the Soviet Union had
reached by the 1930s. After 1960, South Korea fulfilled this criterion admirably.
Most other nonindustrial areas of the world did not clearly make this turn,
though by the 1980s there were important cases of impressive growth. Most areas
did change, however, by their previous standards, and in some cases the change
was considerable.

Several societies, indeed, staked a claim to outright industrialization in the
1980s. Turkey argued that it had entered the ranks of industrial societies. So did
Brazil, now the industrial leader of Latin America. Neither of these societies managed quite as rapid advances in per capita income as the outright industrializers,
in part because of continued rapid population growth, but it was true that the
boundary line between industrialized and not-quite-industrialized economies
was blurring. Simultaneously, several nations close to the Pacific Rim increased
their manufacturing sectors and upgraded their technologies, enjoying rapid
growth that held the promise of full entry into the Pacific Rim's industrial zone.

Several parts of the world continued to serve extensively as raw-materials or
tropical-foods suppliers to industrialized areas, with little manufacturing base of
their own. Most international trade was handled by Western or Japanese companies, and many manufactured goods were imported from other areas. The contrast between these areas and advanced industrial societies grew increasingly
stark. Many observers spoke of a North-South division in the world, because a
disproportionate number of the dependent economies lay in the Southern Hemisphere, in much of Africa and parts of South America.

Countries in a larger part of the world, though still not fully industrialized,
gained greater control over their economies after 1945, partly through greater government planning but partly through a noticeable expansion of their manufacturing sector. India, for example, reduced its dependence on manufacturing imports from the West by providing more of its own needs; it also developed some
manufacturing exports destined mainly for other parts of Asia. The economy of
the Arab Middle East and Iran, though different from India's if only because of
extensive oil revenues, shared some characteristics in the development of an industrialized manufacturing sector, another instance of growth unattended by full
industrialization. China, finally, after several experiments with different industrial policies after the communist revolution—first an imitation of Soviet planning, then a radical Maoist variant—began to experience rapid industrial growth
rates in the 1980s; these likewise occurred in specific sectors rather than across the
economy as a whole.

The industrial revolution still pressed on the economies of every nation in the
world. Some continued largely to be exploited, and a huge range of conditions,
from dire poverty to steadily rising per capita wealth, glaringly revealed the continued inequalities industrialization had furthered. But the array of adaptations

had expanded, and this was one of the most striking characteristics of industrialization's third phase in world history.

The Postindustrial Concept

Established industrial areas clearly built substantially on previous accomplishments. Postwar revival demonstrated that countries that had industrialized had also acquired great resiliency. The German economy was back on its feet, for example, by the 1950s, in what was proudly labeled the nation's *Wirtschaftswunder*, or economic miracle. World War II bombing had not destroyed nearly as much industrial capacity as intended—only 22 percent was hit—and damage, after a few painful recovery years, helped trigger investment in new, up-to-date plants. Further, the knowledge of how to run an industrial economy—the human capital in management and labor—persisted strongly. This was another reason Germany and Japan bounced back surprisingly fast, as did war-torn France and even, though with less dynamism, Great Britain.

The story of the established industrial economies was not simply a resumption of business as usual, however. Although the industrial revolution was long past, fundamental change continued to be the hallmark of longer-run developments. Older industrial sectors began to fade. Not only textiles and coal mines but metallurgy declined as a result of expanding production elsewhere in the world and a slowing of demand. New industries surged forward: computers, electronics, biological products. Higher levels of automation reduced the need for manufacturing labor; in the 1970s growing use of robots in manufacturing accelerated this automation process. A host of other industrial characteristics were modified. In Western Europe and the United States, women began reentering the labor force in massive numbers, creating a watershed in women's lives and another set of profound changes in family functions.

To many observers it seemed that another revolution was taking shape in nations that had already been revolutionized. Experts as well as popularizers tried to define a postindustrial revolution that would prove as sweeping as the industrial revolution less than two centuries before. In this postrevolutionary imagery, the computer became as basic a symbol as the steam engine had been before.

At the same time, participation in change was not uniform across the established industrial economies. Japan moved quickly into a leading role; its earlier lag, based on a later industrial start, disappeared. Western Europe also participated strongly, displaying economic growth rates far higher than it had managed during the first half of the twentieth century and in some cases higher than during the industrial revolution itself. Germany's strength persisted, but France and then Italy were added to the ranks of advanced industrial leaders. The United States helped develop many of the new technologies but in the 1970s seemed to falter slightly; its relative economic standing slipped. Finally, the Soviet Union and satellite economies in Eastern Europe failed to make the turn into the most advanced economic levels for a variety of reasons, including deliberate state policy that blocked the development of a strong consumer-goods sector, unintended clumsiness due to excessive government planning and control, and the burdens of military expenditure in the Cold War. After 1980, for the first time in industrial history, a major industrial economy seemed to be slipping back—not just losing ground relatively but actually shrinking, jettisoning some previously acquired technical capacity. Shifts in the economic balance were an important part of the latest phase of the ongoing history of industrialized societies, and societies that could not rapidly move forward risked falling back.

The International Thrust

The international implications of the industrial revolution emerged ever more strongly from the 1950s onward. New industrial revolutions, expansion of the industrialized economies, and the evolutionary strides elsewhere all added up to more industrialization around the world. International contact was unavoidable. Revealingly, two economies that attempted to isolate themselves from world currents paid the price of lagging technologies: Both the Soviet Union and China had to decide to reenter the international economy.

The new round of technological innovations associated with industrialization had obvious worldwide impact. Satellite communications and computer linkages increased the volume and speed of information flow. High-speed air travel made international business meetings and expert conferences commonplace.

The greatest organizational innovation associated with the contemporary phase of the world's industrial revolution centered on the development of multinational corporations. As in many other aspects of ongoing industrial change, the multinationals built directly on earlier patterns. The true multinational, however, did more than establish subsidiaries in various countries—it set up specialized manufacturing operations almost literally around the world for assembly of completed products from parts manufactured in a host of separate countries. The ability of multinationals to seek cheap factory labor in societies not fully industrialized testified to the spread of industrial work habits and technical capacities well beyond the industrial societies themselves; this same ability obviously extended industrial conditions ever more widely. The operations of multinationals did not equalize conditions around the world, but they increasingly brought equivalent contacts with industrial operations.

Finally, the third phase of world industrialization saw a new movement of labor from lesser developed societies to the highly industrialized nations. Immigration levels in the United States reached higher absolute rates than ever before in the nation's history. Western Europe also had high levels, and even Japan began to depend on a significant number of immigrant workers from other parts of Asia. The immigrant experience offered yet another example of the world's economic inequalities, as the majority of immigrants were kept in a rather separate set of jobs. But the experience also showed the international outreach of industrialization, as some societies came to depend substantially on the earnings their emigrant workers sent home. Here again, the latest phase of the industrial revolution forged a new international context. The industrialization of the world's labor, like that of the world's technology and the world's business, was one of the most prominent features of contemporary world history. What had begun as a series of important effects radiating from the industrialized centers turned into a global experience.

Deepening Diversity

In contrast to the first stage of industrialization (1760–1880), when the industrial revolution was confined to the West though with moderate spillover into the international economy, the second phase (1880–1950) brought the decisive involvement of literally the entire world in the industrialization process. The nature of participation varied widely. Some societies joined the West in industrializing, others were essentially exploited for resources by the industrial centers, and several hovered in between these extremes. The third phase opened in the 1950s and 1960s, and this contemporary stage of world industrialization extended the developments that had taken shape in the previous seventy years. As before, though more modestly, the list of true industrial economies expanded even as the nature of established industrial societies continued to change. The result was the widely commented division between industrial and nonindustrial (developing) nations. These nations, however, continued to change rapidly in their own right. Exploitation persisted as Japan joined the West in seeking resources and cheap labor in other areas. But many regions, aided by political changes that increased their range of economic initiative, built on previous experience with limited factory sectors to establish a wider manufacturing base. As before, the world industrial economy was composed of unequals, but it required recurrent change at all levels, from the societies reluctantly compelled to defend positions as resource suppliers on the one hand, to the world's new high-technology leaders on the other.

   Two theories emerged in the postwar decades to explain international economic patterns by relating industrial history to future prospects. Modernization theory, popular in the United States during the 1950s, held that all societies could establish the political and social bases for an industrialization process like that of the West or Japan. Foreign economic and technical aid could help, but industrial modernization would ultimately carry the day worldwide. As it became clear that many societies were not industrializing fully, and that even substantial change did not necessarily produce a classic industrial revolution, this rather literal use of historical models declined in favor.

The second theory stressed the deep roots of international economic inequalities and especially the dependency certain economies had established on cheap production for the world's industrial giants. Latin America was held up as a classic dependent economy in which real industrial advance might be almost impossible because of poverty, foreign domination, and international debt. This theory emphasized the historical growth of dependency relationships as they had been intensified during the nineteenth and early twentieth centuries. Although dependency theory explained much, it homogenized too many different experiences and ignored the real industrial growth occurring in several (though not all) previously dependent areas.

By the 1990s many historians had concluded that sweeping theories inherently oversimplified both historical and contemporary experience with international industrialization. They argued for more limited generalization and for attention to distinctive features and historical experiences of the various major players in the contemporary world economy. There was no escaping some complexity and a variety of specific stories.

12

New Industrial Revolutions

WHILE DRAMATIC industrial revolutions occurred in parts of East Asia, the expansion of industrial economies included other patterns as well. The integration of parts of southern Europe and Eastern Europe (for example, Romania) with the industrial economies of Western Europe and the Soviet Union, respectively, also multiplied the number of industrialized nations and regions. The process of fanning out showed clearly in Spain. Two Spanish centers (Catalonia in light industry and Bilbao for metallurgy) had industrialized earlier. After 1950 the nation received substantial investment from both the United States and Western Europe and ultimately became a Common Market member. This set the framework for rapid industrialization from the 1970s onward, though Spanish industrial levels continued to lag somewhat. The same pattern emerged in parts of the American South. Before 1900 this region was largely a raw-materials supplier to Europe and the industrial northern states. Then some light industry began to locate in mill towns, drawing on cheap labor. General U.S. industrial expansion during and after World War II created a genuine industrial boom in some southern states, which acquired a label connoting the strong economy—the "New South." Developments of this sort were vitally important, but while they expanded industrial geography, they raised no major new themes. Rather, they extended the process of industrial integration of what had initially been fringe areas of existing industrial regions.

Israel: Development in the Desert

The establishment in 1948 of the new state of Israel also brought an industrial economy to the Middle East for the first time. The pattern was important, but it was also highly unusual in terms of industrial history more generally.

175

During the first half of the twentieth century, Jewish settlers in Palestine had brought with them assumptions about commerce and technology drawn from their European backgrounds. As Zionists they had a deep commitment to Israel and also to a wider range of economic activities than had been common among European Jews. In particular, they worked to extend commercial agriculture in an area where centuries of excessive farming had reduced the fertility of the soil. They drained swamps, established new irrigation systems, and sank new wells. In sum, a major transformation of agriculture had occurred before the formation of the new Israeli state. Extensive commercial production, some of it destined for export sale, was based not only on hard work and cooperation among the settlers but also on advanced agricultural technology and construction. The state of Israel extended commercial agriculture, concentrating on products like fruits, eggs, and cotton that could be sold abroad.

Commercial agriculture laid the groundwork for the development of new industry. This was also furthered by the massive new Jewish immigration, initially mainly from war-torn Europe, which doubled the Jewish population between 1948 and 1953. Many of the new settlers, though ravaged by the Nazi holocaust, brought established craft and commercial skills and moved relatively easily into the task of establishing an industrial economy. In addition, Israeli industrialization was supported by considerable foreign aid, particularly from the U.S. government and from private Jewish organizations in the United States and Western Europe. American assistance, for example, supported the construction of massive water pipelines that brought irrigation to additional parts of the new nation.

Israeli industrialization focused on the production of consumer goods that would supply needs within Israel and be suitable for export as well. Production of construction materials and the development of an armaments industry followed from needs of the Israeli state to settle additional Jewish immigrants and to maintain military preparedness. Some Israeli-manufactured weapons also were sold abroad. Consumer-goods production focused on areas like textiles, household appliances, and precision instruments. An important traditional craft sector, cutting and polishing diamonds, was added to the manufacturing roster. With this base, Israel developed extensive export sales to Western Europe, the United States, Turkey, and parts of Africa. By the 1960s a quarter of the population worked in manufacturing, and while agriculture remained important, Israel by this point constituted the clear industrial leader in the Middle East. The nation depended heavily on imports, particularly of advanced machinery and raw materials for industry. Despite its export energy, it tended to suffer from an adverse balance of payments, which was offset by earnings from tourism and by continued foreign aid. Notwithstanding some distinctive features and the vulnerabilities of operating an industrial economy in such a limited area, there was no doubt about the achievement of industrialization as part of building the Israeli state.

The Pacific Rim

Led by South Korea, the Pacific Rim began to industrialize rapidly during the 1960s. The achievement of these countries was in many ways unexpected. Many of the new centers, including South Korea and the island nation of Taiwan, had little apparent industrial background and few particular advantages in launching an industrial revolution. Many had been devastated by World War II and subsequent events. Japanese occupation had been brutal and costly. Taiwan had subsequently suffered from the communist takeover of mainland China between 1945 and 1949; a new, Nationalist Chinese government, committed to continuing the struggle with the giant communist neighbor, took control of the island. Tensions and some outright hostilities peppered the 1950s. Korea, divided between communist- and Western-controlled zones after 1945, faced recovery not only from the long period of Japanese control but also from the costly war between North and South that broke out in 1949 and that soon involved U.S. and Chinese confrontation on Korean soil. Property damage and loss of life were extensive in a war that came to an end only in 1953 and left lingering tension along the zonal border as well as continued need for substantial military expenditures in both North and South. Few observers in 1950 could have predicted Korea and Taiwan as locations for the world's next decisive set of industrial revolutions. Indeed, most assumed that industrialization would come next in one of the more stable new nations, like India.

South Korea, Taiwan, and other parts of the Pacific Rim certainly matched the classic latecomer industrial model, much as Japan had before them. They faced immense industrial competition from established areas, including a rapidly rebuilding Japan. They needed to develop special advantages to catapult them into the ranks of industrializing powers. Again like Japan and Russia, the previous leaders in latecomer industrial revolutions, Pacific Rim nations relied heavily on state planning and state guidance—this in societies governed by authoritarian leaders who actively supported the process of economic transformation and who were eager to prevent political instability or significant protest. Government direction was supplemented by low-wage labor, which provided opportunities to develop relatively inexpensive factory production in certain sectors despite an initial lack of technological leadership.

Some parts of the Pacific Rim were also able to build on previous if limited experiences with factory industry. Hong Kong, for example, was one of the centers in which British and Chinese business interests had developed extensive commercial institutions and some modern manufacturing from the late nineteenth century onward. Scholars have found the case of South Korea less clear. Japanese occupation after 1910 had been exploitative, and many observers have assumed that the results held down Korean economic development. However, some recent research has suggested that while Japan unquestionably used Korean resources and labor as supplements to its industrial economy, it also provided some significant industrial experience in the peninsula. The Japanese government built railroads. Japanese business invested in some Korean factories with an eye toward sales back home. South Korea thus did not necessarily jump from the status of exploited colony to vigorous industrializer in a single bound.

Explicit government support and some prior factory development do not, however, account for the extraordinary surge of the Pacific Rim after 1960. Many other regions of the world had governments that backed industrialization, and many had gained at least as much experience in modern manufacturing during the 1880–1950 decades. Many, certainly, could and did offer low-wage labor. Two other factors seem to have prompted Pacific Rim industrialization, differentiating this region from the many other areas where the next industrial revolution might instead have occurred. First, most of the areas initially involved enjoyed some special contacts with the West after World War II. Singapore, for example, had been founded by Great Britain in the nineteenth century and had long served as a major military base in Southeast Asia. Even after Singapore gained independence (it became self-governing in 1959), Britain retained a substantial presence. British naval activities brought in their wake significant investments and an opportunity for Chinese business leaders in Singapore, along with some Westerners, to set up industrial and commercial operations. Hong Kong was another British enclave from the imperialist period, and even as it gained growing autonomy in the 1960s, it was able to utilize commercial and technical contacts with Britain and the United States as part of its economic development.

Taiwan became a major Cold War partner of the United States, particularly during the 1950s and 1960s when the United States refused to recognize the communist regime on the mainland. Partnership meant military support, but it also meant considerable economic aid until the late 1960s. Taiwanese capital and also opportunities for technical contacts benefitted accordingly. By the time U.S. aid ended, when Taiwan was developing rapidly on its own and indeed generating some manufacturing competition with the United States, the period of intensive interaction had paid off. Like Russia in the nineteenth century, Taiwan combined its interests in industrial development with extensive imports of funds and technology to a point where self-sustained growth became possible.

The same pattern applied in South Korea. During and after the Korean War, the United States poured substantial economic aid into the nation, hoping to rebuild it as a staunch Cold War ally against the communist regime in the North. Again, not only investment but technological exchange was facilitated. Many Koreans, like many Taiwanese, began to study in the United States, particularly in fields of engineering, management, and agriculture. A 1984 Korean advertisement in *Fortune* magazine extolling the nation's technological prowess pictured three leading executives wearing the sweatshirts of their American universities—the Massachusetts Institute of Technology, the University of Wisconsin, and the California Institute of Technology, respectively. The advertisement angered many Americans because it suggested that American know-how was being used against them in international economic competition, but it correctly reflected the benefits Korean industrialization had derived, in a formative phase, from its hothouse association with the United States.

The second factor distinguishing Pacific Rim industrialization related to important features these societies shared with Japan. The fact of Japanese industrial success, including the nation's striking recovery after World War II, served as some inspiration in the Asian Pacific, even in the nations that had cordially detested Japanese occupation. Commitment to reform through the agency of strong government also revived a pattern from Japan's early industrial decades. Most important, the initial Pacific Rim industrializers shared with Japan a substantial Confucian cultural tradition. Like Japan, they had to modify Confucianism substantially in order to industrialize, providing more attention to scientific and technical training, more defiance of purely traditional learning, than strict Confucianism entailed. But Confucianism also provided special habits of deference and cooperation conducive to forming industrial management strategies, building on group loyalty, and engaging in collective decisionmaking. The same habits encouraged a common bond between workers and managers, promoting a willingness to work hard and sacrifice for the good of the firm or the nation. Confucian culture provided a different context for the industrial revolution from that of Western or Russian culture, and it promoted different patterns of management and labor. It was, however distinctive, demonstrably successful. It had helped anchor an industrial economy in Japan, and it clearly served the industrial revolution of the Pacific Rim more generally. This cultural factor was critical to the region's ability after 1960 to steal a march on the rest of the nonindustrial world and to gain ground on the established industrial giants themselves.

Industrial Growth in the Pacific Rim

South Korea, the most obvious exemplar of Pacific Rim industrial revolutions, emerged in the 1980s as the most important industrial economy in the region after that of Japan. The Korean government rested normally in the hands of a political strongman, usually from army ranks, in a pattern that caused periodic unrest but also yielded extensive periods of stability. One leader was forced out of office by massive student demonstrations in 1960, but in 1961 a military general, Park Chung Hee, seized power, retaining his authority until his assassination in 1979. Then another general took over, yielding to renewed student protest at the end of the 1980s, after which a conservative politician gained control. In South Korea politics took a second place to economic growth.

Government support combined with active business entrepreneurship to create huge industrial firms from about 1960 onward. Exports were actively encouraged, for Korea needed to earn foreign exchange to buy the most modern equipment and some raw materials. By the 1970s, when Korean industrial growth rates began to match those of Japan, Korea was competing successfully in cheap consumer goods, like plastics, but also in steel and automobiles and serving a variety of international markets. Korea based its surge in steel on the most up-to-date technology, a skilled engineering sector, and low wages and indeed pushed past Japan. The same held true in textiles, where Korean growth (along with that of Taiwan) erased almost one-third of the jobs in the same industry in Japan.

Huge industrial groups like Daewoo and Hyundai resembled the great Japanese holding companies before and after World War II, wielding great political influence. Hyundai, created by Chung Ju Yung, had 135,000 employees by the 1980s and offices around the world. The company virtually governed Korea's southeastern coast. It built ships and automobiles. It constructed thousands of housing units for its low-wage labor force, promoting worker stability at relatively modest cost. Its sponsorship of technical schools provided a steady supply of skilled workers and technicians, for South Korea did not import labor from other areas. Hyundai, like other major Korean companies, also built a framework for workers' social life and a series of rituals that helped tie workers to each other and to the company. The similarities to the kinds of labor policies installed in Japan, particularly after 1920, were striking. Company sports facilities included an arena for the practice of the traditional Korean martial art, tae kwon do. Work days began with group exercises and other expressions of solidarity. With their lives carefully organized, Hyundai workers seemed to respond in kind, putting in six-day weeks with three vacation days per year and participating in reverential ceremonies when a fleet of cars was shipped abroad or a new tanker launched.

Korea's industrial revolution did not propel the nation into the top ranks of world industrial leaders. Korea still depended on imports of some of the most modern equipment, including computers. It also continued to experience population pressure, unlike the more established industrial nations that had gone through the demographic transition. By the 1980s Korea had the highest population density on earth, about 1,000 people per square mile. This helped supply a cheap labor force, but it also strained resources in other respects, and considerable Korean emigration continued (primarily to Japan and the United States) even as the industrial revolution gained ground. Population growth and advancing industry combined to generate new pollution problems, particularly air pollution in the major cities. Notwithstanding these limitations, some of them characteristic of earlier industrial newcomers, Korea's economic progress was undeniable. Per capita income rose almost tenfold between 1950 and 1990 despite massive population growth, though Korean living standards still lagged well behind those of Japan. Leading Korean businessmen amassed considerable fortunes. Korean industry competed not only in Japan but also in the United States, where Korean cars made noticeable inroads alongside more massive imports from Japan and where Korean steel even more successfully competed with the ailing steel industry.

Industrialization in Taiwan was slightly less impressive than that of Korea, but many basic trends were similar. Productivity increased in industry and agriculture, the latter spurred by government-sponsored land reforms that benefitted small commercial farmers. In 1960 the government began to concentrate on economic growth as its commitment to military rivalry with communist China declined. An authoritarian government, led by Nationalist Chinese, generated some discontent but also provided considerable political stability; this too paralleled the Korean pattern. Elaborate economic planning mechanisms were designed to make the most of limited capital and resources, though as in Korea government action was compatible with considerable latitude for private business. Increased government funding of education produced rising literacy rates and rapid improvement in levels of technical training.

Taiwanese manufacturing sold widely around the world. Inexpensive consumer items, including plastic products and textiles, became a Taiwanese hallmark. Hothouse export growth included inexpensive copies of Western musical records and books. Taiwan also built important regional contacts with other nations in eastern and southeastern Asia. Japan served as the nation's most important single trading partner, purchasing foodstuffs, manufactured textiles, chemicals, and other industrial goods. Japan's own explosive growth by the 1980s clearly facilitated the further development of Pacific Rim industrialization, as Japan concentrated increasingly on high-technology production, depending on other areas not only for raw materials but also for the less expensive categories of factory goods— some of which had once been Japanese staples when the nation launched its surge into world industrial markets.

The two other centers of Pacific Rim commerce and industry were the city-states of Hong Kong and Singapore. Singapore boasted one of Asia's most single-minded authoritarian rulers, Lee Kuan Yew, who took power in 1959 and held it for three decades. Tight controls over Singapore's population provided not only political stability but also increasing work discipline and urban regulation. With government encouragement, Singapore's status as a major port—it was already the world's fourth largest port under British rule—expanded. Manufacturing and banking services, however, came to surpass shipping as sources of revenue. Oil refineries and textile and electronics factories joined shipbuilding as major sectors. By the 1980s Singapore's population enjoyed the second highest per capita income in Asia, though it remained well behind Japanese levels. Industrial growth plus government regulation and propaganda also began to reduce birthrates, which suggested Singapore's move into a second stage in the development of an industrial society.

Hong Kong, though more flexibly governed than Singapore, also built on its status as a major world port. Its banking services expanded as the city served as a commercial bridge to communist China. Export production in industry, particularly in textiles, combined high-speed technology with low wages and long hours for the labor force to yield highly competitive results. Like the other Pacific Rim nations, Hong Kong experienced rapid population growth that was swelled by flights from its communist Chinese neighbor. The twofold result was agonizing urban crowding but also a flexible, inexpensive labor force. While textiles and clothing formed 39 percent of Hong Kong's exports by the 1980s other sectors, including heavy industry, had developed impressively as well. As in other Pacific Rim industrial nations, a large and prosperous middle class developed, and this group had cosmopolitan links to many other parts of the world, Western and Asian. Hong Kong's technically advanced, dynamic economy and its strong emphasis on competitive exports placed the city-state fully within the larger Pacific Rim industrialization framework.

Expanding the Rim?

By the 1980s the steady industrial development of the Pacific Rim—headed of course by Japan as the oldest and largest industrial power in the region—was beginning to draw in other parts of eastern and southeastern Asia plus Australia. An eastern Pacific economic zone was taking shape, with the most advanced sectors stimulating factory development in outlying areas. During the early 1960s, for example, the Malaysian government launched a program of diversification of its export crops to improve foreign earnings and particularly to fund expansion of the manufacturing sector (then responsible for only about 15 percent of total national income). Raw materials and inexpensive factory goods were targeted toward Japan, while tourist facilities expanded for both Japanese and Western clientele. No industrial revolution occurred, even by 1990, but the range of manufactured products climbed, and standards of living improved as well. By the early 1990s many observers believed that full industrialization was imminent and that with it would come equal Malaysian participation in an expanding Pacific Rim.

Thailand was another entrant to the region's rapid-growth sectors. A significant stream of Thai workers labored in Japan (along with migrant workers from the Philippines and Korea, as Japan's labor force no longer sufficed for all the nation's needs, particularly in the less skilled jobs). Exports from Thailand expanded, mainly in the category of foods and raw materials, but on this basis the manufacturing sector also grew. Frenzied industrial and commercial growth, in what was still a poor society, produced its characteristic concomitant: growing urban pollution. Air and water quality in Bangkok deteriorated rapidly even as Thailand experienced what eventually may prove to be the beginnings of an industrial economy.

The expansion of the Pacific Rim economy embraced Indonesia, where economic growth accelerated though without as much manufacturing as in Thailand or Malaysia. Australia participated actively, expanding its industrial exports but, particularly, serving as Japan's major supplier of foods and raw materials aside from petroleum.

The surge of Japan to a share of world industrial leadership and the independent, rapid industrial revolutions in other parts of the Pacific Rim were clearly transforming economic relationships throughout the Asian Pacific. Just as industrialization earlier had fanned out beyond the initial leaders in Western Europe, generating increased manufacturing on the fringes, so too was a larger Pacific economic zone taking shape. Plans for collaboration in trade policy and investment inevitably followed basic industrial reality. Both South Korea and Japan opened increased economic contacts with communist China, particularly after 1978, and a bit later with Vietnam and Cambodia. Some forecasters projected continued expansion not only of trade but of industrial development should the Pacific Rim, for example, come to include expanding manufacturing centers in coastal China. Even aside from speculations about the future, it was clear that Pacific Rim industrialization had already transformed international economic patterns, creating a major trade and manufacturing zone—the fastest growing zone in the world economically—that rivaled earlier zones carved out by Europe and the United States.

Brazil, Mexico, and Turkey: New Candidates?

The emergence of borderline industrial economies in Mexico, Turkey, and Brazil did not rival the industrialization of the Pacific Rim in importance or drama. It did suggest, however, a pattern of industrial growth that in the future may well become more characteristic than industrial revolutions outright.

Mexico, Turkey, and particularly Brazil entered the ranks of significant industrial exporters by the 1980s. Factory textiles in Turkey, for example, became competitive in world trade, with significant exports to advanced industrial nations such as Germany. Brazil's steel industry exported successfully to the United States, and Brazilian and Korean steel combined to dent American production by the late 1970s. Brazil also became the world's fourth largest exporter of computers, deliberately tapping markets beneath the level of the most sophisticated technology but developing a substantial manufacturing sector in the process.

Governments in Mexico, Turkey, and Brazil eagerly backed industrial development, beginning their support in the 1920s (in Turkey's case) and the 1930s (in Brazil and Mexico). All three nations experienced frequent periods of authoritarian rule and accompanying stability, though a democratic political party system also had some impact. Government sponsorship of industry included carefully negotiated trade arrangements with other regions, active solicitation of foreign aid and investment, and support for technical training and infrastructure. Finally, all three nations had developed sectors of factory industry in the previous period in world industrial history, and these served as the basis for subsequent industrial expansion. In short, none of the three was a newcomer to the industrial game.

At the same time, however, Mexico, Turkey, and Brazil continued to experience rapid population growth. A substantial proportion of the labor force remained rural, and production of agricultural goods for export—including Brazil's traditional cash crops such as coffee and Turkey's newer success in raising fruits and nuts for sale in Europe—served as clear reminders that industrialization had not yet displaced earlier commercial patterns. All three countries contained large and expanding numbers of urban poor, as factory growth could not keep pace with the movement of impoverished people to the cities. Brazil and Mexico, in addition, had a substantial foreign debt, which hampered independent economic growth, while Turkey continued to depend on earnings from Turkish workers in Western Europe. All three countries thus showed various and important symptoms of incomplete industrialization, as older economic patterns and dependencies vied with genuine factory growth. Although authorities in the three nations claimed entry to the ranks of industrial powers, and although industrial expansion was clear and significant, it was not yet possible to discern a full-scale industrial revolution of the classic sort—such as was contemporaneously visible in South Korea and Taiwan. Overall growth rates, correspondingly, lagged, as factory expansion was balanced by the size of the more traditional sectors in agriculture and in the urban slums.

Yet there was change as Mexico, Turkey, and Brazil deliberately expanded modern industry to meet internal needs and produce export earnings. Brazil's computer industry was a striking case in point: A nation well behind the world's industrial leaders deliberately fostered an industry capable of serving the nation's computer needs and so avoiding yet another dependence on expensive imports. Governmental regulations protected this new Brazilian industry, while heavily supported computer engineers at the technical university in São Paulo constructed independent computer prototypes. While the industry itself developed only in the 1970s, it clearly built on Brazil's earlier commitment to industrial growth and technological progress. The engineering group at São Paulo thus stemmed from earlier advances in university science and technology, including nuclear physics; Brazil by the 1970s was producing 3 percent of the scientific articles in international journals. Beginning in 1959 the government had supported computer research directly, in connection with the Brazilian navy. Training in advanced electronics expanded steadily. Imports of advanced Western military equipment spurred growing interest in computers, and collaborative programs were developed with U.S. universities. By 1971 Brazil was ready to develop its own computer model, in partial imitation of European prototypes. A variety of small companies linked to the university center in São Paulo then developed to produce computers. Brazilian computers were deliberately designed not only to serve national needs but to be inexpensive and also compatible with frequent disruptions in electrical power: Although these models were not as advanced as those available from Japan, the United States, and Europe, they were more suitable to many nonindustrial areas (and more affordable as well). Brazilian computer production depended on imports of microchips from other areas, including Japan; this was not an isolated national industry. But it did demonstrate that prior technical progress, careful government sponsorship, and growing awareness of production and export opportunities could produce a genuine industrial breakthrough even in an economy that was, in terms of overall standards, still struggling to industrialize.

New focus on production sectors like computers added to Brazil's earlier manufacturing developments in steel, chemicals, construction products, textiles, and a host of other industries, as the nation generated a wide range of factory production for internal consumption and for an impressive array of industrial exports. While some factory sectors like textiles continued to depend on low wages (as had earlier been the case in textile industrialization elsewhere), the technologically advanced branches like electronics, chemicals, and heavy industries, offered reasonably good pay. With the expansion of factories, Brazil converted increasingly to the innovative technology and the rationalized economic organization characteristic of industrial economies since Britain first had defined the genre. Not surprisingly, this industrial surge, along with an aggressive policy of agricultural expansion that included clearing large stretches of rain forest for cattle grazing, provided Brazil with the highest annual economic growth rates in Latin America—over 6 percent per year by the 1960s and 1970s. Standards of living improved accordingly. By 1990, 22 percent of all Brazilians owned cars, 56 percent had television, and 63 percent had refrigerators. These levels were well below those in the advanced industrial nations, to be sure, but were actually higher than rates in Eastern Europe and South Korea.

Yet Brazil's industrialization seemed shaky in many respects. It was, of course, relatively recent. While manufacturing by 1990 generated 26 percent of the total Brazilian economic product, manufacturing and mining workers constituted only 22 percent of the labor force. Over a quarter of all Brazilians still worked in agriculture, while an amorphous service sector, including large numbers of domestic servants and other poorly paid, "low-tech" urban employees, also loomed large. These figures were characteristic of an industrial economy in its early stages, but they did not guarantee that a fuller industrialization process would take hold. Brazil's economic problems, furthermore, often overshadowed industrial development. Astronomical inflation rates—running between 600 and 900 percent per year in the early 1990s—reflected excessive government spending, including the heavy state investments that spurred the industrial sector. Foreign debt was also high, which necessitated crippling interest payments to Western and Japanese banks and frequent efforts at negotiating some modification of financial strictures from abroad. The Brazilian birthrate remained one of the highest in the world, running about 8 percent above annual world levels. Brazil's economy, despite impressive changes, clearly had problems simply keeping pace with this population surge. Again, this perhaps reflected merely the birth pains implicit in an early industrial revolution until some of the wider impacts, including a demographic transition, could take hold. Many ultimately successful industrial economies were subject to some combination of foreign debt, population pressure plus massive urban poverty, and fiscal uncertainty in their early years.

The obvious point was that in contrast to the much clearer industrial revolutions of the Pacific Rim, Brazil's industrialization had yet to win through; the commitment to industrial innovation, while quite real, was not yet the dominant fact of the Brazilian economy. The result was unusual complexity: Substantial industrial change was undeniable, as significant sectors of the Brazilian economy had been transformed. Many features of a latecomer industrial revolution had emerged, including government guidance and rapid economic growth. Brazil had triumphantly demonstrated that an economy once effectively controlled by European commercial interests could gain a real margin of independence and generate an internal transformation. Whether the long-term result foreshadowed continuing industrialization that would complete some recognizable version of a fully industrial economy was simply unclear. Brazil's case—like Russia's in a different way—suggested a novel pattern, in which industrial change combined with other characteristics to produce an economic amalgam durably different from the industrialization models provided by the West and Japan.

Mexico's claims to industrialization were in most respects shakier than Brazil's, but there was an impressive surge after 1950. The Mexican standard of living, in fact, was higher than Brazil's. Economic growth after 1950 fell a bit short of Brazil's, but still, during the 1960s, it expanded by more than 6 percent per year. Mexican President Miguel Alemán Valdes, whose administration began in 1946, fostered a policy of "import substitution," deliberately promoting the growth of factory production in steel, chemicals, and other industries in order to reduce the need to buy manufactured goods from abroad. Inexpensive government loans were offered to entrepreneurs in these sectors. This policy was combined with stiff tariffs on foreign goods, excepting only the advanced machinery and tools needed to get the modern industries started. Significant factory sectors developed in metallurgy, construction goods, and chemicals, boosting mining and manufacturing to 26 percent of Mexico's total production value.

But Mexico's industrialization had some pronounced constraints besides the fact that its early stages inevitably limited the nation's economy in comparison with advanced industrial areas like the neighboring United States. Real industrial growth did not soak up much of the labor force, for Mexican industrialists utilized advanced technology precisely for the purpose of avoiding high labor costs. Government policies, designed to appease labor unions, of providing extensive welfare benefits increased employer obligations and so limited employment. Industrial jobs did not keep pace with population growth or with factory output—one estimate found jobs increasing by only about 2.3 percent per year. The result was high unemployment—at 8.5 percent of the labor force by the 1980s—and even more substantial underemployment. By 1990 only 11 percent of the labor force worked in factories compared with 24 percent still in agriculture and a massive floating population in the growing cities. Mexico's government also borrowed heavily, partly to finance new industry but partly to enjoy a short-lived oil export boom, the collapse of which in the 1980s left a $98 billion international debt. Other Mexican exports increased, but the fact that major Mexican-run factories did not export widely made the debt all the more intractable. A century before, in the earlier period of growth, Mexico's dictator, Porfiro Díaz, had commented on how economic problems combined with political revolution would prevent an outright industrial revolution. Even after an important series of changes in the twentieth century, his words still seemed prophetic: "Poor Mexico, so far from God, so close to the United States."

Turkey's claim to industrialization by the 1980s legitimately identified substantial industrial growth, but it was perhaps misleading. The Turkish government, bent on reform and modernization from the 1920s, had for decades pushed economic changes with surprisingly little effect. Turkey was long studied as a case in which conscious government policy, unusually open to innovation, bumped against massive poverty and cultural resistance. Expansion of education, laws promoting a more secular lifestyle as opposed to strict Muslim habits, and a host of other measures changed Turkish life, but they did not set the stage for much modern industry. Foreign investors were wary of a Muslim society, and periodic political instability also warned them off.

Government focus on industrialization took shape by the 1930s. State investments expanded the road and railway system, creating the best internal transportation network in the Middle East. A central bank was set up in 1931 to control the monetary system and manage large state investments in factory sectors such as textiles and chemicals. Government mining companies also expanded. Turkey's loyal participation in the Cold War as an American ally brought significant foreign aid—though also high military costs—after 1950. Foreign investments increased, and a state planning agency emerged in 1960 to regulate these investments while also coordinating national planning. Only from about 1970 onward did private-sector industries receive much attention. By this point extensive factory industry that used advanced technology had been established not only in textiles but in automobiles (Turkey assembled some foreign makes but also established a domestic line for internal consumption), metallurgy, and chemicals. According to some measurements, Turkey by 1980 had become the second most industrialized nation in the Middle East after Israel. Yet only 11 percent of the labor force worked in mining and manufacturing combined (the same percentage as in Mexico) compared with a full 49 percent still in agriculture. Rapid population growth drained some resources, though Turkey was not densely populated and many workers, seeking jobs in Western Europe, brought back vital foreign earnings. It was not possible to predict whether massive industrial growth lay in Turkey's future, or whether an important factory sector had been established short of transforming the larger economy and society.

Two Patterns of Innovation

Each of the two previous periods in the world's industrial history had highlighted industrial revolutions in large, complex societies, like those of Western Europe, the United States, Russia, and Japan. The most recent period in industrial history was less impressive in terms of new entrants. Most of the revolutionizing economies were small or at most midsized. Their innovations were striking. The internal transformation of Spain, Israel, and the Pacific Rim was every bit as substantial as in earlier industrial revolutions elsewhere. And the international impact of the new industrializations was also considerable. Israel gained power in the Middle East, and Spain moved up in European status. The industrial newcomers in the Pacific Rim not only realigned economic patterns in eastern Asia and Australia but also participated strongly in the world economy, independent of Japan's even-greater voice.

Yet clear-cut industrial revolutions did not occur in larger societies. What happened in places like Mexico involved genuine change, though a host of limitations and complexities left such nations hovering on the brink of substantial, self-sustaining economic growth but quite capable of continuing to fall short. Of all the substantial societies not already industrialized, Brazil came closest to a genuine revolution through its technological leadership in certain sectors and the sheer expansion of the manufacturing labor force. Even here, however, dynamic change was balanced by an unusually imposing set of economic problems, including foreign debt.

Complex patterns of change of this sort seemed to become more important than the classic industrial revolutions in analyses of world response to industrialization at the end of the twentieth century. That industrial revolutions could still occur was undeniable, and the results of Pacific Rim industrialization would clearly expand further as these economies matured. Yet genuine change short of revolution probably marked the next wave of the future. In this regard, Mexico and Turkey as well as China, India, and a number of other major nations represented a new surge of industrial evolutions in which expanding factories and new technology were balanced against substantial nonindustrial economic sectors and qualified by a host of uncertainties, including the impact of continuing population growth. Pinpointing industrial futures became more difficult—would even Brazil move to the ranks of fully industrial economies within the next half century? This difficulty, in turn, was a measure of how the international impact of the industrial revolution had shifted, despite the hopes of modernization theorists to see history repeat itself. A search for the next industrialization candidates gave way to the more subtle attempt to determine how far a substantial commitment to factory production could move a society toward the industrial ranks.

13

A Postindustrial Revolution?

THE ESTABLISHED industrial societies in the 1950s centered in North America, Western Europe, Australia/New Zealand, Eastern Europe, and Japan. All began to generate explosive further industrial growth during the 1950s. The results followed many of the lines set by the previous industrial revolution—extensions of new technologies, introduction of new products, more sophisticated organizational forms—but sheer expansion created some novel results. Further, it became increasingly apparent—by the 1960s and 1970s—that more fundamental changes were occurring as a new generation of industrial technologies seized center stage; these, too, had widespread social effects, altering yet again the definition of industrialization's wider impact. Finally, amid both growth and change, the balance among the established industrial sectors shifted. Western Europe displayed unexpected new vigor, and Japan surged to the top for the first time.

Except for the new industrial revolution in the Pacific Rim, the changes in the established industrial economies constituted in many ways the leading and certainly the most dramatic developments in the world's industrial history in the late twentieth century. Redefinitions of established industrial technology and work increased the gap between the world's economic leaders and many other countries, even ones, like Brazil, that could point to substantial change in their own right. These same redefinitions, along with the rise of the Pacific Rim, set a framework for the world's industrial economy generally.

Growth Rates

Between 1960 and 1990, manufacturing output in the United States more than doubled, growing by 134 percent—and this was the lowest growth rate of any major industrial nation outside the communist bloc. Manufacturing in Canada expanded 137 percent, in Britain 195 percent, in Sweden 200 percent. Other European countries tripled or quadrupled their output—Germany by 226 percent, France by 323 percent, Italy by 375 percent. Japan, in its own league, posted an almost sevenfold increase—666 percent.

These were astonishing rates by any historical standard. Population increased also, but because output more than outstripped this growth, per capita productivity soared, even in the slightly laggard United States. Several European countries during the 1950s and 1960s saw their gross national product increase by 8 to 10 percent annually; France and Italy, in particular, greatly exceeded their dynamism during the earlier industrial-revolution phase. Growth slowed somewhat during the 1970s, the result of two sharp crises induced by a shortage of petroleum from the Middle East. Nevertheless, performances continued to improve overall, and there were no catastrophic depressions of the sort that had afflicted the industrial economies during the 1870s and 1930s.

Eastern Europe participated strongly in the industrial boom of the 1950s and 1960s. Growth rates in the Soviet Union were reported at 8–10 percent per year, about on a par with the most rapidly expanding areas of Western Europe and ahead of the United States. Indeed, a Soviet leader in the 1950s predicted to an American audience that "we will bury you"—a claim that the Soviet economy was on the verge of beating the United States at its own industrial game. This turned out to be greatly exaggerated, but the industrial surge was impressive nevertheless. Major technological gains included the world's first and most successful space program. By the late 1970s Soviet industrial output was about seven times greater than it had been in the late 1940s. Throughout Eastern Europe employment in agriculture dropped as a result of further agricultural modernization; this freed up additional workers for industry. Strong state investment focused on spurring heavy industry. Some East European regions that had long lagged behind began now to catch up, completing their industrial revolutions and seeming to move forward beyond the minimal industrialization level. In Bulgaria, for example, per capita manufacturing production increased fivefold between 1950 and 1970. Industrial output in Romania rose 120 percent from 1963 to 1970. These gains did not generate the same levels of prosperity that prevailed in most of Western Europe, and they did not match the Japanese explosion, but they nevertheless were significant.

In Western Europe and the United States, rapid industrial expansion often occurred in regions different from the previous centers of factory industry. Coal mining and textiles continued to decline, leaving troubling industrial backwaters in places like northern England or Appalachia. Even in Japan some previous metallurgical centers suffered. But the decline of older centers was more than balanced by the advance of petrochemicals, electronics, and heavy consumer goods such as automobiles and appliances. Regions that were particularly appropriate to some of these newer industries, like the Silicon Valley computer cluster near San Francisco or the London region in England, surged forward.

Soviet laborers in Leningrad wind a stationary set of blades around a turbogenerator. This energy-producing machine can be used to pump water, supply electricity, or propel jet engines. (Courtesy of Independent Picture Service. Reprinted by permission.)

There were several causes of this new round of rapid industrial growth, though of course they varied somewhat from one society to the next. Rising military spending played a role in stimulating armaments industries and aeronautics in the United States and the Soviet Union. In general, further improvements in agricultural methods freed up labor for industry while creating new consumer spending in the countryside. Greater use of mechanical equipment, particularly notable in Western Europe, brought rapid reduction in the size of the rural labor force along with lower food costs. France's peasant population, for example, declined from 16 percent of the nation's total in 1950 to 6 percent by the 1980s. French sociologists wrote of a "vanishing peasantry," not only because of its falling numbers but because of the new fascination with maximizing market production and with mechanical efficiency. Although European agriculture remained somewhat more costly than that of North America, the industrial revolution had definitely come to Europe's countryside.

New government policies stimulated economic growth. The Japanese government resumed its careful planning and coordination, operating in close harmony with business leaders. The state set production and investment goals while lending public revenues to encourage research and capital development projects. The government also reduced the population pressures that had afflicted prewar Japan by actively promoting a campaign for birth control and abortion; Japan's population growth slowed to essentially the same levels as in Western Society and the Soviet Union. The government also sponsored technological research in state laboratories while carefully developing foreign trade policies designed to spur exports. By the 1970s Japan was turning out more engineers than many larger nations such as the United States—the result of ongoing government interest in promoting education. Overall, Japan's orchestration between government and the leading business giants prompted the half-mocking, half-envious label from the West of "Japan, Incorporated."

Government policies shifted rapidly in Western Europe, though they fell short of Japanese coordination. West European governments late in the 1940s made a fuller turn toward the welfare state, providing state-sponsored health programs or health insurance, payments to families with numerous children, and a host of other benefits such as construction of low-cost housing. Canada, Australia, and New Zealand also expanded their welfare provisions. Many programs were financed in part from tax revenues, which offered some cushion for those most poorly paid. Not all welfare programs worked well, and some drew protests from various groups. On balance, however, the European welfare state won great popularity. It helped integrate certain groups, notably from the working class, more firmly in the national political structure. It reduced the worst material misery and, by providing some income floors for the poorest groups, stimulated consumer demand. At the same time, many European governments complemented the welfare state with an active planning effort. Various sectors were nationalized outright; most states, for example, took over the railroad system and improved its efficiency. More generally, planning mechanisms aimed to stimulate industrial growth in backward regions and spur more rapid technological development. France went furthest here, establishing a national planning office, the Commissariat du Plan, in 1946 to steer capital toward economic sectors deemed significant for long-term growth. Private enterprises remained free to run their firms as they saw fit, but the French government orchestrated its powers to guide investment and credit. Not all European governments moved quite so far. Germany, for example, emphasized market competition as an alternative to its statist experience under Nazism. All governments undertook planning, however, and the impressive economic growth rates suggested that the initiatives were paying off.

Government planning in Eastern Europe was by far the most extensive, as the Soviet system of a command economy, directed from the central government, was spread to the new communist regimes in the region. State planning committees allocated resources, set prices and wages, and determined production goals. After 1968 certain governments, as in Hungary, modified this rigid planning by providing some autonomy for individual enterprises. By this point some suspicion was developing that rigid state planning, effective in mobilizing resources for early industrialization, perhaps was not best suited for further development. Major changes in direction, however, occurred only after the industrial collapse of the region in 1985.

Only the United States did not extend new government measures in any systematic way, though increased military spending involved the government more heavily in economic issues than ever before. Welfare programs did not greatly expand, though there was some growth in the late 1960s: The United States was one of the only industrial countries actually to shrink welfare efforts in the 1980s; this move accompanied great increases in income inequality within the nation. The United States was also unique in having no economic planning office, though the Federal Reserve Board coordinated fiscal policy in the interest of economic growth. American lack of major policy initiatives seemed irrelevant in the 1950s and 1960s when economic demand was fueled by rising wages and high consumer expectations. As growth eased in the 1970s, many experts began to urge a shift in the American policy framework but without major result into the 1990s.

Diplomatic shifts contributed to the industrial surge. The active foreign policy of the United States, including various international gifts and loans, helped stimulate American exports, particularly in the 1950s and 1960s. The United States also participated in a number of international efforts to lower tariff barriers, and trade among industrial nations increased in part as a result of these initiatives. The Soviet Union built a separate economic bloc with its East European satellites, which helped coordinate exports and resource allocation within the bloc. In the long run the isolation of the communist economic grouping reduced the flow of technical information necessary for a vigorous economy, but in the short run certain industries were aided by easier access to resources such as the Soviet Union's vast petroleum supplies. The greatest shift in market policies occurred in Western Europe with the formation, from 1956 onward, of the European Economic Community, or Common Market. This group, ultimately embracing most of the West European nations, progressively reduced trade barriers internally, gradually creating the world's wealthiest total market. Full economic unity was proclaimed in 1992, but well before then the Common Market had helped stimulate internal economic growth.

Rapid industrial growth in the established industrial areas had several major consequences. First, it greatly increased the standard-of-living gap with most of the rest of the world. Even regions that improved their economic performance, like India, saw themselves falling further behind the material levels of the industrial zones. Only an outright industrial revolution, as in South Korea, enabled a nation to catch up at all.

Within the industrial societies, rapid economic growth paid off in improvements in living standards. Consumer goods remained scarce in Eastern Europe, and there were long lines for many items and often shoddy products. Nevertheless, growth had some impact. East-bloc countries like Hungary fared particularly well; by the 1980s one family in three had a private car in Hungary, well below Western levels but a thirtyfold increase in the nation since 1960. Many people in the communist nations also enjoyed improved vacation possibilities because of state-organized resorts in such areas as the Black Sea coast.

Japan made a clearer turn toward a real consumer economy, though this evolution was slowed by Japan's lower economic level in the 1950s and by state policies and personal habits that promoted high rates of personal saving over spending. Inflation by the 1980s further limited buying power, even though wages were rising considerably. Basic items such as food and housing remained expensive. Even so, Japan's standard of living grew close to Western levels by the 1980s. Purchase of a variety of consumer goods, including appliances and automobiles, increased steadily. By the 1980s over half of all families had cars, and 95 percent had washing machines and refrigerators. A joke as early as 1970 held that the "three sacred objects" in Japanese society had become a color television, a car, and an air conditioner. Huge department stores, called *depato*, were by this point providing an immense variety of standardized goods, including cameras, audio equipment, and other delights of a high-tech consumerism in whose production Japanese factories participated strongly.

Western Europe became a consumerist paradise as living standards in some countries, like Germany and Switzerland, pushed beyond those of the United States. Ownership of automobiles, televisions, and a variety of household appliances became commonplace. Many French homes were filled with gadgets. At the same time, vacation time increased, reaching an average of five weeks a year for many groups. Europeans swarmed to the sunny beaches of Spain and Italy, ventured widely into Eastern Europe and parts of the Middle East, and began to visit the United States and Latin America in increasing numbers as a memorable vacation became one of the hallmarks of the European version of mass culture in an affluent age.

Finally, sheer industrial growth raised a new set of environmental issues. Larger factories meant more potential emissions into air and water. Substantial consumer goods generated their own pollution potential through use of electricity and the belching exhausts of automobiles. Chemicals industries expanded rapidly, building on an earlier trend, with new kinds of artificial fertilizers and pesticides, a huge plastics industry, and other branches including weaponry. Chemical emissions and spills contributed disproportionately to environmental problems. Greater demands on energy and the obvious limits to petroleum production prompted growing interest in nuclear energy. Nuclear power stations spread in the United States but particularly in Eastern Europe and the energy-short nations of Western Europe, where nuclear generation accounted for a substantial fraction of all power. Nuclear wastes and accidents, like the Three Mile Island burst in Pennsylvania and the 1980s partial meltdown of a reactor in Chernobyl, in the Soviet Union, drew particular attention to the environmental hazards of advanced industrial societies. So did frequent oil spills, which fouled many coastlines and killed a great deal of oceanic life.

New environmental devastation occurred throughout the industrial world. Acid rain from coal-using factories spread widely. Ironically, tall smokestacks, used to control damage locally, dispersed damaging chemicals more widely than ever before. Forests in Scandinavia suffered from the industry in Germany's Ruhr region. Forests in Canada and New England dwindled under the pall of chemicals from the American Midwest. Many rivers and lakes effectively died as a result of chemical pollution; some occasionally even caught on fire.

Japan suffered heavily from the environmental byproducts of its rapid industrial surge and the attendant growth of cities. By the 1970s traffic policemen in Tokyo often had to wear protective masks simply to breathe safely. Offshore pollution endangered the fishing industry. Several episodes of industrial poisoning . occurred; the famous case was a series of illnesses resulting from methyl mercury that became known as Minimata disease (from the town in which it occurred).

Pollution problems in the West and Japan were partially counterbalanced by increasing legislation, though many activists urged that the regulations fell short of needs. Some industrial waterways, long fouled by factory and urban wastes, were cleaned up. In the Thames River in London, for example, fish returned after decades of pollution-induced absence. New standards of fuel use aided cleanup of grimy factory cities like Pittsburgh. Japan's worst pollution problems eased after the 1970s as the government became pressed by public opinion to take a stronger stand. A protest against expansion of Tokyo's airport, for example, proved to be one of the most successful popular movements in recent Japanese history. Discovery of the Minimata disease also sparked a successful grassroots movement. In a number of countries public uneasiness and nuclear accidents combined to slow the growth of nuclear power.

The established industrial region with the most agonizing environmental problems proved to be the Soviet Union and Eastern Europe. Industrial growth and the fierce arms race with the United States, in which the Soviet bloc participated successfully but with great strain given a lower industrial base, prompted tremendous neglect of environmental consequences. Safety precautions were ignored because of their cost, and this led to chemical spills and waste dumping. According to Soviet estimates, half of all the rivers in the Soviet Union were severely polluted and over 40 percent of agricultural land was endangered by the late 1980s. Over 20 percent of Soviet citizens lived in regions of "ecological disaster." Huge natural resources like the Aral Sea were rendered unfit for use. Rates and severity of respiratory and other diseases rose, impairing both morale and economic performance;

infant mortality figures also began to climb. Problems that existed also in the West but on a much more limited regional basis (in the United States in some petrochemical areas in the south, for example, as measured by per capita cancer incidence) occurred in Eastern Europe on a massive scale. Until political changes opened Eastern Europe to freer discussion and political opposition, no effective countermeasures existed; governments, bent on maximizing short-term growth, stood idly by.

Obviously, rapid industrial growth proved to be a mixed blessing by creating new opportunities but also new problems in the established industrial areas. Many developments had been foreshadowed during the industrial-revolution period, but expansion magnified their intensity, whether the focus was on new heights of consumerism or the threats to the natural environment.

Structural Changes: The Postindustrial Thesis

Sheer growth had obvious impact, but the advanced industrial economies also introduced some important new features. These features could not have been predicted from earlier industrial patterns save as these had already assured recurrent basic change. The United States and Western Europe led the way in these advances, but Japan was quickly engaged as well. The Soviet Union and its satellites lagged, more rooted in an earlier version of the industrial economy.

As always, a series of technological changes lay at the heart of the new economy. Development of automatic circuitry helped reduce the hands-on labor necessary on certain kinds of assembly lines. New materials like plastics could be automatically poured into molds. Workers in many petrochemicals plants became more like technicians, supervising automatic processes, than workers in the traditional style of factory industry. The creation of computers soon added an even more powerful innovation. A German engineer, Konrad Zuse, had devised an electromagnetic computer before World War II, but American firms, headed by IBM (International Business Machines), led in further development during the 1940s and 1950s. Huge computers began to be installed for information processing. The transistor, a major advance by Bell Laboratories in 1948, greatly improved reliability of computers and cut their size. Accounting, inventory control, and other procedures began to be computerized. The technology was applied to manufacturing processes as well. The development of robotics, from the 1960s onward, replaced many assembly-line workers with machines that could perform repetitious processes like drilling and assembly. By the 1980s 20 percent of French industry and about 10 percent of American manufacturing depended on robots. Finally, genetic engineering began to have a tangential effect on manufacturing in the 1960s: The emphasis was less on new manufacturing methods than on new products, including new medicinal drugs, but some genetic technology also operated under the supervision of technicians rather than machine-aided manual laborers.

The new technologies lay behind a host of new products, including sophisticated sound equipment. More important, they spurred greatly increased productivity that reduced the need for blue-collar labor. The manufacturing labor force reached its peak size in the 1950s in the United States and Western Europe and then began to shrink—a reversal of one of the staple trends of the industrial revolution. Many hardships resulted from the displacement of industrial workers in industries like steel and automobiles, victims of increasingly automated technology as well as, in many cases, heightened foreign competition. But employment in the service sector grew rapidly, and these jobs by the 1950s commanded a full half of the labor force in the West. This was the continuation of a trend that had begun in the late nineteenth century, but it now reached new proportions. The typical worker was an employee in insurance, government, a hospital, a school, an office, or a hotel or restaurant. Some of these service jobs were attractive and gave people upward mobility from the working class. A full fourth of the traditional French working class moved up to white-collar work during the 1950s. Canada's labor force included a 46 percent share for service workers by the late 1950s, and many came from farmer or working-class backgrounds. But low-level service jobs also were created in fast-food restaurants, custodial services, and security jobs.

Associated with the new technologies were some changes in management. Corporations continued to grow. In 1940, for example, about 100 companies accounted for 30 percent of all manufacturing in the United States; by the 1950s the figure was nearly 70 percent, as a host of new mergers developed and as government purchasers during the war favored big business. In Western Europe many old-line manufacturing families died out or were displaced because of dubious activities during the Nazi years. The giant Krupp firm, for example, shifted away from tight family control. A new breed of managers from middle-class backgrounds and with substantial technical training came to the fore. These people were friendlier to business-government cooperation and to long-range planning than their predecessors had been, and they worked also to stabilize labor relations. New technologies supported growing emphasis on abilities to master information and use specialized knowledge; some observers argued that control of knowledge was replacing control of property as the cornerstone of the industrial elite. Japanese management changed less than its West European counterpart, but it worked more consistently to foster careful relations with labor than had been the case before the war. Efforts to assure about 50 percent of the labor force lifetime job security and to consult workers about potential improvements in methods showed a more effective use of Japan's tradition of group spirit than in the prewar years.

Some authorities contended that new technologies and management forms added up to a decisively new economy; they heralded a postindustrial revolution and argued that it was as sweeping in its implications as the industrial revolution before it. They pointed of course to the shift away from manufacturing jobs and from traditional management styles. They also predicted that with robotics and computers the nature of work would shift. Products could become more individ-ualized. Work could be decentralized, even located in the home, and supervision would accordingly lighten. Time constraints would decrease, as workers could log onto their computers whenever they so desired. These were interesting visions, but they did not in the main accord with reality. Most service jobs became more, not less, routinized. New equipment enabled management to speed up the work of secretaries and bank personnel; work tensions increased in many cases. Super-vision could be enhanced by computer checks. And while jobs did move away from center cities and the traditional factory declined in importance, group work settings continued to predominate. New management did not necessarily mean a new freedom from regimen. An American oil company's recruiting pamphlet noted that "personal views can cause a lot of trouble" and suggested that moder-ate or conservative ideas were preferred. Airlines trained flight attendants to smile courteously at all times, suppressing their emotions; annoyance, their personnel authorities urged, not only was bad business but also was bad for one's health. Growing conformity and coordination at work increased for many people, and this new age in many respects constituted an intensification, albeit in new specific forms, of work trends that had been associated with the industrial revolution from the outset.

Two additional shifts accompanied the larger changes in industrial structure, however; these occurred particularly in Western society, though there were some echoes in Japan. First, women began to reenter the labor force in large number. Adult working-class women started taking jobs during the 1950s, and a middle-class surge followed a decade later. Young women actually reduced their work levels, instead staying in school longer. But the typical adult woman now expected to work not only after marriage but after childbearing. By the 1970s over 40 per-cent of the labor force in Western Europe, Canada, and the United States was fe-male. At the root of this historic shift in Western industrial trends—the reversal of women's removal from the labor force—were several factors. A key ingredient was the rise of service jobs, for which women seemed particularly suited and for which relatively cheap labor was often preferred. Women's hold on key occupa-tional sectors intensified; whereas about 60 percent of all American secretaries were women before 1960, over 90 percent were female by the 1980s. Women's em-ployment, in other words, was not spread over industrial jobs evenly but concen-trated in the service sector. Women provided a vital increase in available workers at a time when growing economies were crying out for new help and when older workers were increasingly choosing (or being forced to choose) formal retirement rather than remaining active. The result was major shift not only in women's lives but also in the larger relationship of family to the economy. The attempt during the first century or more of industrialization in the West had been to provide nec-essary industrial labor while keeping the family somewhat separate, under wom-en's tutelage. In the new setting the family was diluted; the rise of day-care facili-ties for children, particularly rapid in Western Europe, was an obvious result of the new evaluation of the work-family equation for adults. Japan lagged somewhat in this trend, with a smaller percentage of married women at work and more emphasis on mother-intensive childrearing. But women's work roles shifted somewhat in this case as well by the 1970s, and many observers expected that as Japan's service sector grew and its labor needs increased (because of population limitation and aging), the country would follow the Western trend.

Finally, and in many ways surprisingly, the class warfare so characteristic of the industrial revolution and ensuing decades declined after a peak in the 1950s. It did not disappear, and a surge of protest around 1968 included a series of intense labor strikes. On the whole, however, agitation directly surrounding workplace issues dropped off. This was particularly true in the United States and Western Europe: In Japan labor agitation also remained low. Trade union membership in the United States and Western Europe began to plummet after the late 1950s, and many union members reduced their effective commitment. French unions found many workers too busy with their new motorcycle or car—or with overtime work by which to pay for such items—to attend meetings. Strikes trailed off as well. Average annual strike rates in the United States during the 1960s were down approximately 15 percent from their 1950s rate, and while levels rose again in the 1970s, they still barely approximated those in the 1950s—despite a massive growth in the size of the labor force. German workers, who had maintained an active political and trade union protest current before the triumph of Nazism, now acquiesced in a very cooperative labor movement. Specifics varied, but the overall trend was the same: The class-based protest that had risen with the industrial revolution was fading.

Prosperity and welfare programs helped explain the change. But some puzzles remained. U.S. workers began to experience a drop in real wages from 1973 onward into the 1990s as prices rose faster than wages did. Furthermore, hours of work went up, partly to compensate for falling standards of living. By 1992 American workers put in 140 hours a year more than their counterparts had in the early 1970s. Yet protest did not respond to these growing pressures. Changes in the industrial structure helped explain the relative silence. Many blue-collar workers feared for their jobs as their numbers shrank. Service-sector employees, including women, had never been as active in formal protest, and now they predominated. Families with wives as well as husbands working often lacked the time to devote to organizational efforts.

Furthermore, the new forms of protest that did arise drew mainly on white-collar groups whose concerns were directly related to the new industrial structure. Feminist protest focused heavily on issues of better treatment of women at work; it gained ground both in the United States and in Western Europe, though interestingly, save for a few voices, not in Japan. Environmental protests against nuclear power and other industrial targets gathered momentum throughout the industrialized world, including Eastern Europe after the liberation currents of the mid-1980s. In Western Europe "green" parties pushed environmental issues directly into the political spectrum. Much of the passion and moral outrage previously applied to working life moved to this new industrial arena.

Whether the structural changes in the industrial economies of the West and Japan added up to a new revolution was unclear. They certainly changed a host of basic patterns, impacting on politics and personal life alike. As with previous changes within the industrial scene, the evolving trends prompted a new and difficult set of adaptations. They also set important challenges for societies struggling to enter the industrial arena in the first place, as the definition of catching up shifted ground.

The New Industrial Balance

Growth and structural alterations in the established industrial societies produced new balances. The economic preponderance of the United States during the 1950s—when at one point the nation produced almost 50 percent of all factory-manufactured goods in the world—almost inevitably declined.

Industrial leadership by the 1980s centered increasingly on Western Europe and Japan. West European nations collectively generated the greatest industrial output. They included some fringe areas still incompletely industrialized, such as Portugal and Ireland, but most of the European industrial economies demonstrated considerable dynamism. This group included established participants such as Sweden or Germany as well as relative newcomers such as Spain. Japan's industrial economy was smaller than Europe's or North America's, but it was growing most rapidly. Japan and Western Europe continued to demonstrate important differences in specific industrial modes. Japan's emphasis on cooperative group management and worker security was not matched in Europe. Europeans managed their impressive economic growth even as they posted noticeable increases in leisure time, particularly the extensive annual vacations. Japanese workers of all sorts put in much longer hours; group pressure and an internal work ethic often inhibited Japanese office workers from even taking vacation time to which they were entitled. Whether differences of these sorts would narrow in societies that could legitimately claim industrial success was an important question for the future.

The United States, though still an industrial giant, lagged somewhat. Many American inventions were most fully exploited by the Japanese; the compact disc was a case in point. American growth rates lagged behind those in both Western Europe and Japan. American recessions, including the downturn around 1990 that brought substantial unemployment, tended to be more severe than those elsewhere. Americans themselves began worrying that something fundamental was wrong, and as previously noted, growing work pressures after 1973 made it clear that the problems of the American economy included more than relative international standing—they had direct bearing on people's standard of living and

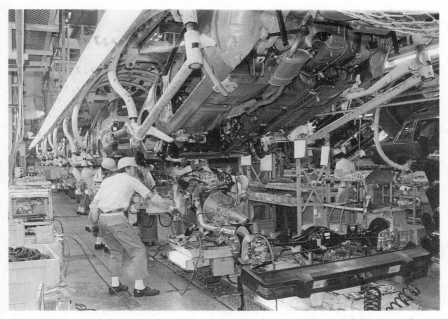

Workers in a Japanese automobile plant as Japan became one of the world's leading industrial nations. Goods manufactured there include steel, motor vehicles, chemicals, and electronic products. (Courtesy AP/Wide World Photos. Reprinted by permission.)

work load. Canadian growth, extremely rapid until the 1960s, also lagged, in part because of the close relationship of Canadian exports to U.S. economic performance.

A number of explanations for the North American industrial slippage circulated. Japanese critics, taking some delight in criticizing American backwardness after years of being given lessons by the United States on how to run a modern society, sometimes denounced what they viewed as a shoddy American work ethic. Given increased work time and substantial improvements in per worker productivity in manufacturing, this criticism seemed implausible. A more logical target was the size of the American service sector and the undeniable problems in generating productivity improvements in this sector that could match manufacturing gains. Advances in health technology, for example, in which U.S. leadership persisted, tended to increase costs, not raise medical "output," whatever their other desirable results.

Amid a host of ingredients in a complex situation, two factors stood out. First, unlike Western Europe and Japan, the United States had shouldered massive military expenditures from World War II onward. Its major industrial rivals, sometimes boasting that they had reoriented their societies to civilian purposes, spent only a fraction of their gross national product on defense. The remainder went to more elaborate welfare provisions and to industrial research and development, in which Japanese and West European investments vastly exceeded those of the United States. Second, American executives seemed demonstrably more concerned than their European or Japanese analogues with high short-term profits. Their incomes were higher compared with average wages—and the gap within the United States tripled from 1970 to 1990. The focus on high stock payments rather than longer-term earnings prospects prompted different kinds of decisions about labor investments, consumer relations, and product selection. Slow responses in the 1950s and 1960s to change in key industries such as steel and automobiles translated some general management problems into direct competitive decline. There was a lag in new methods and new products in many large industries in the United States compared with not only Japan and Germany but also France and other European countries. No one expected the United States to drop out of the industrial picture, and future upturns in fortune were by no means out of the question. By 1993 the United States was in fact pulling out of recession faster than Western Europe or Japan. Nevertheless, many experts compared the failure of the United States to keep full pace with the world's new industrial leaders with the relative decline of Britain in the late nineteenth century after its decades-long leadership in the industrial game.

The most striking balance shift among the established industrial nations, however, focused on Eastern Europe, where industrialization had forged ahead so notably in the immediate postwar decades. Here there was not just a relative decline but an effective industrial collapse after 1980. No clear precedent for this phenomenon existed in industrial history, and prospects for the future were correspondingly unclear.

By the mid-1970s the Soviet Union and most of the East European nations had completed the basic construction of an industrial economy. They had reached a situation where, earlier, Western nations had begun to make a turn toward greater consumer affluence, basing further industrial growth and workplace motivation on a growing proliferation of goods. The communist economies did not make that turn. Absence of consumer goods forced many East European workers to use massive amounts of time shopping, and it reduced incentives for strong work performance. Along with growing health and environmental problems, the result was a measurable reversal of the region's industrial progress. Industrial production began to stagnate, and after about 1980 it actually dropped. Worker productivity declined, in part because of poor morale and related alcoholism. Falling production forced the Soviet regime to commit so much to the military program to keep up in the Cold War by matching U.S. spending that other initiatives were starved for resources. By the mid-1980s up to a third of all Soviet GNP was targeted for military spending.

Basic problems included the costs of the arms race, which constrained the United States but now literally overwhelmed the smaller industrial economy of the Soviet bloc. Rigid state planning, which failed to allocate supplies flexibly and encouraged mismanagement and false reporting, contributed strongly as well. The larger failure to devise a communist version of a second-phase industrial economy that would deal with ongoing issues of worker motivation and the challenge of new information-exchange technologies set the wider context in which these more specific failures brought unprecedented industrial collapse.

Soviet leaders began to acknowledge the problems under Mikhail Gorbachev from 1985 onward. Efforts to introduce greater flexibility into the system ran into entrenched bureaucratic opposition and widespread popular anxiety about potential price increases on basic staples once government control was removed. Movement toward a more market-oriented economy was widely hailed, but practical implementation lagged. Meanwhile, in 1989, most East European countries broke away from the communist orbit, installing varying versions of looser planning or (in Poland) a market economy outright. Some of these experiments were limited; others (as in Poland by 1992) provoked resistance from people thrown out of work from units that collapsed because of economic inefficiency. The Soviet Union dissolved, and leaders in successor states, including Russia, vowed to introduce a market economy to jump start the industrial engine once again. But the future was impossible to discern.

Forecasts for the world's economic future into the twenty-first century built mainly on the lively industrial centers. The orbits around Western Europe, Japan, and North America drew particular attention. Western Europe, newly unified, seemed assured of further industrial development. Japan and newly industrializing areas on the Pacific Rim had powerful momentum. The resiliency of the United States was more questionable, but great industrial strength would long persist. Uncertainty surrounded the fourth established industrial center, and many observers predicted a long period of troubles for Eastern Europe and the former Soviet Union, leavened perhaps by inroads from other industrial powers eager to take advantage of vast natural resources. Limitations on Soviet industrialization even earlier, plus the recent collapse, made it impossible to forecast a speedy recovery. Yet the absence of any historical precedent and the fact that other industrial societies had bounced back from periods of lethargy seemed to offer some relevant encouragement. Forecasts for some smaller economies, like those of Hungary and the Czech Republic, were bright. What was clear was that the balance among industrial powers, which had been unstable ever since the first challenges to British preeminence, continued to shift. In this as in other ways, the aftermath of the industrial revolution remained fluid even in the areas that had passed through the fundamental transition.

14

The Less Industrial World:
Evolution and Exploitation

Economic development experts (including, in their separate fashions, both modernization and dependency theorists), politicians, and large segments of the general public became accustomed after 1950 to thinking of a world economically divided in two: There were industrialized societies and there were others—underdeveloped or developing. A society either had it or did not. Other terms came into play. "Third World" was initially a Cold War concept designed to identify societies that were neither permanently aligned with the West (capitalist democracy) or with the Soviet bloc (communism), but because most of the Third World countries were also not completely industrialized, the term survived the Cold War and meant simply underdeveloped. Finally, in the 1980s the North-South dualism became popular: The "North" meant industrial, the "South" mainly the nonindustrial Southern Hemisphere but also Northern Hemisphere nations, like those on the Indian subcontinent, where great poverty persisted and industrialization seemed to lag.

The dualistic distinction accurately described one definable gap: Some parts of the world had experienced an industrial revolution or, like South Korea, were clearly in the process of experiencing one, and some parts had not. Industrialized countries had, by definition, more manufacturing, more advanced technology, and (except for Eastern Europe) higher living standards on average than less industrial ones. Beyond this real but rather gross distinction, however, the "Third World" label was almost completely misleading in implying some uniform, barely changing condition for the majority of the world's population that lived in "nonindustrial" economies. Ironically, the distinction would have been considerably more valid in the two previous phases of the world's industrial history, when a large number of societies developed very little factory industry of their own and seemed helpless to launch a process of significant change save insofar as this was forced on them by established industrial powers.

After 1950 there were in fact two major trends operating in the vast stretches of the world, embracing the bulk of the global populations, in which an industrial revolution had not occurred. The first trend continued a theme that had been present from the onset of the industrial revolution in Britain: Significant economic change occurred on the basis of economic penetration by industrialized areas in search of resources, markets, and labor. The second theme, however, involved the increasing ability of a large number of nations to regain some control over the national economy, sufficient at least to launch a measurable process of industrial evolution. This second process enabled many major nations, including India and China, to surpass the more modest experiments with factory industry of earlier periods that focused on factories for cheap export goods or isolated sectors of advanced technology. Most nonindustrial/Third World/developing/Southern regions combined elements of both major trends, continuing to be subject to considerable economic dominance by the established industrial powers but generating an important range of industrial initiatives short of full commitment to an industrialization process. The differences among these regions followed from different combinations of the two trends.

The Long Reach of the Industrial Powers

In 1992 the U.S. Department of Labor charged several American clothing manufacturers with major abuses of factory workers on the Mariana islands, an American protectorate in the western Pacific 1,500 miles from the Philippines. Subcontractors producing men's clothing for some stylish American brands had for years been importing workers from China and the Philippines, putting them to work in sweatshops complete with sewing machines but few other amenities. The workers were compelled to labor eleven hours a day, seven days a week, for a salary of $1.50 an hour. Any hint of discontent or ill-discipline was controlled by the threat of returning the workers home.

Effectively forced labor had long been a concomitant of the industrial revolution. In the first phase, it had been a feature in the West—the orphan gangs recruited in Britain, for example. Later, new systems of forced labor spread to other parts of the world where, even after the abolition of formal slavery, cheap workers seemed essential to produce volumes of low-cost goods. Here, the system had initially been applied mainly to foods and minerals, but even by 1900 it was extending to factory industries in which equipment was relatively simple, such as rope making in the Yucatan peninsula of Mexico. Clearly, this type of extension was alive and well in some parts of the world in the late twentieth century, as mechanization was combined with abusive labor controls to keep costs down.

Exploitation of nonindustrial areas to serve needs in industrialized societies persisted in the late twentieth century, although its dimensions changed somewhat. On the one hand, exploitation was encouraged by the sheer growth of the industrial sector in Western Europe, the United States, Japan, and the Pacific Rim. Industries needed more raw materials than ever before. The search for cheap labor was intensified by improving wages at home, by government-enforced welfare programs that increased the cost of domestic labor still further, and by the slowing rate of population growth in most of the industrial world that inevitably increased competition for workers. At the same time, population explosions in much of Asia, Africa, and Latin America extended the possibility of finding workers whose desperation could drive them to accept abusive conditions. The workers recruited for the Marianas sweatshops resisted being sent home because finding jobs in the Philippines amid rapid population growth was so difficult. It was small wonder that many of the unequal relationships between industrial and nonindustrial economies endured or even expanded after 1950.

On the other hand, there were two new constraints, at least in certain areas, that complicated the simplest kind of exploitative relationship. First, political independence resulting from decolonization and, in the case of Latin America, increasingly effective governments in nations that had long been nominally independent enabled many regions to cut back foreign economic intervention by force of law or at least to regulate it. Strong, independent governments in places like India, China, Brazil, and Malaysia progressively removed these regions from the simplest kind of economic dependency on the industrial world—even though, except perhaps for Brazil, a full industrial revolution remained elusive. China, for example, sold many low-cost factory products to the West after 1978, but these were produced by Chinese companies operating under regulations of their government. Governments in several Latin American countries, including Chile and Cuba, were able to take over foreign concerns (such as American-owned mines and plantations), encouraging local management and in certain cases improving conditions of labor.

Second, in some of these same areas considerable local industry, building on the more halting expansion of manufacturing developed before 1950, reduced the need for massive imports of standard manufactured items from the West or Japan. Regions like China or India thus produced most of the textile goods required in the domestic market, reversing—particularly in India's case—more than a century of submission to Western-made goods. Other import needs, of course, remained considerable; these areas depended extensively on higher-technology products made in Japan and the West. Still, part of the pressure to pay for basic items by cheap-labor exports had been relieved, and some nations built up considerable foreign exchange surpluses in their dealings with industrialized giants. China, for example, ran second only to Japan in the foreign trade advantage with the United States, running a $40 billion annual surplus by the early 1990s.

More than in the previous two periods of the world's industrial history, then, relationships between industrial and nonindustrial regions varied greatly. Many areas, though still lagging behind in outright industrialization, pulled away from the starkest kind of inequality; others seemed locked in the more familiar dependency.

Fortune clearly turned in favor of the oil-producing regions of the Middle East and North Africa after 1950. Industrial needs for oil expanded steadily. Western Europe and Japan depended heavily on Middle Eastern oil; the United States also came to rely on Middle Eastern imports for a growing percentage of its petroleum needs. At the same time, Middle Eastern nations won new political independence. There were attendant problems: Internal strife made considerable foreign manipulation still possible; thus an Iranian effort in the 1950s to seize Western oil companies was thwarted by an American-engineered political coup. Further, intense national rivalries complicated decisions about oil in the region, and by increasing reliance on industrial nations for arms supplies, military buildups led to a new version of economic dependency. Nevertheless, Middle East oil states steadily amassed gigantic revenues and simultaneously gained increasing control over their national oil policies. Many Western companies were nationalized, others heavily regulated. In 1961 Iran, Iraq, and Saudi Arabia took the lead in forming the Organization of Petroleum Exporting Countries (OPEC) to improve coordination of price and production policies and reduce the market voice of the industrial importers. OPEC included other members, notably Venezuela, Nigeria, and Indonesia, but it was primarily a Middle Eastern/North African entity. Finally, because decades of experience had produced not only increasing political acumen in dealing with the West but also a growing body of technical expertise, Arabs and Iranians could, with at most modest advice from Western technicians, run the oil fields themselves.

The altered relationship between the Middle East and the industrial regions showed dramatically in the two oil crises of the 1970s. In 1973 OPEC cut oil production in order to force a substantial price increase. Western economies suffered as the vital fluid of modern industry drained away; huge gasoline lines formed at service stations in the United States and Western Europe. Oil prices rose in response as OPEC won a signal victory. A second, less deliberate oil crisis occurred in 1979 as revolution in Iran and then warfare between Iran and Iraq reduced the oil flow again.

The Middle East did not retain a persistent ability to raise oil prices. Internal competition, both economic and political, prompted many nations to increase production even at the risk of lower prices. The West and Japan adopted stringent conservation measures that reduced industrial demand. Oil prices did not continue to escalate during the 1980s, and several oil-rich nations in the Middle East and elsewhere suffered declining revenues. Clearly, industrial importers continued to hold important bargaining chips, including their ability to sell advanced weaponry to the Middle East in order to earn back some of the oil payments. Yet key Middle Eastern oil producers continued to accumulate great wealth. Some of the small Gulf states boasted the highest per capita incomes in the world— $16,000 per person in Kuwait in 1976. A region that initially developed under

Western industrial control had shaken off the most direct kinds of exploitation. Many Arab businessmen in fact began to invest heavily in the West, amplifying their oil revenues with a wider industrial portfolio.

The leading oil producers also developed a version of an industrial economy based on oil. Saudi Arabia and the small states of the Persian Gulf expanded their major cities, building huge refinery centers that combined advanced technology with hundreds of thousands of workers (up to 80 percent of the labor force in some instances) imported from other parts of the Middle East and Pakistan. Modern transportation and communications facilities developed, along with technical universities. By 1980 the annual development budget of Saudi Arabia reached $70 billion. Industry continued to focus on petroleum refining, and it remained uncertain whether a wider industrial base would emerge; many Gulf states continued to have less than 10 percent of their labor force in manufacturing, with the bulk in service sectors (including finance) and construction. Nevertheless, with most of the population living in cities and a substantial foreign labor contingent, the oil-producing states of the Gulf had parlayed their special wealth in a vital resource into a version of an industrial economy. Certainly, reliance on resource exports no longer guaranteed subservience in the larger world economy.

Unusually abundant resources and use of advanced technology assured other resource-exporting regions of considerable economic bargaining power, even outside the oil-producing areas. Australia maintained an essentially industrial standard of living on the basis of agricultural and mineral exports and substantial local industry. As in the Gulf states, efficient production of resources made possible substantial earnings from industrial importers (Japan, Western Europe, the United States) whose own growing prosperity yielded an expanding basis to pay. Resource exploitation by no means uniformly meant poverty and constraint.

Yet benign relationships were not the whole story. A number of parts of Africa and some in Latin America continued to depend so heavily on Western purchases of raw materials that they imposed few effective controls. Even after independence from Belgium, for example, Zaire (the former Belgian Congo) continued to be dominated by Western mining concerns. The most abusive labor practices were modified, but African miners still received low pay amid rigorous working conditions. Expanding exploitation of copper and uranium brought profits to the Western companies and some wealth for local businesses and politicians but little improvement in living standards or funding for a larger program of industrial development. Several Caribbean and Central American countries continued to find it difficult to shake loose from cash-crop dependency, supplemented in some instances by foreign tourism. Efforts to diversify sugar economies, even in revolutionary Cuba, won scant success. Yet sugar was overproduced on the world market, which led to declining prices and continued economic marginality for many of the sugar-growing regions. A few dependent areas sought to diversify their exports to the industrial West by growing illicit drugs, in what was in fact a variant on a classic cash-crop export. Impoverished Bolivian and Ecuadoran peasants produced opium that was then handled by a small number of high-living local merchants, whose profits soared without much wider impact on the regional economy.

As industrial demand for resources and tropical crops continued, expanding low-paid wage labor in many parts of Africa and Latin America, these same regions continued to rely heavily on imports of industrial goods from other areas—from Brazil and the Pacific Rim as well as Japan and the West. Growing need for advanced machinery plus a middle-class taste for automobiles and computers expanded the list of items that were sought from the outside; the result was a persistent and highly traditional tendency for imbalance in foreign trade. Even some oil exporters like Nigeria, once prices stabilized again in the 1980s, found that their need for equipment imports exceeded their capacity to pay, and this imbalance created heavy foreign debts that further constrained the national economy.

Thus, elements of the industrialized world's advantage over many resource-producing areas endured in a pattern that had been sketched in the early decades of Europe's industrial revolution. The greatest innovation in this relationship after 1950 involved the increasing quest by American, Japanese, and European firms for cheap labor in factory industry. Appliance manufacturers, electronics firms, and other businesses established branch factories in many parts of the world with the primary objective of reexporting production back to the industrial regions. In a few instances, assembly plants also issued goods for local consumption and thus reduced the transport and tariff costs of shipments from the industrialized world directly. More commonly, however, the expansion factories looked for cheap labor (much of it female) in regions where population growth generated endemic underemployment and scant bargaining power. These companies looked for inexpensive or nonexistent benefit programs and, in some instances, for loose environmental regulations. They thus sought a basket of advantage that would enable them to undercut the costs of production in the United States, Europe, or Japan. They expanded the geographical range of modern technology and the factory system in the process—major change was involved for the receiving areas—but not necessarily with any intent to generate a full range of industrialization.

A variety of areas were drawn into factory industry on this basis, including parts of North Africa, the Caribbean, and Pacific Oceania. One of the most striking examples was along Mexico's border with the United States, where what was called *maquiladora* industry expanded dramatically from the 1980s onward. Hundreds of foreign firms, mostly from the United States, set up assembly factories in northern Mexico, transforming regions around cities like Juarez (the border town next to El Paso, Texas) in a fashion reminiscent of a true industrial revolution. Thousands of workers were drawn in, 85 percent of them young women between the ages of fifteen and twenty-four. Industrial refuse was in many cases released without precaution, which created barren wastelands behind many factories and amid worker housing.

As in earlier interactions between industrial economies and other regions, an exploitative relationship brought some benefits in its wake. A growing number of Mexicans learned factory skills, extending Mexico's own nascent industrialization. Wages, though low, brought vital relief to some families amid massive underemployment. At the same time, the spread of industrial operations under foreign control spelled only limited benefits for the host countries. The bulk of the profits were often exported rather than reinvested locally, and the larger impact of the search for additional labor outside the industrialized world per se was extremely difficult to calculate. As in the early days of industrialization elsewhere, many employers blatantly intimidated workers, encouraging the government to arrest potential union leaders and firing dissidents. Overall, only 15 percent of the *maquiladora* workers were unionized. Observers in Mexico and elsewhere debated the long-run consequences of this new industrial growth, which some claimed simply institutionalized poverty. What was clear was the transformative impact industrialization could still bring to bear, changing the lives of thousands of families and the physical face of whole regions when it was exported to new locales.

The Process of Evolution: Semiindustrial Economies

In the decades after 1950, many areas of the world participated in several relationships to industrialization. Mexico was representative of one type of connection. It developed a growing industrial sector, expanded export agriculture, and of course participated extensively as a site of foreign factories seeking inexpensive labor. It also embraced pockets of more customary agriculture and craft manufacturing in which essentially traditional techniques and habits prevailed.

Very few countries failed to generate some growth in factory industry after 1950 even if they remained very poor because of extensive foreign commercial penetration and/or sectors of a traditional economy. Newly independent African nations like Ghana and Nigeria embarked on a process of what they called "indigenization," in which foreign ownership was discouraged in favor of local business interests. This had some results similar to those generated by Brazil's earlier policy of import substitution, such as spurring some factory industry to produce consumer goods for the national market and thus replace imports of foreign textiles, metal products, construction goods, and the like. Most African economies continued to depend on imports of more complex equipment. Correspondingly, most also promoted exports of cash crops and natural resources, including oil in the case of Nigeria. Finally, most included pockets of traditional village agriculture fairly remote from world commerce and modern technology save for a few bicycles, an occasional truck, and some radios. A few African nations that were resource-poor actually reduced their commitment to a commercial economy. Most, however, including leaders such as Nigeria and Kenya, displayed the typical elements: growing local manufacturing that featured power technology and fairly

This man uses a soldering iron to work on central telex equipment in Abidjan, Ivory Coast, in 1967. Telex systems are very helpful in international trade and communications. (Courtesy of the United Nations. Reprinted by permission.)

typical factory conditions; encouragement to exports in search of the vital foreign exchange needed because of continued dependence on foreign technology; and important traditionalist remnants.

These mixtures defied easy categorization, which is one reason simple labels like "Third World" proved so misleading. Some countries by the 1990s perhaps were in the early stages of outright industrialization. After all, previous early industrializers also had developed special low-wage export sectors (like Japanese silk) and had maintained important traditionalist pockets (like the slow-moving villages in midnineteenth-century France). It was not possible, however, to predict a triumph of modern industry in light of other impediments like lingering commitment to preindustrial economic habits or vulnerability to economic initiatives from abroad. The inability of both Nigeria and Mexico to translate oil revenues in the 1970s into permanent industrial growth—instead leaving both countries indebted and open to new foreign schemes like *maquiladora* factories—complicated future projections. Several African countries, many in Latin America, and even Asian nations like Thailand, on the fringe of the Pacific Rim, were developing industrial potential but amid a number of major uncertainties.

What was common to all of these specific economic combinations was the experience of considerable change, most of it now generated internally. Significant industrial evolution described all but the most impoverished nations by the 1970s and 1980s.

Partial industrial economies clearly developed in the two giants of Asia—India and China. India moved to an active policy of economic development after gaining independence in 1947. Notwithstanding some antiindustrial sentiments on the part of Mohandas Gandhi, India's great nationalist leader, who opposed the squalor and exploitation of modern industry and foresaw an India of crafts and agriculture, most leaders of the new nation judged industrial growth a precondition of economic independence. The government did provide some support for craft production and small-scale rural industries, including hand weaving, but the major attention went to urban industrial growth. Five-year plans were developed that focused on factory development above all. Despite massive poverty and crushing population pressure, India was generating industrial growth rates of as much as 5 percent per year by the 1950s. Advanced technology was introduced or expanded in metallurgy and chemicals, which created islands of extremely productive factory industry having well-trained engineering staffs amid a still agricultural nation. Rich deposits of iron ore encouraged growth in metallurgy, in which India had established a significant industrial sector earlier in the twentieth century. By the 1970s a successful space program emerged from this same policy of selective technological promotion.

India's growth faltered in the 1960s as the population explosion exceeded agricultural output. However, new agricultural technology and more productive seeds—the so called "green revolution," backed by U.S. and West European agricultural expertise—restored India's agricultural self-sufficiency. Economic growth resumed in the 1970s even though the bulk of the population remained in the countryside and much of it, rural and urban, was extremely poor. Growth rates in the 1980s, at 3 percent per year, exceeded those of the United States.

Indian industrial growth relied heavily on government intervention, and complaints mounted that rules and regulations complicated economic life. Government experts guided the use of scarce foreign exchange, seeking to restrict imports to two categories India could not supply: advanced technology and oil. Indian exports boomed as well with sales of factory-produced goods particularly to the Middle East and Southeast Asia. India did not sell industrial products widely to the industrialized countries, but it enjoyed marked success as a regional economic leader in southern Asia. Government regulation limiting imports of consumer goods created some discontent—automobiles, for example, were hard to come by, for India's automobile production, featuring two compact models designed for fuel efficiency, did not keep pace with demand. But the historical dependence on Britain for basic factory goods was a thing of the past.

India was not, however, industrialized. It continued to house significant foreign economic activity, not all of it well designed. A tragic chemicals explosion in an American-owned plant in Bhopal constituted the world's second worst environmental disaster in the 1980s; over 2,000 people were killed immediately and literally hundreds of thousands maimed. Indian growth rates lagged in the 1980s compared with the clear industrial surge of the Pacific Rim, and many experts worried that initially successful government planning had become too cumbersome. Rapid population growth continued despite government campaigns to stem the tide, though the rate abated slightly. Rural development lagged behind the leading industrial centers. A fully industrial economy was not yet in sight.

China provided a second though very different case of industrial growth without full industrialization in Asia. After some consolidation following communist victory on the mainland, China's leader, Mao Zedong, launched a period of rapid industrialization in the 1950s based on earlier Stalinist models in the Soviet Union. Heavy industry was emphasized in a rapid-growth program backed by Soviet advisers and limited economic aid. Then in 1958 Mao shifted gears, touting a "great leap forward" that emphasized the formation of rural communes combining farming with some small-scale industry. The idea was to generate a distinctively Chinese version of communist industrialization—to rely on masses of people rather than high technology. Technical universities were dismantled. Backyard steel furnaces sprang up over the countryside. Mao boasted that his "great leap" would enable China to overtake Britain in industrial output through the united efforts of a galvanized people organized for mass labor but in largely nonfactory settings.

The experiment was a disaster, and China's industrialization was actually set back, by as much as 30 percent. Most of the industrial output was of a quality too poor to be usable. Yet through the 1960s Mao continued to emphasize small-scale industrial development for meeting local needs with rural industry in such sectors as iron, cement, chemicals, and electric power. The ideal was noble: to avoid the huge, exploitative factories of the rest of the industrialized world and to limit pollution and strain on transportation facilities. But the industrial output in fact proved unpredictable and expensive, for advanced technology and economy of scale were deliberately absent. Politics and a heroic vision of an alternative to standard industrialization held China back for almost fifteen years.

Policy shifted after Mao's death, and in 1978 China began to adopt a more flexible and conventional industrialization strategy. Exports were promoted, and foreign technical advice was eagerly sought. Despite commitment to communism, including considerable state planning, and a fiercely authoritarian government, private business sectors were encouraged in agriculture and industry. Some rural industry persisted, but urban production was emphasized as China worked to recover familiarity with advanced technology. Economic growth rates boomed in the 1980s, and China, thanks to its size, became a considerable industrial force. Not only factories but also roads and railroads expanded rapidly.

Late in the Mao regime a woman drives a tractor of the People's Corporation in Peking. Even today, however, much farm work is done without the aid of machinery. (Courtesy of AP/Wide World Photos. Reprinted by permission.)

Industrial growth in China and other evolving economies brought new wealth to many people. A new group of rich entrepreneurs surfaced in China complete with symbols of high consumer standards, including televisions and tape recorders. Even many villagers enjoyed bicycles and other new products. Other industrial fruits were less palatable. Pollution levels in many countries surpassed those of the West and Japan. Chinese cities were choked with industrial gases, called the "Yellow Dragon," and chemical pollution of water sources was considerable. Mexico City boasted probably the world's worst pollution record. In 1992 factories were periodically required to cut production simply because of the poisons in the city's thin mountainous air, as pollution levels routinely hit levels triple those accepted as maximum in the United States. Plans were generated to use giant fans to expel smog, but the costs were probably prohibitive. Industrial evolution had more than local pollution effects. China's industrial advance combined with its huge population placed China in third position as a world contributor to the chemical emissions causing global warming by 1992. China contributed 9 percent of total world emission compared with 5 percent for Japan, 14 percent for the former Soviet Union, and a booming 18 percent for the United States. Growing use of coal for fuel (as China became the world's largest coal-mining nation) promised a further Chinese advance on this dubious achievement scale for the future, as Chinese policy frankly placed economic growth ahead of environmental concerns.

In general, semiindustrial countries, still poor but also desperate to expand, were precisely those least able to afford pollution control. Still, pollution itself was a measure, however murky, of industrialization's new international outreach as virtually every major nation in the world and many smaller centers in Asia, Latin America, and Africa developed a substantial industrial sector. Specific patterns varied widely, from India's steady planning policies to China's industrial zigzags, but the fact of evolutionary change was almost universal wherever an industrial revolution itself had not (at least as yet) taken hold.

The Ambiguity of Change

Outside the industrialized regions, the variety of economic situations, including the degree of commitment to factory industry and its related attributes, was immense. The fact that new industrial revolutions proved to be rare after 1950 misled some observers into lumping all nonindustrial societies into a then common "developing-nations" category. Yet the nonindustrial societies were not simply waiting around after 1900, avoiding the industrial revolution. Any single label—"nonindustrial," for example, describing these societies collectively by what they were not—not only conceals the tremendous variety among them but also downplays significant industrial change. The amount of factory industry increased enormously in places like India and China, compared with the previous period of the world's industrial history. Thus, a concept of evolution—which allows for important innovation short of revolution and also allows for different specific patterns and degrees—proves most accurate.

Because it is impossible to characterize regions like China or the Middle East through simple formulas—they neither industrialized in the classic Western or Pacific Rim sense nor stagnated—evaluations of trends inevitably vary. Partly this reflects decisions as to which nonindustrial societies to use as examples; levels of factory industry, population pressure, and poverty varied widely outside the industrialized societies. But partly it reflects the ambiguousness of developments within key societies. Gloom is clearly justified: Mexico and India continue to suffer from severe poverty; population pressure or foreign indebtedness or traditionalism may continue to prevent a full industrial breakthrough; the contrasts with the dynamism of Western Europe or the Pacific Rim remain vivid. Modest optimism may also be justified: Mexico and India have established significant industrial sectors; standards of living have improved; the degree of change since the early twentieth century, when these same economies were much more fully open to foreign exploitation, is impressive. No single lens captures the complex reality of major regions of the world still not fully industrialized but committed to substantial development efforts. While much of the world has departed from any single standard of industrial revolution in the decades since 1950, societies in evolution have built on the previous global impact of industrialization to increase massively the industrial component of the world's economies.

15

International Industry

T HE INTERNATIONAL implications of industrialization became much clearer after 1950, creating what might legitimately be termed a global economic revolution. In addition to innovations in specific societies, and atop the great variety of industrial situations, an international industrial apparatus took shape. International links and combinations built on previous developments, including transoceanic shipping and communication and the formation of foreign subsidiaries by leading companies. Nevertheless, the sheer complexity of international industry had important new qualities in the last half of the twentieth century.

The two basic features of the industrial revolution—technology and organization—began to apply on a world scale. International technology included routine air travel that enabled business leaders and technical experts to meet regularly and thus form something of an international community in their fields across political and ideological boundaries. With advances in computer linkages and satellite communication that greatly speeded the flow and volume of messages came literally instant access to developments on the other side of the world. The organizational revolution showed most clearly in the emergence of multinational corporations (stemming mainly from Western Europe, the United States, and the Pacific Rim, including Japan) that had complicated manufacturing operations around the globe. Some authorities argued that multinationals were replacing established governments as the most influential organizations in contemporary life.

International organization and technology were complemented by new flows of labor from Latin America, Africa, and Asia into the industrialized regions. The result was creation of an almost unprecedented mixture of civilizations around a common industrial base. Attending this development as well were new global problems of industrial pollution that required, though did not then receive, another kind of international response.

Finally, the transcendence of international economic links showed in the increasing realization that no economy could successfully isolate itself from global industrial contacts. During the second phase of industrialization several nations understandably sought to establish policies that would insulate them from outside economic interference. The Soviet Union under Stalin managed successfully to isolate its industrial development, reversing previous openness to foreign capital and technology. Even after 1950 Mao's "great leap forward" and cultural revolution policies sought a distinctive Chinese path to industrial development that ironically revived older Chinese impulses to isolation. By the 1970s isolationist policies in the world's leading communist nations had broken down. The cost, in terms of lagging behind technological developments elsewhere and failing to take advantage of organizational innovations, was simply too great. Hence post-Mao China sought to manage a new economic openness to the world, while the Soviet Union built massive international contacts into its reform movement in the late 1980s. Going it alone had, seemingly, become impossible.

The Multinationals

Corporations that developed massive stakes in economic operations outside their home country—the multinationals—expanded from previous international interests on the part of industrial firms. There was no magic dividing line between the internationally minded corporations of the 1920s and the multinationals that spread from 1950 onward—the differences were sheer scale on the one hand and overall international impact on the other. Multinational corporations fanned out from the United States and Canada, from Western Europe, and from Japan, with other areas of the Pacific Rim increasingly chiming in. They were consequences, in other words, of the general advancement of industrial economies in the three major centers of industrialization.

U.S. firms had $7.2 billion invested abroad in 1946; this figure rose to $78.18 billion in 1970 and to $133 billion in 1976. American corporations invested and operated in other industrial countries, exhibiting particular interest in Western Europe. They also expanded operations in nonindustrial countries, particularly in mining and transportation but also, increasingly, in factory industry. By the 1980s foreign operations of U.S.-based firms were generating between 25 percent and 40 percent of all corporate profits. Major oil companies, computer companies, and some consumer-products firms regularly earned over 50 percent of their totals from foreign operations, while American commercial banks in some instances reaped over 60 percent of their annual profits from activities abroad. The foreign stake of American companies expanded steadily, as did their impact on various regions of the world.

Multinational operations increased more rapidly from Western Europe and Japan than from the United States. Between 1965 and 1971 German and Japanese foreign investment rose at triple the rate of growth in American overseas commitments. Japan held over $4.5 billion in foreign investment by 1973, a fifteenfold increase in a decade. Initial Japanese investments focused on mining and other raw-materials sources in countries like Brazil and Australia, a logical target given Japan's import needs. Germany long emphasized manufacturing and high-technology branches, setting up automobile and chemicals factories in several countries. Japan in the 1980s also began to expand its foreign manufacturing interests, opening a number of automobile-manufacturing branches in parts of the United States and elsewhere. European and Japanese investment in the United States, correspondingly, increased rapidly—even by 1975 direct foreign investment (with Britain in the lead, followed by other parts of Western Europe, Japan, and oil-rich Arab states) had almost quintupled over 1960. German cars, Japanese cars, French tires, German chemicals and pharmaceuticals, and Dutch petroleum all had substantial American operations.

The advantages of multinational activities on the part of big firms like Mitsubishi, Royal Dutch Shell, Bayer Chemicals, General Motors, and IBM were multifold. Many companies of course established foreign operations to obtain vital raw materials, such as uranium, iron, and, inevitably, oil. This interest was one of the oldest inducements to international expansion. It was constrained after 1950 by the increasing success of many countries in controlling foreign extraction operations—for example, in the Middle Eastern oil fields—but it continued to be extensive nevertheless. In time-tested fashion, many multinationals were able to take the bulk of their profits on resource production out of the countries of extraction, making the rich nations richer and the gap between industrial and nonindustrial ever wider.

Branch factories were also a way to save on transportation costs. Japanese automobile assembly plants in Kentucky and California boosted earnings because the cars did not entail heavy shipping charges and also escaped import duties. Branch operations in Latin America, the Middle East, and various parts of Asia carried the same benefits for multinationals from all of the major industrial centers. Not only cars but also medicinal drugs, household appliances, processed foods, and a host of other products spread through many parts of the world by virtue of multinational operations.

A third motivation involved a worldwide search for capital and for high returns on investments. Multinational corporations drew investments from many different countries, which allowed them to attract capital from regions with temporary overabundance and apply it to opportunities in other areas. One reason for extensive European and Japanese investment in the United States during the 1970s and 1980s was relatively high American interest rates, which meant by the same token that many American firms were drawing capital from places where it was easier and cheaper to find than if they had been confined to competition for investment funds in the high-interest American market.

An increasing search for cheap labor provided a fourth reason for the expansion of multinational corporations. Plants set up in low-wage areas like the Caribbean allowed multinationals to farm out some of the simpler manufacturing operations, such as producing computer chips or assembling household appliances. Most of these products were then reimported to the home country or to other industrial markets.

Finally—and this was the newest facet of the multinationals after 1950 or 1960, aside from the sheer expansion of scale—multinational operations resulted in an almost global specialization. Final products were assembled from components made in several different countries, each with specialist factories capable of benefiting from massive economies of scale in turning out far more parts than the home economy required. Cars sold in Japan and in the United States, for example, whether officially "made" in one country or the other, routinely were composed of parts originally produced in Japan, the United States, possibly Korea, Mexico, and sometimes other places besides. Japanese cars imported into the United States sometimes had fewer Japanese-made parts than did cars made in Detroit.

What the multinationals were doing, clearly, was creating a world economic system through which coordination of various business functions—production, finance, and distribution—could take place without regard to the conditions or policies of any individual nation-state. The globe was treated as a single industrial unit, a factory, that could achieve maximum efficiencies through international coordination of all aspects of manufacturing operations. Specialization, in particular, became a worldwide operation. Only a few carefully controlled economies were partially exempt, but even in these the future seemed to lie with the multinationals. Indeed, substantial multinational penetration followed the collapse of the Soviet system in the 1980s and the opening of China after 1978.

Multinational corporations raised a host of new problems. Because they found it relatively easy to move operations in response to unfavorable government policies or labor conditions, the power of a given nation to regulate or of a particular trade union to bargain came under new constraints. Multinationals' management policies varied, and some granted considerable autonomy to local branch operations. Some multinationals, however, insisted on tighter controls from the center, distrusting local managers and trying to install labor practices and other procedures imported intact from experiences in the home country. Most obviously, the power of multinationals frequently exceeded that of the governments in many of the host societies, particularly of course in smaller and less industrialized nations. The largest multinationals, like General Motors or Toyota, had annual revenues far greater than the total tax intake of many of the countries in which they operated, and their bargaining power was accordingly high. The scale of economic organization, thanks to the international expansion of industrialization, exceeded that of political authority. This disparity, in turn, created abundant possibilities for quarrels over responsibility and for clashes over appropriate taxation, labor, and environmental policies.

Labor Migration

The explosion of multinationals and their increasing ability to operate a variety of economic activities, from resource extraction to capital transfers, in almost every part of the world constituted the clearest sign that the industrial revolution had entered a new, global phase after 1950. Other industrially based contacts occurred as well, and like the multinationals they demonstrated the increased ability of industrial development to pull people from widely different cultural backgrounds into contact that defied not only purely national boundaries but the often more deeply rooted distinctions among major civilizations as well. Unprecedented movements of people constituted a second major international force operating under the umbrella of industrialization.

Movements of labor were a constant feature of the industrial revolution. Immigration into the United States and Canada fed the factory and mining labor force taking shape around 1900, providing relatively cheap workers willing to accept not only modest wages but also novel working conditions in hopes of earning enough to return home or simply because they saw little alternative. West European, Japanese, and Russian industrial growth depended on similar movements of displaced rural inhabitants into the factory centers. Most of these came from within the nation—unlike the immigration in North America—but a minority spilled over from neighboring areas in which population pressure limited local options. Thus French industrialization was aided by Belgian migrants, while around 1900 numerous Poles and Italians sought work in French and German factories. The British industrial labor force was supplemented, particularly among the unskilled, by migration from Ireland.

Industry's need for new workers and its success in recruiting migrants—some of them drawn to the city but more of them pressured to migrate by changes in rural life—were basic to the industrialization process. Before 1950, however, most industrial migration drew workers from a background somewhat similar to the host society. Poles in France faced some discrimination and culture shock, but they were partially cushioned by common Catholic religious traditions. Eastern and southern European immigrants to industrializing North America faced greater barriers as they moved into countries whose dominant culture was Protestant. This helped account for harsh measures U.S. employers adopted to police immigrant workers and for the patronizing "Americanization" campaigns designed to convert "inferior" peoples into good American workers. The cultural factor also helped generate internal conflict within the U.S. working class: Native-born workers were often reluctant to associate with unskilled immigrants, immigrants clashed with each other along ethnic lines, and white workers of various origins displayed a general tendency to look down on African Americans in the cities. One industrial immigrant group—the Chinese workers recruited to the

American West by railroad companies seeking cheap construction labor—faced unusual barriers of cultural unfamiliarity and massive racism on the part of both employers and workers.

After 1950 the experience of immigrant labor shifted, as most of the labor needs of industrial areas were filled by migrants from other cultures. The recruitment of industrial labor internationalized. Major industrial regions continued to need additional workers, particularly for lower-paid, unskilled jobs deemed unsatisfactory by the native-born working class. Declining rates of population growth and rising expectations on the part of the native-born combined to create the new labor needs in a context of considerable economic expansion. At the same time, the combination of population pressures in various nonindustrial parts of the world, improved transportation and growing information about industrial life, and in some instances prior experience with commercial work settings in the home country produced a growing potential immigrant pool.

Japan was least affected by labor migration from outside its boundaries. Nevertheless, Japanese expansion, plus the falling birthrate, created an unprecedented interest in foreign workers by the 1970s. Immigrants were recruited from Korea, the Philippines, and Thailand to work on construction crews and on the docks primarily. By the early 1990s approximately 600,000 foreigners were laboring in Japan, a country with considerable cultural suspicion of outsiders.

The United States began to receive substantial immigration from several nonindustrial areas. By the 1970s, in fact, the nation was experiencing the highest absolute rate of immigration in its history. Immigrant groups included some trained professionals from parts of Europe and Asia, but the largest numbers were unskilled workers from Korea, the Philippines, Mexico, and the Caribbean. A significant flow of illegal immigrants, particularly from Mexico and Central America, added to the official total. Over 6 million Mexican workers, both legal and illegal, provided agricultural, construction, and factory labor in the Southwest and in major midwestern centers like Chicago. Many found it difficult to obtain anything more than low-paying, unskilled positions, though they were in some instances able to compete favorably with native-born inner-city African Americans, whose economic position became exceptionally marginal.

A new immigrant "underclass" also took shape in Western Europe as industrial prosperity and growing opportunities for the native-born working class created new needs in the unskilled ranks. Initial migration came from relatively established sources, particularly southern Italy and Spain, but the industrialization of these countries quickly reduced this flow. The major migrant sources then shifted to include Yugoslavia, Turkey, North Africa, Pakistan, and the West Indies. These immigrants, euphemistically labeled guest workers in West Germany, typically were residentially segregated, poorly paid, and victims of prejudice, racial violence, and job discrimination. They formed something of a separate labor force, confined for the most part to unskilled factory and construction jobs and transportation slots like bus conducting. By 1990 legal and illegal immigration had brought over 12 million immigrants into the economy of the European Common Market. Islam became the second religion of countries like France.

The development of racial and cultural minorities in the industrial labor force increased immensely through the internationalization of the industrial experience after 1950. Pressures to seek work continued in many nonindustrial regions as economic growth failed to provide fully for an expanding population. Industrialized societies, though hardly welcoming the new migrants, also benefited from their cheap labor. In the short run, something like a dual labor force resulted, with native-born people competing for the better-paying jobs, the racial minorities for the stubborn residuum of low-paid work. Service-sector jobs, particularly, were hard to come by for groups that looked distinctive and seemed to behave distinctively as well—yet service-sector jobs were the most rapidly growing category in these same economies. Racial tensions with other workers added new political issues to the agenda of Western Europe and complicated politics in the United States as well. Antiimmigrant movements began to flourish in Europe by the 1980s, combining concerns about job security with long-standing racial fears and prejudices. At the same time, immigrant workers themselves became increasingly restive. Between 1980 and 1985 a series of race riots involving mainly workers of West Indian origin occurred in British cities. In 1990 a North African neighborhood in Lyons, France, rioted for four days after a young man died in a motorcycle crash with a police car.

Clearly, international industrialization introduced a new component in the ongoing formation of the urban labor force. Equally clearly, the expansion of the sources of labor, as it spilled into diverse, often hostile cultures, posed new problems of identity and tolerance in the most established industrial centers. Finally, the industrial centers were not alone in being affected. Many societies, like Turkey or Algeria, depended considerably on the earnings sent back by immigrant workers in Europe. They benefited also from the industrial experience of immigrants who ultimately returned. Thus, international economic links, though generating suspicion and inequality, also increasingly bound a number of parts of the world.

The Environment

The environmental impact of industrialization turned visibly international after 1950. The expansion of industry in established centers, including new ventures such as nuclear power, and the frenzied growth efforts in other regions contributed to new levels of global concern. Persistent industrial pollution from factory centers regularly carried across national boundaries; acid rain in northern Europe and in Canada came from sources in nations to the south. Accidents spilled over as well. The partial nuclear meltdown at Chernobyl, in the Soviet Union, not only devastated the immediate region but also increased levels of radioactivity in a wide swath of eastern and central Europe. The operations of multinational firms had similarly far-reaching effects. Oil spills knew no clear boundaries. Operations of foreign chemical plants in places like India and Mexico, sometimes established in part to take advantage of lax environmental regulation, altered the regional environment. In a few tragicomic cases, industrial companies from the West successfully won contracts in poor African nations to dump dangerous industrial waste for which no acceptable place could be found at home. Finally, industrial growth in the cities of China and Latin America brought substantial pollution not only to each regional environment but to international waterways. Increasing poison in many ocean fish, including high mercury levels, resulted from industrial pollution from advanced industrial areas as well as newcomers. The expansion of mining and commercial agriculture in many tropical countries, including Brazil, curtailed oxygen-producing rain forests. Worldwide growth in the use of hydrocarbon fuels produced growing impact on the global climate, including the prospect of an increase in average temperatures, while the emission of certain chemicals (particularly, in this case, from the leading industrial centers) reduced the ozone layer protecting the earth from damaging rays from the sun.

The list of global environmental hazards expanded steadily. The problem was complicated by the fact that most policy agencies remained resolutely national, inclined to focus on local environmental issues above all. Several individual industrial nations demonstrated that environmental protection was consistent with continued industrial growth. Energy conservation and other measures in Japan reduced once-severe pollution levels without dampening the world's most impressive industrial progress. Through new environmental policies, the average Japanese citizen by the early 1990s was contributing over 90 percent less to environmental degradation than his or her U.S. counterpart. But success in one nation was hard to carry to the international arena. Further, some of the most rapidly growing polluters were not the wealthy nations but those, like China and Brazil, just struggling to enter the industrial ranks. These nations understandably argued that their struggle to compete was too difficult to add special environmental concerns to their list of goals to achieve. They further argued, understandably if not necessarily effectively, that it was up to the industrialized nations to contribute disproportionately to an international regulatory operation and thus compensate the newer industrial regions for some of the expenses a sound environment required.

Even more than in the case of labor, the internationalization of industrial impact on the environment created issues with which existing governments could not keep pace. The global framework could not be missed. An increasing number of international conferences were called to seek agreement on protecting the ozone layer or reducing industrial emissions. Whether international remediation was possible remained unclear.

Regionalism and International Forces

The internationalization of industrialization created new tensions between people's loyalties and most established governments on the one hand and the framework needed for effective economic operations on the other. Even as industrial issues took on global dimensions and multinational organizations gained ground, many political developments suggested the importance of purely regional identities.

Regionalism showed in strong separatist movements in places like Canada, where pressure for autonomy or independence for French-speaking Quebec displayed new muscle from the 1960s onward. The trend showed in the collapse of multiethnic states like Yugoslavia in the early 1990s and in new separatist movements in well-established nations like Spain and Britain. In Spain, Catalonian cultural identity generated renewed vigor, while in Britain a potent surge for a separate Scotland challenged a unity over three centuries old. The collapse of the Soviet Union in 1991 eclipsed the lesser centripetal regional displays: Several central Asian republics and several independent Slavic states maintained the loosest of connections, while the three small Baltic republics split off entirely. Some of these developments reflected economic discontents, particularly when minority ethnic regions felt their resources had been abused by a larger neighbor within the nation; thus nationalistic Scots accused England of exploiting North Sea oil reserves to Scotland's detriment. None of the separatist movements claimed industrial advantage as a major motive, however, and most of the movements defied the strictest kind of economic rationality. In a world where international industrialization called for larger, more global combinations, the widespread impulse toward splintering revealed a different set of passions.

The two trends were not entirely incompatible, of course. The very pressure of anonymous global economic forces encouraged some people to feel more intensely about their local identity. It was also possible that regional autonomy could combine successfully with larger economic frameworks. Scottish and Catalonian nationalists, for example, pointed out that separate political or cultural institutions would operate under the common economic umbrella provided by the European Economic Community. Precisely because the nation was no longer a central economic unit, having been transcended by international industrialism, local cultures could be indulged along with supranational economic policies. Many former Soviet leaders hoped that economic ties could be preserved within most of the dissolved state even as formal political institutions were carved up regionally, though the durability of the first makeshift coordinating device, awkwardly named the Commonwealth of Independent States, was not at all clear. Other regional coordination frameworks were even more loosely sketched. By the 1990s Pacific Rim states were holding various coordination discussions concerning tariff and development policies. They included not only the Asian industrial leaders but also governments like Mongolia and China that were newly open to international economic contacts. Some discussions also embraced Australia, New Zealand, Canada, the United States, and the Latin American nations bordering the Pacific. The possibility of a Pacific basin economic group, paralleling the European Economic Community's new Atlantic group, was outlined by some forecasters. Finally, tariff coordination between the United States and Canada increased trade freedom, and leaders of both countries joined Mexico and other Latin American nations in discussing a more effective trading zone composed of North and South America.

Some of these possibilities seemed remote. Furthermore, even regional trading blocs omitted certain areas (where were the Middle East and South Asia to fit, for example?). And even these blocs, if realized, would fall short of the international scale of industrialization. The fact remained that international business organizations and international industrial problems had outstripped the scale of effective politics and culture. Whether the gap was permanent, and whether it was harmful or potentially creative, were issues ripe for debate. But that the gap existed seemed indisputable—another, if very recent, result of the speed of industrial transformations.

16

Conclusion

SINCE ITS INCEPTION, the industrial revolution has raised vital issues of analysis. While these issues have changed as the technology and organization associated with the revolution have advanced and as additional societies have been drawn into the process, historical assessment remains essential not simply to understand the past but to grasp what the industrial economy now is and what its implications are. Causation remains a fundamental concern. Explaining why Britain or Japan generated an industrial revolution remains a challenging historical exercise. Explaining what basic factors were involved and how they might be replicated even today merges history with contemporary concerns. Asking why some societies continue to face difficulties in making a turn to industrialization (or why some societies may not wholeheartedly wish an industrial revolution because of its threat to their more important values) involves a serious understanding of what causation has entailed for the past 200 years.

Precedent as Guide to Prediction

Since the industrial revolution spread from Britain to other parts of Europe and then well beyond, a balance between commonality and diversity has been central to comparative analysis: this, too, continues to be true. Industrial revolutions that have transpired had some essential common features. They obviously involved not only massive technological and organizational change but also redefinition of family function and alteration of the nature of work and leisure. Cities invariably grew and agricultural groups were reassessed, their status diminished though usually amid persistent clamor. Yet industrial revolutions also varied greatly. They differed according to geography and available resources. They differed according to timing—latecomers inevitably emphasized different features from earlier industrializers, and some of these distinctions have proved long lasting. They differed, finally, according to prior culture and institutions. Various cultures proved suitable for industrialization, but they also created different definitions of management structure, government involvement, attitudes toward consumerism, and labor relations. Thus, juggling the relationship between standard patterns and vital variants is a significant interpretive challenge. It particularly directs attention to the need to avoid equating Western versions of industrial society with some sort of inevitable product. This simplification, one of the weaknesses of the modernization model, has become less common in the 1990s because of the obvious success of Japan's distinctive industrial enterprise, but it can still intrude in historical judgments.

The theme of variety also extends to experience within any individual industrial process. One of the great advances in knowledge in recent years has been a fuller appreciation of the immense differences in the impact of industrial revolutions on workers and employers, urbanites and farmers. Gender is now seen as crucial. In many instances industrialization has reduced economic roles for women—this is true not only in industrializing societies but also in many other areas, such as large parts of Africa, where industrial pressures from the West have unseated the balance of traditional agricultural economies. In the West many aspects of contemporary history (including feminism but also debates over retirement policies) relate directly to the ongoing attempt to assimilate and rearrange the differential results industrial revolutions have brought to various segments of the population.

The various facets of historical analysis concerning industrialization pertain directly to assessments of probable future developments. Will industrial societies and experiences become more alike over time? Many people expect Japan ultimately to develop a larger number of Western traits because of continued imitation and contact and because of the dynamic of industrialization itself. Surely, this argument goes, the Japanese will soon turn to a greater interest in leisure time, as Westerners began to do a century ago after their initial industrial achievement seemed complete. Surely Japanese women will insist on a fuller work role, creating conditions for a larger feminist movement centered around the economic issues industrialization has forced to prominence in redefining family roles. Yet perhaps distinctive patterns will persist amid substantially different approaches to some common industrial issues. And it is possible that Japanese success will impel Western industrialization toward greater emphasis on links between state and private enterprise and toward new attention to group harmony in management and labor relations. Many Americans, for example, urge that the Japanese example is argument for a relaxation of the antitrust laws that for a century have posed some legal limitations on the growth of big business: Japan had prospered amid less enforced internal competition, and world conditions may make big firms essential to survival on the international scene. This, of course, is a reincarnation of the idea of a single industrial model toward which all industrial societies should flow, but the model is not Western. Yet the quest for a single set of industrial trends may by misleading, for history certainly indicates that a tension between commonalities and diversities best describes what has happened in the evolution of industrial societies during the past 200 years.

The range of impacts of industrialization constitutes a compelling analytical category. How exactly will further industrialization replicate the impact that has historically followed from the industrial revolution process, and in what order must developments occur? Demography is a crucial case in point. Every industrial revolution so far had yielded a dramatic turn toward slower population growth through lower birthrates resulting from the reduced utility of children's work. The precise process has varied according to region and social class—methods used have ranged from sexual abstinence to widespread abortion—but the birthrate revolution has been a fairly uniform result. Will this always be true? Can other societies industrialize without this movement toward birthrate reduction, and must they (as many Western observers have argued) indeed launch this reduction in order to industrialize in the first place? China's Mao Zedong in the 1960s claimed that China's huge and growing population was an industrial asset by providing more abundant labor, but after 1978 new leadership worked more assiduously for birth control as a means of reducing general demands on capital and resources and so permitting an industrial revolution. No fuller answer to the question of the population-industrialization relationship is yet forthcoming, but knowledge of historical relationships raises questions and influences not only predictions but also policies.

In the 1980s a similar set of issues arose concerning political structure. What political systems were compatible with the ongoing development of industrial societies? Before 1980 the answer seemed obvious if messy: Various systems had worked, depending on specific conditions and cultures. Western industrial revolutions had arisen amid governments that usually recognized some formal limits to their functions and had some openness to parliamentary institutions. The process fairly quickly generated pressures for more political democracy (which in the United States had been established before industrialization). Votes helped give workers an outlet for demands and reduced, or seemed to reduce, radical pressures. Some analysts have argued that the accumulation in cities of workers having a number of important grievances about their working conditions requires either democracy or a repressive totalitarian system. The West for the most part opted for democracy, though Nazi Germany briefly demonstrated that a repressive state could function industrially until it self-destructed through the folly of war. The Soviet experience proved that a controlled economy and a strong police state could promote rapid industrial development. The recent examples of Japan and, after World War II, of Korea and Taiwan suggest that while traditional governments must change in order to industrialize, giving new groups some access to power and developing new functions for the state, authoritarian systems with strong state involvement may be quite compatible with early industrialization and perhaps in some cultures even very useful.

In the 1980s, however, economic stagnation in several societies prompted a new belief that installing democracies might be essential to keep industrialization going. Workers and others needed outlets for grievances and some sense of responsive political system, else they would simply stop working hard. Advanced industrial technology, notably the computer, required so much information exchange that maintenance of rigid police controls over ideas was impossible. As a wave of democratic change developed in Latin America after the mid-1970s, many leaders associated their political reforms with hopes for more rapid industrial growth, though there were other motives as well. The Soviet Union, under Gorbachev, clearly if haltingly moved toward a position that more democracy and political openness (glasnost) was an essential concomitant of economic reform and industrial progress (perestroika). In fact, of course, political change proved easier to achieve in Eastern Europe than did movement toward renewed economic growth and a more advanced industrial economy, but the experiment continued into the 1990s. China and Vietnam, struggling to industrialize in the first place, dissented. In their view a command state, free from the distraction and inefficiency of political protest, was still the best context for industrial revolution. But even these countries granted that a redefinition of the economic system, toward a reduction of state control and admission of greater economic competition and more consumer choices, was essential. From these precedents a question clearly arises: Is a single basic political system an inevitable international result of the push to industrialize further? Even though the answer is clearly negative in terms of history—given the success of various combinations of government involvement—the changing conditions of industrial society, including ever tighter international links and the imitation possibly resulting from these contacts, may make the answer affirmative for the future.

How much must follow from an industrial revolution? Will further industrialization create greater world uniformities not only in technology and urban styles, which has already occurred, but also in political values and even basic beliefs? Or will the industrial revolution, like the agricultural revolution that replaced hunting and gathering societies, prove compatible with a host of different translations?

The Balance Sheet

Finally, assessment of the industrial revolution in its many manifestations raises vital questions about gains and losses. These questions are not simply historical, as they involve the values of the observer as well as objective data, but they should not be avoided simply because they must be debated.

Very few people living in an industrial society could or would readily trade places with someone in their society's preindustrial past. Too much would seem strange—too many material comforts would be lacking. A significant handful of Westerners, to be sure, have deliberately sought lives in agricultural or herding societies, finding greater truth and beauty there than in the industrial context. During the 1960s, for example, some American and European youths journeyed to places like Nepal in a quest for a more natural existence. Far more Westerners occasionally use industrial means of transport to take brief visits to nonindustrial locations, and even there they more often than not surround themselves with industrial artifacts, in their luxury hotels, to cushion the shock.

This tendency to seek the familiar is understandable because the industrial revolution brought great change, which makes it difficult to contemplate alternatives. Its benefits have been quite real. Industrial societies have curtailed infant death, making it a rare experience for the first time in human history. They have reduced the impact of vagaries of nature and thus improved the reliability of food supplies. These advantages, greatest in fully industrialized societies, have had significant impact on the world at large. Certainly industrialization has enabled many societies to support far larger numbers of people than ever before, though economic imbalances have ironically generated the greatest population concentrations in societies where industrialization is at best incomplete. Industrialization has been associated with new opportunities, as it has shaken established social hierarchies and created new kinds of work.

At the same time, like any major transformation in the human experience, the industrial revolution has had its very real costs, and some of these continue as well. It has led to unprecedented opportunities to damage the environment, and here its impact seems to increase exponentially over time.The process has created new sources of social tension and perhaps has narrowed basic life experiences, particularly in work, for many people. It has challenged and in some instances clearly defeated basic family cohesion. Industrialization steadily has tightened the links that bind societies to each other around the globe. Expanding transportation, communication, and commerce have, as the trite but true saying goes, progressively shrunk the globe, making international relations far more immediately important in world history than ever before. Yet the same industrial revolution has created or enhanced among societies deep-seated imbalances in fundamental material conditions. These imbalances have been preserved in part by force, but they are nonetheless real and may embitter participants as international relations intensify.

The final tally of the industrial revolution has yet to be reckoned. People have been debating its balance sheet since the process began—not only scholars but also the businesspeople and workers directly involved. This widespread participation is not surprising because the industrial revolution has shaped lives and even consumed souls. The analysis is not simply a historical exercise, for the process is ongoing. The most fearsome toll of the industrial revolution may still await us in the form of greater environmental degradation or new kinds of conflicts between the haves and have-nots at the industrial table. Great opportunities may also beckon as various societies become increasingly able to make adjustments to the industrial world if not to industrialize outright. The industrial revolution, caused by an unusual set of circumstances in world history, unleashed forces that have been hard to control. The one certainty is that the process has not slowed. It continues to shape world history, from the societies seeking higher industrial achievement to societies desperately striving to preserve a newly challenged industrial lead.

Suggestions for Further Reading

THE LITERATURE on the history of the industrial revolution is considerable. A disproportionate amount focuses on Western Europe and in particular Britain, but there is good reading on most areas. At the same time, many topics are incompletely explored; some, like industrialization and women, are currently being recast, with much analysis still to be completed. Furthermore, opportunities for comparative work are limited by the current supply. Still, a host of topics can be pursued in greater depth.

Europe as Crucible

A useful compendium for the European side of this is Derek Aldcroft, ed., *Bibliography of European Economic and Social History* (Manchester, England, 1984). See also the essays in Carlo Cipolla, ed., *Industrial Revolution, 1700–1914* (London, 1973); and see David Landes, *The Unbound Prometheus: Technological Change and Industrial Development in Western Europe from 1750 to the Present* (Cambridge, England, 1969).

On proto-industrialization and the origins of the industrial revolution, see P. Kriedte, H. Medick, and J. Schlumbom, eds., *Industrialization Before Industrialization* (Cambridge, England, 1981)—in particular Medick's essay, "The Proto-Industrial Family Economy," and Kriedte's contribution, "Proto-Industrialization Between Industrialization and De-Industrialization"; for a critique, see D. C. Coleman, "Proto-Industrialization: A Concept Too Many," *Economic History Review*, 2d ser., 36 (1983): 435–448. A fine recent study using the proto-industrial concept is Gay L. Gullickson, *Spinners and Weavers of Auffray* (Cambridge, England, 1986); see also Carlo Cipolla, *Before the Industrial Revolution: European Society and Economy, 1000–1700* (New York, 1980); Rudolph Brauns, *Industrielisierung und Volskleben* (Winterthur, Switzerland, 1960); Dolores Greenberg, "Reassessing the Power Patterns of the Industrial Revolution: An Anglo-American Comparison," *American Historical Review* 87 (1982): 1237–1261; and Charles Tilly, *Big Structures, Large Processes, Huge Comparisons* (New York, 1985).

The term "industrial revolution" was introduced in Arnold Toynbee, *Lectures on the Industrial Revolution* (New York, 1884; reprint 1979). Older and/or conventional treatments of the industrial revolution, focusing mainly on Britain and Western Europe, are legion, and some still serve as a useful introduction to many basic features. See Paul Mantoux, *The Industrial Revolution in the Eighteenth Century* (New York, 1961; first English edition, 1928); J. H. Clapham, *An Economic History of Modern Britain* (Cambridge, England, 1930–1938) and

An Economic History of France and Germany (Cambridge, England, 1961); T. S. Ashton, *The Industrial Revolution, 1760–1830* (New York, 1948); Karl Polanyi, *The Great Transformation* (Boston, 1944); W. O. Henderson, *Britain and Industrial Europe, 1750–1870* (London, 1972) and *The State and the Industrial Revolution in Prussia* (Liverpool, England, 1958); Arthur Dunham, *The Industrial Revolution in France, 1815–1848* (New York, 1955); Rondo Cameron, *France and the Economic Development of Europe* (Princeton, N.J., 1981); Phyllis Deane, *The First Industrial Revolution* (Cambridge, England, 1969); Eric Pawson, *The Early Industrial Revolution* (New York, 1979); A. E. Musson, *Growth of British Industry* (New York, 1978); Robin Reeve, *Industrial Revolution, 1750–1850* (London, 1971).

A bold effort at historical modeling, now somewhat discredited, is W. W. Rostow, *The Stages of Economic Growth* (Cambridge, England, 1960); see also his "The Beginnings of Modern Economic Growth in Europe: An Essay in Synthesis," *Journal of Economic History* 33 (1973): 547–580, and *How It All Began* (New York, 1975). A useful discussion of whether the industrial revolution is a useful term and whether the debate is worth attention, with citations of other recent work, is Rondo Cameron, *"La révolution industrielle manquée,"* and R. M. Hartwell, "Was There an Industrial Revolution?" *Social Science History* 14 (1990): 559–566 and 567–576. For other definitional work, see R. Roehl, "French Industrialization: A Reconsideration," *Explorations in Economic History* 12 (1967): 230–281; M. W. Flinn, *Origins of the Industrial Revolution* (London, 1967); François Crouzet, "Western Europe and Great Britain: Catching Up in the First Half of the Nineteenth Century," in A. J. Youngson, ed., *Economic Development in the Long Run* (New York, 1967); Crouzet, "England and France in the Eighteenth Century: A Comparative Analysis of Two Economic Growths," in R. M. Hartwell, ed., *The Causes of the Industrial Revolution in England* (London, 1967); Crouzet, "Essai de construction d'un indice annuel de la production industrielle française au XIXe siècle," *Annales: Economies, sociétés, civilisations* (1970): 56–101; see also Charles Kindleberger, *Economic Growth in France and Britain, 1851–1950* (New York, 1964). For the more traditional disparagement of nineteenth-century French business, see David Landes, "French Entrepreneurship and Industrial Growth in the Nineteenth Century," *Journal of Economic History* 9 (1949): 49–61.

For an extremely useful introduction to newer economic history analyses, see Joel Mokyr, ed., *The Economics of the Industrial Revolution* (London, 1985) and the rich bibliography. Substantive contributions are François Crouzet, ed., *Capital Formation in the Industrial Revolution* (London, 1965), including Crouzet's essay, "Capital Formation in Great Britain During the Industrial Revolution," 162–222, originally published in *The Proceedings of the Second International Conference of Economic History* (The Hague, Netherlands, 1965); Phyllis Deane, "New Estimates of Gross National Product for the United Kingdom, 1830–1914," *Review of Income and Wealth* 14 (1968): 104–105, and "The Role of Capital in the Industrial Revolution," *Explorations in Economic History* 10 (1962): 349–364; Deane and W. A. Cole, *British Economic Growth, 1688–1959* (Cambridge, England, 1969); J. Mokyr, "Capital, Labour, and the Delay of Industrial Revolution in the Netherlands," *Economic History Yearbook* 38 (1975): 280–299, and *Industrialization in the Low Countries* (New Haven, Conn., 1976). See also Robert W. Fogel, *Railroads and American Economic Growth: Essays in Econometric History* (Baltimore, Md., 1970), a classic of the "cliometric" approach; J. G. Williamson, "Regional Inequality and the Process of National Development: A Description of the Patterns," *Economic Development and Cultural Change* 13 (1964–65): 1–82; E. F. Denison, *Why Growth Rates Differ* (Washington, D.C., 1967); R. M. Hartwell, ed., *The Industrial Revolution and Economic Growth* (London, 1971); J.R.T. Hughes, *Industrialization and Economic*

History (New York, 1970); N.F.R. Crafts, "English Economic Growth in the Eighteenth Century," *Economic History Review* 29 (1967): 226–235.

On the technological component, see Melvin Kranzberg, "Prerequisites for Industrialization," in M. Kranzberg and C. W. Pursell, Jr., eds., *Technology in Western Civilization*, 2 vols. (New York, 1967); Daniel Headrick, *The Tentacles of Progress: Technology Transfer in the Age of Imperialism, 1850–1940* (New York, 1988), an important recent work on dissemination; A. E. Musson, ed., *Science, Technology, and Economic Growth* (London, 1972); A. E Musson and E. Robinson, *Science and Technology in the Industrial Revolution* (Manchester, England, 1969); N. Rosenberg, "Technological Change in the Machine Tool Industry, 1840–1910," *Journal of Economic History* 33 (1963): 414–443; Rosenberg, "Factors Affecting the Diffusion of Technology," *Economic Journal* 84 (1972): 90–108; Rosenberg, *Perspectives in Technology* (Cambridge, England, 1976); H. J. Habbakuk, *American and British Technology in the Nineteenth Century: The Search for Labor-Saving Inventions* (Cambridge, England, 1962); and David Hounshell, *From the American System to Mass Production, 1800–1932: The Development of Manufacturing Technology in the United States* (Baltimore, Md., 1985).

Social Impact: Western Europe and the United States

On overall social impacts, see Peter N. Stearns and Herrick Chapman, *European Society in Upheaval*, 3d ed., (New York, 1991), and the extensive bibliography. A good introduction to artisanal developments is John M. Merriman, ed., *Consciousness and Class Experience in Nineteenth-Century Europe* (New York, 1979); William Sewell, *Work and Revolution in France: The Language of Labor from the Old Regime to 1848* (Cambridge, England, 1980); Joan W. Scott, *The Glassworkers of Carmaux* (Cambridge, Mass., 1974); and Lee Shai Weissbach, "Artisanal Responses to Artistic Decline: The Cabinetmakers of Paris in the Era of Industrialization," *Journal of Social History* 16 (1982): 67–81; on another key traditional urban group, see Philip G. Nord, *Paris Shopkeepers and the Politics of Resentment* (Princeton, N.J., 1986).

On labor relations in European industrialization, see Sidney Pollard, *The Genesis of Modern Management: A Study of Industrial Revolution in Great Britain* (Cambridge, Mass., 1965); Reinhard Bendix, *Work and Authority in Industry: Ideologies of Management in the Course of Industrialization* (Berkeley, Calif., 1974); Peter N. Stearns, *Paths to Authority: The Middle Class and the Industrial Labor Force in France, 1820–1848* (Urbana, Ill., 1978). The classic study of management history per se is Alfred Chandler, *The Visible Hand: The Managerial Revolution in American Business* (Cambridge, Mass., 1977). See also Katrina Honeyman, *Origins of Enterprise: Business Leadership in the Industrial Revolution* (Manchester, England, 1983); François Crouzet, *The First Industrialists: The Problem of Origins* (Cambridge, England, 1985); W. D. Rubinstein, *Men of Property: The Very Wealthy in Britain Since the Industrial Revolution* (New Brunswick, N.J., 1981); Anthony Howe, *The Cotton Masters, 1830–1860* (New York, 1984); Hartmut Kaelble, *Social Mobility in the Nineteenth and Twentieth Centuries: Europe and America in Comparative Perspective* (New York, 1986).

On white-collar development, see Susan Porter Benson, *Counter Cultures, Saleswomen, Managers, and Customers in American Department Stores, 1890–1940* (Urbana, Ill., 1986); Michael Miller, *The Bon Marché: Bourgeois Culture and the Department Store* (Princeton, N.J., 1981); David Lockwood, *The Black-coated Worker: A Study in Class Consciousness* (London, 1958; rev. ed., 1990); Jürgen Kocka, *Unternehmenensverwaltung und Angestelltenschaft am Beispiel Siemens, 1849–1914* (Stuttgart, Germany, 1969), a pioneering empirical study, and his useful synthesis, *White-Collar Workers in America, 1890–1940: Social-Political History in International Perspective* (Beverly Hills, Calif., 1980); Mario König, Hannes Siegrist, and Rudolf Vetterli, *Warten und Aufrücken. Die Angestellten in der Schweiz, 1870–1950* (Zurich, 1985).

On the impact on family, see Michael Anderson, *Family Structure in Nineteenth-Century Lancashire* (Cambridge, England, 1971); Peter N. Stearns, *Be a Man! Males in Modern Society* (New York, 1979). For a good recent synthesis on family change, see Steven Mintz and Susan Kellogg, *Domestic Revolutions: A Social History of American Family Life* (New York, 1988), which has a useful bibliography.

For conventional coverage on children in industry, see Ivy Pinchbeck and Margaret Hewitt, *Children in English Society*, 2 vols. (London, 1969–1973). Distinctive approaches include Neil J. Smelser, *Social Change in the Industrial Revolution: An Application of Theory to the British Cotton Industry* (Chicago, 1959); John R. Gillis, *Youth and History: Tradition and Change in European Age Relations, 1770–Present* (New York, 1974); L. Narindelli, "Child Labor and the Factory Acts," *Journal of Economic History* 40 (1980): 739–755; Katherine Lynch, *Family, Class, and Ideology in Early Industrial France: Social Policy and the Working-Class Family, 1815–1848* (Madison, Wis., 1988); Colin Heywood, *Childhood in Nineteenth-Century France: Work, Health, and Education Among the "Classes Populaires"* (Cambridge, England, 1988).

On women and European industrialization, see Louise Tilly and Joan W. Scott, *Women, Work, and Family* (New York, 1978); see also Patricia Branca, "A New Perspective on Women's Work: A Comparative Typology," *Journal of Social History* 9 (1975): 129–153; Mariana Valverde, "'Giving the Female a Domestic Turn': The Social, Legal, and Moral Regulation of Women's Work in British Cotton Mills, 1820–1850," *Journal of Social History* 21 (1988): 619–634—the article has useful additional references on recent feminist scholarship. A pathbreaking study is Christine Stansell, *City of Women: Sex and Class in New York, 1789–1860* (New York, 1986); see also Daniel Sutherland, *Americans and Their Servants: Domestic Service in the United States from 1800–1920* (Baton Rouge, La., 1981); Theresa McBride, *The Domestic Revolution: The Modernization of Household Service in England and France, 1820–1920* (New York, 1976); Mary P. Ryan, *Cradle of the Middle Class: The Family in Oneida County, New York, 1790–1865* (Cambridge, England, 1981); Nancy F. Cott, *The Bonds of Womanhood: "Women's Sphere" in New England, 1780–1835* (New Haven, Conn., 1977); Patricia Branca, *Silent Sisterhood: Middle-Class Women in the Victorian Homes* (Pittsburgh, Pa., 1975).

A fine introduction to the standard-of-living debate is A.J.P. Taylor, ed., *The Standard of Living in the Industrial Revolution* (London, 1975), in particular the articles by Eric Hobsbawm and R. M. Hartwell; see also Hobsbawm and Hartwell, "The Standard of Living During the Industrial Revolution: A Discussion," *Economic History Review*, 2d ser., 16 (1963–64): 119–146.

On factory workers and protest, see Patrick Joyce, *Work, Society, and Politics: The Culture of the Factory in Later Victorian England* (New Brunswick, N.J., 1980); David Crew, *Town in the Ruhr: A Social History of Bochum, 1860–1914* (New York, 1979). Lenard R. Berlanstein, *The Working People of Paris, 1871–1914* (Baltimore, Md., 1984), is one of the most interesting recent monographs in opening new facets to the history of the working classes and their conditions; see also Peter N. Stearns, *Lives of Labor: Work in a Maturing Industrial Society* (New York, 1975); Yves Lequin, *Les Ouvriers de la région lyonnaise*, 2 vols. (Lyons, France,

1977); Standish Meacham, *A Life Apart: The English Working Class, 1890–1914* (Cambridge, Mass., 1977); Eric Hobsbawm, *The Age of Capital, 1848–1875* (New York, 1975); E. P. Thompson, "Time, Work-Discipline, and Industrial Capitalism," *Past and Present* 38 (1967): 56–97; see also his *The Making of the English Working Class* (Harmondsworth, England, 1968) and "The Moral Economy of the English Crowd in the Eighteenth Century," *Past and Present* 50 (1971): 76–136. See Charles Tilly, *The Contentious French* (Cambridge, Mass., 1986), for his most recent of many studies on patterns of worker protest; see also William M. Reddy, *Money and Liberty in Modern Europe* (Cambridge, England, 1987).

For developments in leisure, James Walvin, *Leisure and Society, 1830–1950* (London, 1978), and Hugh Cunningham, *Leisure in the Industrial Revolution* (London, 1980), are good introductions, the second with a fine bibliography. See also Roy Rosenzweig, *Eight Hours for What We Will: Workers and Leisure in an Industrial City, 1870–1920* (Cambridge, England, 1983); William J. Baker, *Sports in the Western World* (Totowa, N.J., 1982); Benjamin G. Rader, *American Sports: From the Age of Folk Games to the Age of Spectators* (Englewood Cliffs, N.J., 1983); Gareth Stedman Jones, *Languages of Class: Studies in English Working-Class History* (Cambridge, England, 1983), and "Working-Class Culture and Working-Class Politics in London, 1890–1900—Notes on the Remaking of a Working Class," *Journal of Social History* 7 (1974): 460–508.

On the demographic transition, E. A. Wrigley, *Population and History* (New York, 1969), remains a useful introduction; see also Charles Tilly, ed., *Historical Studies of Changing Fertility* (Princeton, N.J., 1978); E. A. Wrigley and Roger Schofield, *The Population History of England* (Cambridge, England, 1981); Richard Easterlin, *Population, Labor Force, and Long Swings in Economic Growth: The American Experience* (New York, 1968); Maris Vinovskis, "Recent Trends in American Historical Demography," *American Review of Sociology* 47 (1978): 736–759. See also Michael Drake, ed., *Population in Industrialization* (New York, 1969); the much-debated Thomas McKeown, *The Rise of Modern Population* (New York, 1976); Robert Rotberg et al., eds., *Population and Economy* (Cambridge, England, 1986); and Esther Boserup, *Population and Technological Change* (New York, 1981).

On migrations, see Stephen Castles, *Immigrant Workers and Class Structure in Western Europe*, 2d ed. (Oxford, England, 1985), and *Migrant Workers and the Transformation of Western Societies* (Ithaca, N.Y., 1989); and Michael Piore, *Birds of Passage: Migrant Labor and Industrial Societies* (Cambridge, England, 1979).

There has been increased attention to certain other variables in relation to industrialization. Some important quantitative work focusing on literacy discusses whether measurable advances in literacy and schooling played a causal role in encouraging Western industrialization. There is considerable agreement (as in the case of Germany) that while correlation for initial industrialization is scant, literacy gains salience in advancing the industrial process. A fine recent survey with good bibliography is Harvey J. Graff, *The Legacies of Literacy: Continuities and Contradictions in Western Culture and Society* (Bloomington, Ind., 1987). See also Carlo Cipolla, *Literacy and Development in the West* (Harmondsworth, England, 1969). Peter Lundgreen offers an interesting case study, *Bildung und Wirtschaftswachstum in Industrialisierungprozess des 19 Jahrhunderts* (Berlin, 1973); see also his "Industrialization and the Educational Formation of Manpower in Germany," *Journal of Social History* 9 (1975): 64–80.

Beyond Western Europe

On international impacts of Western industrialization, see Immannuel Wallerstein, *The Modern World-System,* 2 vols. (New York, 1980), and ed. with Terence Hopkins, *Processes of the World System* (Beverly Hills, Calif., 1980); see also Albert Bergeson, ed., *Studies of the Modern World System* (New York, 1980); D. K. Fieldhouse, *Economics and Empire, 1830–1914* (New York, 1970); and Tony Smith, *The Pattern of Imperialism* (Cambridge, England, 1981). Classic statements are J. A. Hobson, *Imperialism: A Study* (Ann Arbor, Mich., 1965), and V. I. Lenin, *Imperialism, the Highest Stage of Capitalism* (Moscow, 1975). An important recent study is Michael P. Adas, *Machines as the Measure of Men: Science, Technology, and Ideologies of Western Dominance* (Ithaca, N.Y., 1989). See also Daniel R. Headrick, "The Tools of Imperialism: Technology and the Expansion of European Colonial Empire in the Nineteenth Century," *Journal of Modern History* 51 (1971): 231–263, and *The Tools of Empire: Technology and European Imperialism* (New York, 1981); Damodar R. Sar Desai, *British Trade and Expansion in Southeast Asia* (Columbia, Mo., 1977).

On the industrial revolution in the United States, see Thomas Cochran and William Miller, *The Age of Enterprise: A Social History of Industrial America* (New York, 1962); George R. Taylor, *The Transportation Revolution, 1815–1860* (New York, 1951); Albert W. Niemi, Jr., *United States Economic History* (Washington, D.C., 1987); Douglas North and Terry Anderson, *Growth and Welfare in the American Past* (Englewood Cliffs, N.J., 1984). Jonathan Prude, *The Coming of Industrial Order: Town and Factory Life in Rural Massachusetts, 1810–1860* (Cambridge, Mass., 1983) is one of the best recent case studies. See also David Montgomery, *Workers' Control in America: Studies in the History of Work, Technology, and Labor Struggles* (Cambridge, England, 1979); Sean Wilentz, *Chants Democratic: New York City and the Rise of the American Working Class, 1788–1850* (New York, 1984); David Grimsted, "Ante-Bellum Labor: Violence, Strike, and Communal Arbitration," *Journal of Social History* 19 (1985): 5–28; Loren Baritz, *The Servants of Power* (Middletown, Conn., 1960); Daniel Nelson, *Managers and Workers: Origins of the New Factory System in the United States, 1880–1920* (Madison, Wis., 1975); Herbert Gutman, *Work, Culture, and Society in Industrializing America* (New York, 1976); Alan Dawley, *Class and Community: The Industrial Revolution in Lynn* (Cambridge, Mass., 1976); Michael H. Frisch and Daniel Walkowitz, eds., *Working-Class America* (Urbana, Ill., 1983).

On the industrialization of Russia and the Soviet Union, see John McKay, *Pioneers for Profit: Foreign Entrepreneurship and Russian Industrialization* (Chicago, 1970); William Blackwell, *The Beginnings of Russian Industrialization, 1800–1860* (Princeton, N.J., 1968); Ben Eklof, *Russian Peasant Schools: Officialdom, Village Culture, and Popular Pedagogy, 1864–1914* (Berkeley, Calif., 1986); John Bushnell, *Mutiny Amid Repression: Russian Soldiers and the Revolution of 1905–1906* (Bloomington, Ind., 1985); Rose L. Glickman, *Russian Factory Women: Workplace and Society, 1880–1914* (Berkeley, Calif., 1984); Victoria E. Bonnell, *Roots of Rebellion: Workers' Politics and Organizations in St. Petersburg and Moscow, 1900–1914* (Berkeley, Calif., 1983); Reginald E. Zelnik, *Labor and Society in Tsarist Russia: The Factory Workers of St. Petersburg, 1855–1870* (Stanford, Calif., 1971); Diane Koenker, *Moscow Workers and the 1917 Revolution* (Princeton, N.J., 1981); Moshe Lewin, *The Making of the Soviet System: Essays in the Social History of Interwar Russia* (New York, 1985); William J. Chase, *Workers, Society, and the Soviet States: Labor and Life in Moscow, 1918–1929* (Urbana,

Ill., 1987); Ann D. Rassweiler, "Soviet Labor History of the 1920s and 1930s," *Journal of Social History* 17 (1983): 147–158; Hiroaki Kuromiya, *Stalin's Industrial Revolution: Politics and Workers, 1928–1932* (Cambridge, England, 1988).

On Japan, see R. P. Dore, ed., *Aspects of Social Change in Modern Japan* (Princeton, N.J., 1968); Marius B. Jansen and Gilbert Rozman, *Japan in Transition, from Tokugawa to Meiji* (Princeton, N.J., 1986); Johannes Hirschmeier and Tsunehiko Yui, *The Development of Japanese Business, 1900–1980*, 2d ed. (London, 1981); Kazushi Ohkawa, *The Growth Rate of the Japanese Economy Since 1878* (Tokyo, 1957); G. C. Allen, *A Short Economic History of Modern Japan* (New York, 1981); James W. Abegglen, *The Strategy of Japanese Business* (Cambridge, Mass., 1984); William W. Lockwood, *The Economic Development of Japan: Growth and Structural Change*, rev. ed. (Princeton, N.J., 1968); Andrew Gordon, *The Evolution of Labor Relations in Japan: Heavy Industry* (Cambridge, Mass., 1985); Thomas Smith, *Political Change and Industrial Development in Japan: Governmental Enterprise, 1868–1880* (Stanford, 1955). See also Hugh Patrick, ed., *Japanese Industrialization and Its Social Consequences* (Seattle, Wash., 1973), an excellent collection; Jon Halliday, *A Political History of Japanese Capitalism* (New York, 1975); Kozo Yamamura, *A Study of Samurai Income and Entrepreneurship* (Cambridge, Mass., 1974); W. Dean Kinzley, *Industrial Harmony in Modern Japan: The Invention of a Tradition* (London, 1991); Kazuo Okochi, Bernard Karsh, and Solomon B. Levine, eds., *Workers and Employers in Japan: The Japanese Employment Relations System* (Princeton, N.J., 1974); and Koji Taira, *Economic Development and the Labor Market in Japan* (New York, 1970).

On fringe areas in Europe, see Alexander Gerschenkron, *Economic Backwardness in Historical Perspective: A Book of Essays* (Cambridge, Mass., 1962), a classic study. See also I. T. Berend and G. Ranki, *The European Periphery and Industrialization, 1780–1914* (Cambridge, England, 1982); Charles W. Anderson, *The Political Economy of Modern Spain: Policy Making in an Authoritarian System* (Madison, Wis., 1970); George H. Hildebrand, *Growth and Structure in the Economy of Modern Italy* (Cambridge, Mass., 1965); Jane Horowitz, *Economic Development in Sicily* (New York, 1978); K. J. Allen and G. Stevenson, *Introduction to the Italian Economy* (New Haven, Conn., 1976); Charles Kindleberger, *Europe's Postwar Growth* (New York, 1973); and Daniel Chirot, *Social Change in Peripheral Society: The Creation of a Balkan Colony* (New York, 1976).

On the Pacific Rim, see Robert L. Downen and Bruce Dickson, *The Emerging Pacific Community: A Regional Perspective* (Boulder, Colo., 1984); *Pacific Basin Economic Handbook* (New York, 1987); Douglas Philips and Steven Lei, *Pacific Rim* (Los Angeles, 1988). On the Pacific Rim concept and its implications in terms of the world economy, see David Aikman, *Pacific Rim: Area of Change, Area of Opportunity* (Boston, 1986); Philip West et al., eds., *The Pacific Rim and the Western World: Strategic, Economic, and Cultural Perspectives* (Boulder, Colo., 1987); Stephan Haggard and Chung-in Moon, *Pacific Dynamics: The International Politics of Industrial Change* (Boulder, Colo., 1989); Ronald A. Morse et al., *Pacific Basin: Concept and Challenge* (Washington, D.C., 1986); and Staffan B. Linder, *The Pacific Century: Economic and Political Consequences of Asian Pacific Dynamism* (Stanford, Calif., 1986). Excellent introductions to recent Korean history are Bruce Cumings, *The Two Koreas* (New York, 1984), and David Rees, *A Short History of Modern Korea* (New York, 1988). A variety of special topics are addressed in Marshall R. Pihl, ed., *Listening to Korea: A Korean Anthology* (New York, 1973). See also David Steinberg, *The Republic of Korea: Economic Transformation* and Social Change (Boulder, Colo., 1989); Paul Kuznets, Economic Growth and Structure in the Republic of Korea (New Haven, Conn., 1977); and Dennis McNamara, The Colonial Origins of Korean Enterprise 1910–1945 (Cambridge, England, 1990). See also Robert N. Kearney, ed., Politics and Modernization in South and Southeast Asia (Cambridge, Mass., 1975); Edwin Winckler and Susan Greenhalgh, eds., Contending Approaches to the Political Economy of Taiwan (Armonk, N.Y., 1988); Robert Wade, Governing the Market: Economic Theory and the Role of the Government in East Asian Industrialization (Princeton, N.J., 1990). On Singapore, Janet W. Salaff, State and Family in Singapore (Ithaca, N.Y., 1988), is an excellent study.

On industrialization in Latin America, Leslie Bethell, ed., The Cambridge History of Latin America, vol. 6 (Cambridge, England, 1986), is the most useful general recent survey, in particular essays by William Glade, Rosemary Thorp, and Colin M. Lewis. An old classic is Roberto Cortes Conde, The First Stage of Modernization in Spanish America (New York, 1974). There are also a number of excellent national studies, among them Warren Dean, The Industrialization of São Paulo, 1880–1891 (Austin, Tex., 1969); Barbara Weinstein, The Brazilian Rubber Boom, 1850–1920 (Stanford, Calif., 1983); Thomas F. O'Brien, Jr., The Nitrate Industry and Chile's Critical Transition, 1870–1891 (New York, 1982); Rosemary Thorp and Geoffrey Bertram, Peru 1890–1977: Growth and Policy in an Open Economy (London, 1978); John H. Coatsworth, Growth Against Development: The Economic Impact of Railroads in Porfirian Mexico (De Kalb, Ill., 1982); Marcos Palacios, Coffee in Colombia 1870–1970: An Economic, Social, and Political History (Cambridge, England, 1980); Stephen H. Haber, Industry and Development: The Industrialization of Mexico, 1890–1940 (Stanford, Calif., 1989); Erick D. Langer, "Generations of Scientists and Engineers: Origins of the Computer Industry in Brazil," Latin American Research Review 24 (1989): 95–111; Charles Bergquist, Labor in Latin America: Comparative Essays on Chile, Argentina, Venezuela, and Colombia (Stanford, Calif., 1986). On maquiladora industry in Mexico, see Maria Patricia Fernandez-Kelly, For We Are Sold, I and My People: Women and Industry in Mexico's Frontier (Albany, N.Y., 1984); Clark W. Raynolds, The Mexican Economy: Twentieth-Century Structure and Growth (New Haven, Conn., 1970). On other major nations, see Laura Randall, An Economic History of Argentina in the Twentieth Century (New York, 1978); and Peter Evans, Dependent Development: The Alliance of Multinational, State, and Local Capital in Brazil (Princeton, N.J., 1979). See also Catherine M. Conaghan, Restructuring Domination: Industrialists and the State in Ecuador (Pittsburgh, Pa., 1988); Miguel D. Ramirez, Mexico's Economic Crisis: Its Origins and Consequences (New York, 1989); and Newell G. Roberto and Rubio F. Luis, Mexico's Dilemma: The Political Origins of Economic Crisis (Boulder, Colo., 1984).

On the Middle East, see Charles Issawi, Economic History of the Middle East and North Africa (New York, 1982) and, as editor, The Economic History of Turkey, 1800–1914 (Chicago, 1980); Donald Quataert, "Machine Breaking and the Changing Carpet Industry of Western Anatolia, 1860–1908," Journal of Social History 19 (1986): 473–490. See also Ragaei El-Mallakh, Saudi Arabia, Rush to Development (Baltimore, Md., 1982) and The Economic Development of the United Arab Emirates (New York, 1981); Charles Issawi, ed., Economic History of the Middle East, 1800–1914 (Chicago, Ill., 1966); Roger Owen, The Middle East in the World Economy, 1800–1914 (New York, 1987); and Peter R. O'Dell, Oil and World Power, 5th ed. (London, 1981).

On India, see S. D. Mehta, The Cotton Mills of India, 1854 to 1954 (Bombay, 1954); Francine R. Frandel, India's Political Economy, 1947–1977: The Gradual Revolution (Princeton, N.J., 1978); Thomas A. Tinberg, The Marwaris: From Traders to Industrialists (New Delhi, 1978); Lester Brown, Seeds of Change: The Green Revolution and Development in the 1970s (New

York, 1970); A. Vasudevan, *The Strategy of Planning in India* (Meerut, 1970); Wilfred Malenbaum, *Prospects for Indian Development* (London, 1962); and B.L.C. Johnson, *Development in South Asia* (New York, 1983).

On Africa, see Frederick Cooper, *On the African Waterfront: Urban Disorder and the Transformation of Work in Colonial Mombasa* (New Haven, Conn., 1987) and *Struggle for the City: Migrant Labor, Capital, and the State in Urban Africa* (Beverly Hills, Calif., 1983); Allen Isaacman, "Peasants, Work, and Labor Process: Forced Cotton Cultivation in Colonial Mozambique, 1938–1961," *Journal of Social History* 25 (1992): 815–855. For a discussion on vent for surplus theory, see J. S. Hogendorn, "Economic Initiative and African Cash Farming: Pre-Colonial Origins and Early Colonial Developments," in Peter Duignan and L. H. Gann, eds., *Colonialism in Africa: 1870–1960*, 5 vols. (London, 1969–1975); vol. 2 (1971): 283–328; Anthony Hopkins, *An Economic History of West Africa* (London, 1973). For critiques of vent for surplus theory, see Frederick Cooper, "Africa and the World Economy," *African Studies Review* 24 (1981): 2–6; Megan Vaughan, "Food Production and Family Labour in Southern Malawi: The Shire Highlands and Upper Shire Valley in the Early Colonial Period," *Journal of African History* 23 (1982): 351–364; S. Martin, "Gender and Innovation: Farming, Cooking, and Palm Processing in the Ngwa Region, Southeast Nigeria, 1900–1930," *Journal of African History* 25 (1984): 441–427. For a discussion of the staple theory, see Carville Early, "A Staple Interpretation of Slavery and Free Labour," *Geographical Review* 68 (1978): 51–65; Ralph Shlomowitz, "Plantations and Smallholders: Comparative Perspectives from the World of Cotton and Sugar Cane Economies, 1865–1939," *Agricultural History* 58 (1984): 1–16. See also J. Forbes Munro, *Africa and the International Economy, 1800–1960* (London, 1976); Brian Bowles, "Export Crops and Underdevelopment in Tanganyika, 1929–1961," *Utafiti* 1 (1976): 71–85; E. A. Brett, *Colonialism and Underdevelopment in Kenya: The Political Economy of Neo-Colonialism* (Berkeley, Calif., 1974); D.M.P. McCarthy, *Colonial Bureaucracy and Creating Underdevelopment: Tanganyika, 1919–1940* (Ames, Iowa, 1982).

On China, see Gilbert Rozman and Thomas P. Bernstein, *The Modernization of China* (New York, 1981); Michael Gasster, *China's Struggle to Modernize*, 2d ed. (New York, 1983); Roderick MacFarquhar, *The Great Leap Forward, 1958–1960*, vol. 2 of *The Origins of the Cultural Revolution* (New York, 1983); Gilbert Rozman, ed., *The East Asian Region: Confucian Heritage and Its Modern Adaptation* (Princeton, N.J., 1991); Thomas G. Rawski, *Economic Growth in Prewar China* (Berkeley, Calif., 1989); Emily Hong, *Sisters and Strangers: Women in the Shanghai Cotton Mills, 1919–1949* (Stanford, Calif., 1986); Gail Hershatter, *The Wonders of Tianjin, 1900–1949* (Stanford, Calif., 1986); Jean Chesnaux, *The Chinese Labor Movement, 1919–1927* (Stanford, Calif., 1968); Alexander Eckstein, *China's Economic Revolution* (Cambridge, England, 1977); Dwight Perkins, *China, Asia's Next Economic Giant?* (Seattle, Wash., 1986); Andrew Walder, *Communist Neo-Traditionalism: Work and Authority in Chinese Society* (Berkeley, Calif., 1986); Frances V. Moulder, *Japan, China, and the Modern World Economy: Toward a Reinterpretation of East Asian Development Circa 1600 to Circa 1918* (Cambridge, England, 1977); and Albert Feuerwerker, *China's Early Industrialization: Sheng Hsuan-Huai (1844–1916) and Mandarin Enterprise* (Cambridge, Mass., 1958).

On recent international developments and prospects, several serious books (as well as many more simplistic popularized efforts) attempt to sketch the world's or the West's future. On the postindustrial society concept, see Daniel Bell, *The Coming of the Post-Industrial Society* (New York, 1973). For other projections, consult Robert L. Heilbroner, *An Inquiry into the Human Prospect* (New York, 1974), and Lefton Stavrianos, *The Promise of the Coming Dark Age* (San Francisco, 1976). On environment and resource issues, D. H. Meadows and D. L. Meadows, *The Limits of Growth* (New York, 1974), and Murray Bookchin, *Our Synthetic Environment* (New York, 1962), are worthwhile. M. ul Haq, *The Poverty Curtain: Choices for the Third World* (New York, 1976), and Lewis D. Solomon, *Multinational Corporations and the Emerging World Order* (Port Washington, N.Y., 1978), cover economic issues, in part from a non-Western perspective.

About the Book and Author

THE INDUSTRIAL REVOLUTION is generally recognized as a major development in world history. Even so, the study of it is routinely handled as simply part of Western European history or as part of individual national histories.

Peter Stearns offers a genuinely world-historical approach, looking at the international factors that touched off the industrial revolution and at its global spread and impact. Stearns begins with an examination of industrialization in the West, but he also treats later cases in other societies—including Russia, Japan, and the United States—providing the comparative analysis usually lacking in single-nation treatments. Although Stearns defines the essence of industrialization in terms of technology and economic organization, he pays substantial attention to larger social results, especially changes in the experience of work and shifts in family functions and gender roles.

The Industrial Revolution in World History seeks to build on recent scholarly advances to include more fully international and more human views in our understanding of the industrial revolution. This book will be particularly useful for students of world history and economics as well as for those seeking to know more about the global implications of what is arguably the defining socioeconomic event of modern times.

PETER N. STEARNS is Heinz Professor of History at Carnegie Mellon University. He is editor of the *Journal of Social History* and the author of many books, including *The Other Side of Western Civilization* and *World Civilizations*.

Index